continued on back

D0780253

MULTIDIMENSIONAL SCALING

MULTIDIMENSIONAL SCALING

036568

MARK L. DAVISON
University of Minnesota

JOHN WILEY & SONS

New York · Chichester · Brisbane · Toronto · Singapore

Library of Congress Cataloging in Publication Data:

Davison, Mark, L. (Mark Leonard), 1947–
   Multidimensional scaling·

   (Wiley series on probability & mathematical
statistics. Applied probability & statistics,
ISSN 0271-6356)
   Bibliography: p.
   Includes indexes.
   1. Multidimensional scaling.   2. Psychometrics.
I. Title.   II. Series: Wiley series in probability and
mathematical statistics. Applied probability and
statistics section.

BF39.D323   1983   300′.72   82-17403
ISBN 0-471-86417-X

Printed in the United States of America

10 9 8 7 6 5 4 3 2 1

To

LESLIE, JACK, and ANDREW

Preface

In teaching a course on multidimensional scaling (MDS), it is very difficult to assemble primary sources that form a coherent, comprehensive, and integrated set of readings for students. Consequently, I decided to write this book. I had three purposes in writing it: to show what MDS is, to explain how to use the major techniques, and to prepare researchers to read the more technical literature in the field. The book was designed primarily as a textbook for graduate students in the behavioral sciences, the social sciences, and statistics. To aid instructors, problems and answers are included with every chapter except the last. The book was also designed as a reference for researchers in the social and behavioral sciences.

I have tried to illustrate each MDS method with two kinds of examples: There are hypothetical examples constructed to illustrate the major features of the technique, and there are real examples drawn from the published literature. The various examples come from a variety of fields, including acoustics, education, industrial relations, psychology, and sociology. More than any explanation I could give, these examples show what MDS is and why it is important.

Rather than giving a brief description of every technique that could fit under the term MDS, this book focuses on the major ones. Narrowing the focus in this manner makes it possible to describe methods in some depth, to extensively illustrate their application, and to detail the technical problems encountered in their use without making an overly long book. After finishing, readers should be able to read the growing number of studies that employ MDS, to read (though not with ease) much of the technical literature on the subject, to apply MDS in their own research, and to understand how the major MDS analyses work.

For purposes of this book, MDS is defined as a set of multivariate, statistical methods for estimating the parameters in and assessing the fit of various spatial distance models for proximity data. This definition is narrower than that used by some authors, who choose not to restrict the term MDS to methods based on spatial distance models. A broader definition would encompass techniques such as factor analysis and cluster analysis, which are covered extensively in multiple other works. I chose the narrower definition of MDS to avoid covering old ground and to permit a more extensive explanation of those techniques that are not thoroughly described elsewhere.

Chapter 7 discusses MDS methods for analyzing preference data—but *only* those methods consistent with the above definition of MDS. There are several methods for analyzing preference data that are often called MDS, but these methods are simply variations of factor analysis applied to preference responses rather than to correlation coefficients. I decided to exclude these techniques because the mathematical basis for them is so thoroughly described in the numerous sources on factor analysis.

The reader of this book is presumed to have a sophisticated user's knowledge of the statistical techniques commonly used in the behavioral and social sciences up to and including multiple regression. The first and last chapters mention factor analysis and cluster analysis, but a reader need not have any knowledge of these methods in order to understand those chapters. No calculus is used anywhere. The book does assume a knowledge of at least one computer package commonly used in the social and behavioral sciences. Various problems at the ends of chapters ask students to use one of the computer packages or one of the commonly available MDS programs.

Chapter 1 gives a brief introduction to MDS. It describes MDS's origins in experimental psychology and the kinds of research questions for which MDS is appropriate.

Without some minimal knowledge of matrix algebra, researchers cannot read much of the MDS literature. Consequently, Chapter 2 contains a brief introduction to matrix algebra. To prevent the chapter from becoming too burdensome for the less mathematically inclined, however, it discusses only those matrix concepts absolutely essential to an understanding of the MDS literature. All matrix concepts used in this book are explained here.

Many sources on MDS simply describe how one uses the technique to analyze the collected data. Applied researchers need some information about planning research and collecting data in studies that employ MDS. Chapter 3 provides such information.

Chapters 4–7 describe how to use and interpret results from the major MDS techniques. These chapters also contain proofs and descriptions of algorithms that some readers may wish to skip. They may do so without loss of continuity. Asterisks designate the more technical sections that may be omitted without loss of continuity.

Chapter 8 explains how one can use MDS to formally examine hypotheses, and it explains how one can compare results across different studies.

Chapter 9 compares MDS to factor analysis and cluster analysis. A list of major symbols in the book is included at the end.

I would like to thank anonymous reviewers and students, particularly Michael Petkovitch, Janet Schmidt, Stephen Thoma, and Phillip Wood, for their helpful comments on earlier drafts. The Graduate School and the University Computer Center at the University of Minnesota and the Spencer Foundation provided financial support for research from which examples where drawn. I would also like to thank Beatrice Shube, who shepherded this book through the publication process. The major typing was handled by Cathy Marfiz, whose careful eye helped put some polishing touches on the book. Professors Nancy Hirschberg, Lloyd Humphreys, Lawrence Jones, Charles Lewis, and Ledyard Tucker of the University of Illinois provided my early training in psychometrics. Professor David J. Weiss of the University of Minnesota encouraged me throughout this project. Most of all, I would like to thank my wife, Leslie, and our two boys, Jack and Andrew, for their loving understanding of my long working hours. These people and institutions deserve much of the credit for this book. Any of its shortcomings are solely my responsibility.

MARK L. DAVISON

Minneapolis, Minnesota
October 1982

Contents

CHAPTER 1

Introduction

Multidimensional scaling (MDS) is a technique developed in the behavioral and social sciences for studying the structure of objects or people. It has been used to study such things as the social structure of people in an organization, the semantic structure of words, and the logical structure of job tasks for a given occupation. MDS has proven useful to researchers in many fields, including anthropology, education, geography, history, marketing, psychology, political science, and sociology. In that MDS is used to describe structure, it is similar to factor analysis and cluster analysis. The assumptions of MDS differ from those of factor analysis and cluster analysis and, consequently, MDS usually leads to a description of the structure which differs in one or more respects from the description provided by the other two techniques. Furthermore, MDS is applicable to data for which the most common factor techniques are inappropriate. Chapter 9 contains a more extensive comparison between MDS, factor analysis, and cluster analysis.

The basic data in MDS are measures of proximity between pairs of objects. A *proximity measure* is an index defined over pairs of objects that quantifies the degree to which the two objects are alike. Correlation coefficients and joint probabilities are two common examples of proximity measures. Let δ_{ij} refer to the proximity measurement on stimulus pair (i, j). If a proximity measure is scored so that the highest values of δ_{ij} correspond to stimulus pairs that are most alike, then δ_{ij} is a *measure of similarity*. If the proximity measure is scored so that the highest values correspond to stimulus pairs that are least alike, then it is a *measure of dissimilarity*. Unless otherwise specified, readers should assume throughout this book that δ_{ij} refers to a dissimilarity measure. Chapter 3 explains some methods by which social and behavioral scientists collect proximity data.

1

Carroll and Arabie (1980, p. 608) list two definitions of MDS. According to the broader of the two definitions, MDS is "a family of geometric models for multidimensional representation of data and a corresponding set of methods for fitting such models to actual data."[†] Most multivariate statistics, including factor analysis and cluster analysis, would fit so broad a definition. In this book, MDS has a much narrower definition. MDS refers to a set of multivariate statistical methods for estimating the parameters in and assessing the fit of various spatial distance models for proximity data.

THE DISTANCE MODEL FOR DISSIMILARITY

As hinted by the phrase "spatial distance model" in the above definition, MDS assumes an analogy proposed by Richardson (1938) between the psychological concept of similarity and the geometric concept of distance. Strictly speaking, the analogy involves the psychological concept of *dis*similarity, not similarity. The parallels between dissimilarity and distance can be seen by examining the distance axioms. In order for a mathematical function d defined over pairs of objects (a, b) to be a Euclidean distance function, it must satisfy the following four axioms:

$$d(a, b) \geqslant 0, \tag{1.1}$$

$$d(a, a) = 0, \tag{1.2}$$

$$d(a, b) = d(b, a), \tag{1.3}$$

$$d(a, b) + d(b, c) \geqslant d(a, c). \tag{1.4}$$

As applied to the concept of dissimilarity, the first axiom implies that either two objects are identical to each other, in which case their dissimilarity is 0, or they are different from each other in some respect, in which case their dissimilarity is greater than 0. The second axiom suggests that an object is identical to itself. The third axiom implies that an object a must be as dissimilar from a second object b as b is from a.

Although the first three axioms seem intuitively quite plausible, there is nothing about psychological dissimilarity to suggest that measures of dissimilarity would or would not satisfy the fourth axiom, called the *triangular*

[†]Reproduced with permission from the *Annual Review of Psychology* Volume 31. Copyright 1980 by Annual Reviews Inc.

inequality axiom. In the social and behavioral sciences, however, three axioms out of four is not bad, so the analogy caught on.

More formally, the distance model for dissimilarity data can be stated as follows. Let δ_{ij} represent the measured dissimilarity between objects i and j. These objects might be cars, occupations, or political candidates. According to the model, the dissimilarity measures are functionally related to K attributes of the objects. If the objects are cars, the attributes might be such things as price, gas mileage, and sportiness. If the objects are occupations, the attributes might be such things as prestige, salary, and working conditions. Let x_{ik} and x_{jk} be the level of attribute k possessed by objects i and j, respectively. For instance, if the objects are cars and the attribute is gas mileage, then x_{ik} and x_{jk} would represent the gas mileage of two cars. Or if the objects are occupations and dimension k is prestige, then x_{ik} and x_{jk} would represent the amount of prestige associated with occupations i and j.

According to the strictest form of the Euclidean distance model, the dissimilarity measures are related to the attribute levels by the following function:

$$\delta_{ij} = d_{ij} = \left[\sum_{k=1}^{K} (x_{ik} - x_{jk})^2 \right]^{1/2}. \qquad (1.5)$$

Throughout this book δ_{ij} refers to a datum, a quantitative, empirical observation on object pair (i, j). On the other hand, d_{ij}, x_{ik}, and x_{jk} are theoretical quantities in the statistical model for dissimilarity data. These theoretical quantities cannot be observed directly and must be estimated from data.

Richardson (1938) began to wonder whether one could begin from a subject's subjective judgments of the dissimilarity between pairs of objects, and then work backward to determine what attributes were considered in making those judgments and to determine the locations of the stimuli along those dimensions. In so doing, Richardson defined the statistical estimation problem out of which multidimensional scaling grew, the problem of estimating the stimulus coordinates x_{ik} and x_{jk} from measures of dissimilarity.

EXPERIMENTAL EVALUATIONS OF THE DISTANCE MODEL

Experimental psychologists have not been content to assume the distance model for dissimilarity data. They have devised various experimental tests of the model (Beals et al., 1968; Carroll and Wish, 1974a; Krantz and

Tversky, 1975; Krumhansl, 1979; Monahan and Lockhead, 1977; Nygren, 1978, 1979; Wiener-Ehrlich, 1978). One such set of tests is based on the axioms in Eqs. (1.1)–(1.4). Since Euclidean distances must satisfy the axioms, then dissimilarity data that satisfy the Euclidean distance model in Eq. (1.5) should also satisfy the axioms.

To illustrate tests of the axioms, consider an experiment reported by Rothkopf (1957). In an experimental trial, Rothkopf presented two Morse code signals, one after another, to a subject. Then he asked the subject to indicate whether the signals were the "same" or "different." All possible pairs of signals were presented approximately an equal number of times. In approximately half of the trials involving signals i and j, signal j followed i; in the other half i followed j. The number of trials in which stimulus pair (i, j) was presented and the subject responded "different" can be taken as a measure of the auditory dissimilarity between stimuli i and j.

The axiom in Eq. (1.1) implies that the frequency with which two identical signals evoke the "different" response should be the same no matter which signals are presented. The "different" response occurred on only 3% of the trials in which the Morse code signal E was presented twice, but it occurred on 17% of the trials in which the signal P was presented. Experimental psychologists have interpreted such findings as a violation of the distance axiom in Eq. (1.1) (Tversky, 1977).

Taken together, the axioms in Eqs. (1.1) and (1.2) imply that two nonidentical signals should never evoke the "different" response less frequently than two identical signals. In the Rothkopf data, there is one very minor violation of this principle. When the signal P was presented twice, the "different" response occurred on 17% of the trials. When the signal X followed B, the "different" response occurred on only 16% of the trials. Experimental psychologists have interpreted results of this kind as evidence that dissimilarity data do not satisfy the first two distance axioms (Tversky, 1977).

The third axiom leads one to expect that the "different" response should occur as often when signal j follows i as when i follows j. That is, it leads one to expect that the order of stimulus presentation will not influence the response. The Rothkopf data do not meet this expectation. For instance, when the signal U followed A, the "different" response occurred on 63% of the trials. When A followed U, the "different" response occurred 86% of the time. Experimental psychologists have interpreted results of this kind to mean that dissimilarity data do not satisfy the third distance axiom (Tversky, 1977; Zinnes and Wolff, 1977).

Rothkopf's data generally satisfy the last axiom. For most sets of three stimuli (h, i, j), $\delta_{hi} + \delta_{ij} \geq \delta_{hj}$. For instance, when signal pairs (X, Y), (Y, Z), and (X, Z) were presented, the "different" response occurred on 52,

77, and 74% of the trials, respectively. Clearly, $\delta_{XY} = .52$ plus $\delta_{YZ} = .77$ is greater than $\delta_{XY} = .74$, and hence the triangular inequality axiom is satisfied for this set of three stimuli.

If the triangular inequality is violated but the other three axioms are satisfied, it is possible to transform the data so that the triangular inequality is satisfied. Let

$$c = \max(\delta_{hj} - \delta_{hi} - \delta_{ij}) \quad \text{over all } (h, i, j). \tag{1.6}$$

Then one can create new dissimilarity measures γ_{ij} as follows:

$$\begin{aligned} \gamma_{ij} &= 0 && \text{if } i = j \\ \gamma_{ij} &= \delta_{ij} + c && \text{if } i \neq j. \end{aligned} \tag{1.7}$$

If δ_{ij} satisfies the first three axioms, γ_{ij} will satisfy all four distance axioms.

Despite the intuitive appeal of the distance model for dissimilarity, experimental tests of the model fail to consistently support it. These failures have not kept statisticians from developing MDS analyses based on the distance model. There may be several reasons for this. First, some statisticians may be unaware of the experimental studies. Second, even where the model does not hold exactly, MDS analyses may be sufficiently robust to warrant their continued use. Third, as MDS has been used in a wider array of fields, it has been applied to many kinds of data other than the dissimilarity judgments studied by psychologists. Hence the criticisms of the distance model arising from the experimental studies do not apply to all MDS research. Readers interested in a more thorough discussion of the experimental evidence on the distance model for dissimilarity judgments should consult Carroll and Wish (1974).

The conclusions drawn in experimental studies of dissimilarity judgments cannot be extended to other types of proximity measures. Nevertheless, the axiomatic tests of the experimental psychologists can be applied to any potential proximity index. For instance, the correlation coefficient r_{ij} is one possible measure of proximity, and $(2 - 2r_{ij})^{1/2} = \delta_{ij}$ is a possible measure of dissimilarity. From the properties of the correlation coefficient, it follows that δ_{ij} will satisfy the first three axioms. That is, $\delta_{ij} = 0$ if $i = j$, because $r_{ij} = 1$ if $i = j$; $\delta_{ij} \geqslant 0$ for all (i, j), because r_{ij} ranges between -1 and 1; and $\delta_{ij} = \delta_{ji}$ because $r_{ij} = r_{ji}$. It is not immediately clear whether δ_{ij} would satisfy the triangular inequality axiom. Since $\delta_{ij} = (2 - 2r_{ij})^{1/2}$ does not obviously violate any of the four distance axioms, however, it remains a plausible measure of dissimilarity for use in a MDS study. In a similar manner, the axioms in Eqs. (1.1)–(1.4) provide a basis for evaluating the suitability of any proximity measure for analysis by MDS.

APPLICATIONS OF MDS

This author is aware of MDS applications in acoustics (Soli and Arabie, 1979), anthropology (Swann, 1978), education (Johnson et al., 1970; Subkoviak, 1975; Wainer and Berg, 1972), geography (Hanham, 1976), history (Kendall, 1971), marketing (Cooper, 1973; Green and Carmone, 1972), psychology (Davison and Jones, 1976; Rummelhart and Abrahamson, 1973), political science (Mauser, 1972), and sociology (Coxon and Jones, 1974). Since MDS is applied somewhat differently in various fields, readers may wish to consult the above references for examples of applications in their own areas. Shepard's (1980) *Science* article contains a discussion of MDS and its application in acoustics, psychophysics, and learning.

Applications of MDS can be grouped into three categories, each marked by a different purpose. The first class of applications is what will be called dimensional applications. Before a researcher can understand why an organism reacts to a stimulus as it does, the researcher must first understand what aspects of the stimulus are attended to by the organism. In *dimensional applications*, the researcher applies MDS in order to understand the stimulus dimensions to which the organism attends. The dimensions recovered in the MDS are taken to be the salient aspects for the organism, and the stimulus coordinates recovered in the scaling are interpreted as the locations of the objects along the salient aspects.

As examples of this approach, Davison and Jones (1976) employed MDS to derive dimensions of interpersonal perception in a military unit. The dimensions were then used to develop models of sociometric choice among members of that unit. Rummelhart and Abrahamson (1973) used MDS to derive dimensions of animal names. These dimensions were used to derive a model for analogical reasoning problems of the form: dog; puppy; cat; (kitten). Borman et al. (1976) derived dimensions of job performance that were considered for subsequent use in employee performance evaluations.

MDS is not the only way to derive stimulus dimensions, and indeed it is not always the best way. In the application cited above, Borman et al. (1976) compared MDS and a critical incidents technique for deriving dimensions of job performance. They concluded that the MDS solution was not the best. Ultimately, the usefulness of the MDS dimensions depends on their utility in accounting for social and behavioral phenomena such as the sociometric data in the Davison and Jones (1976) study or the analogical reasoning in the Rummelhart and Abrahamson (1973) study.

In *data reduction* applications, the user's intent is to reduce the complex interrelationships between stimuli represented in the proximity matrix to a simpler, more readily comprehended, and more easily communicated form. If three or fewer dimensions are used to represent the similarity data, then the interrelationships between the stimuli can be visually displayed in a one-, two-, or three-dimensional graphical plot of the MDS coordinates x_{ik}. Shepard (1972a, p. 10) seems to have had data reduction in mind when he wrote " ... the [stimulus] representation should be readily visualizable, and so confined whenever possible to two or, at most, three spatial dimensions."

Quite often in data reduction applications, no interpretation is given to the dimensions. In their scaling of numbers, Shepard et al. (1975) make little attempt to give any psychological interpretation to their two dimensions. Their discussion focuses on clusters of stimuli found within their plot of the MDS dimensions. The scaling serves only as a device for reducing the data to a form in which the stimulus clusters can be readily displayed graphically.

The last type of application will be called the *configural verification* type. In such applications, the user begins from an hypothesis that specifies the number of dimensions that should be obtained if the proximity measure is submitted to a nonmetric MDS, and it specifies the configuration that should be formed by the stimulus points. Rounds et al. (1979) began from Holland's (1973) theory of careers. The theory suggests that if the intercorrelations between scales in either the Strong–Campbell Interest Inventory (Campbell, 1977) or the Holland Vocational Preference Inventory (Holland, 1965) are submitted to a nonmetric MDS analysis, the points corresponding to the interest scales should fall along a hexagon in a two-dimensional space. The order of the points along the hexagon is specified by Holland's (1973) theory. Although he presents no specific application, Hubert (1974) discusses a configural verification application of MDS to attitudinal and developmental data.

To better understand the wide ranging applications of MDS, readers are strongly urged to examine one example cited above for each type of application. Each type of application will be illustrated in later chapters.

THE DISTANCE MODEL FOR PREFERENCE

Coombs (1964) proposed a distance model for preference data, often called the unfolding model. In this model, person s is characterized by a set of parameters x_{sk} which are his or her ideal point coordinates. According to the model, the more closely a stimulus resembles the ideal, the more it will be preferred. The coordinate x_{sk} represents that level along dimension k that the subject considers ideal. Taken together, the K ideal coordinates for subject s specify that combination of stimulus attributes that the subject considers the ideal.

Let δ_{is} represent the degree of person s' preference for stimulus i. It will be assumed that higher values of δ designate the lesser amounts of preference. In other words, δ is a measure of dislike for stimulus i, rather than a measure of liking. In one version of the unfolding model, preferences are assumed to be of the following form, except for error:

$$\delta_{is} = d_{is} = \left[\sum_{k=1}^{K} (x_{ik} - x_{sk})^2 \right]^{1/2}. \qquad (1.8)$$

As before, x_{ik} refers to the location of stimulus i along attribute k. In this model, it is as if the subject arrives at a preference judgment by comparing the stimulus to his or her ideal on K object dimensions. Those stimuli whose coordinates place them farthest from the ideal are the least liked.

Because of the obvious parallels between the distance model for dissimilarity and the distance model for preferences, some of the same algorithms can be used to solve for the stimulus coordinates in both; the algorithms can be used to solve for the ideal point coordinates in the distance model for preference data. In Chapter 7, MDS algorithms for preference data will be considered.

Before launching into a discussion of the various MDS algorithms, mathematical concepts fundamental to all MDS will be introduced. In Chapter 2, basic matrix concepts are discussed and given geometric interpretations. Chapter 3 contains a discussion of the more common kinds of proximity data and methods for collecting such data. Having covered this preliminary ground, the various MDS algorithms can be introduced in Chapters 4–7.

PROBLEMS

1. Figure 1.1 displays the gas mileage and cost of three cars. The coordinates for each car are given in parentheses. The first figure in parenthe-

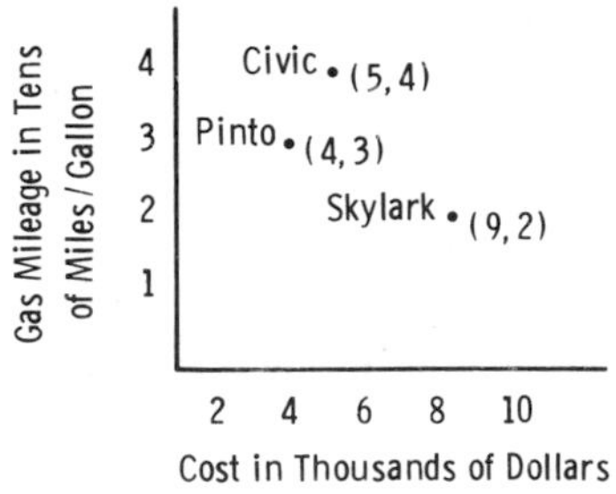

Figure 1.1. Cost and gas mileage of three cars.

ses is the coordinate along the horizontal axis. The second figure is the coordinate along the vertical axis. In answering questions a–d below, assume that a subject will judge the dissimilarity between two stimuli to be equal to distances in the figure.

    a. How dissimilar would the Pinto and Skylark be judged?

    b. How dissimilar would the Civic and Pinto be judged?

    c. If a subject ignored the gas mileage dimension, how dissimilar would the Pinto and Civic be judged?

    d. If a subject ignored the cost dimension, which would be judged more similar to the Civic, the Pinto or the Skylark? Why?

2.   Figure 1.2 shows the temperature of and the number of sugar lumps in four tea cups: A, B, C, D. It also shows the ideal point locations of two people. In answering questions a–d below, assume that a subject's stated preference for a stimulus would correspond to the distance between the stimulus and his or her ideal point in the figure.

    a. How much should Jane dislike stimulus B?

    b. Which should Jim prefer more, stimulus A or stimulus C? Defend your answer.

    c. If Jim were to ignore the temperature dimension, how much would he dislike D?

    d. If Jane were to ignore the sugar dimension, would she more prefer stimulus B or D? Why?

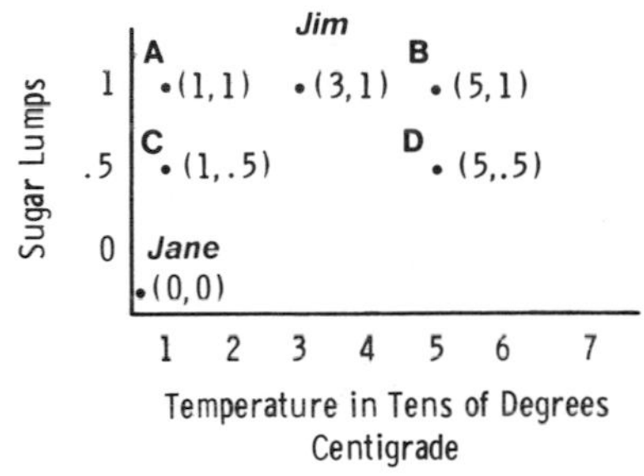

Figure 1.2. Teacups and subject ideal points.

Answers

1. a. $\delta = 5.10$

    b. $\delta = 1.41$

    c. $\delta = 1.00$

    d. The Pinto. Along the mileage dimension, the Pinto is 1 unit away from the Civic; the Skylark is 2 units away.

2. a. $\delta = 5.10$

    b. Stimuls A. A is only 2 units from his ideal. C is 2.06 units from his ideal.

    c. $\delta = .50$

    d. She would be indifferent between B and D, since both are equally distant (5 units) from her ideal along the temperature dimension.

CHAPTER 2

Matrix Concepts

Much of the literature on MDS uses matrix algebra to describe the methods and the rationales behind the methods. Without a minimal knowledge of matrix algebra, researchers will have difficulty updating their knowledge by reading further about MDS. Consequently, this chapter presents matrix concepts essential to an understanding of the MDS literature, and it presents geometric interpretations of matrix concepts. The geometric interpretations make it possible to display abstract matrix concepts in concrete graphical form. In this chapter, little attempt will be made to explain how or why matrix concepts are important in MDS. That will become apparent in Chapters 4–9. For now, suffice it to say that the reason for using matrix algebra in MDS is the same as in other areas. Many things can be stated much more concisely with matrices than without them.

MATRICES, VECTORS, AND SCALARS

A *matrix* is a two-dimensional display of numbers arranged into rows and columns. Figure 2.1 displays two such matrices. In discussing a matrix, the number of rows and columns are designated as follows: $(R \times C)$. Here R the first element refers to the number of rows in the matrix, and the second element C refers to the number of columns. A matrix may have any number of rows and columns

Throughout this book, matrices will be designated by capital letters in boldface type. For instance, the matrices in Figure 2.1 are designated by the capital letters **A** and **B** set in boldface type. Often you will see something in the form $\mathbf{A}_{(3 \times 3)}$ to indicate that matrix **A** has three rows and three columns.

Elements of matrices are represented by lower case letters in italics. For instance, the symbol a_{13} refers to the element in row 1 and column 3 of matrix **A**. For matrix **A** of Figure 2.1, $a_{13} = 7$. The element in the second

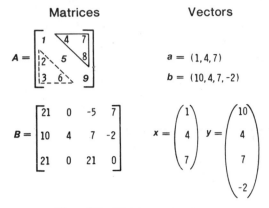

Figure 2.1. Matrices and vectors.

row, and fourth column of matrix **B** is b_{24}. In Figure 2.1, $b_{24} = -2$. In general, something of the form a_{rc} indicates the element in row r, column c of matrix **A**.

Several special kinds of matrices are of particular interest. First, a matrix is said to be a *square matrix* if the number of rows equals the number of columns, that is, $R = C$. Matrix **A** in Figure 2.1 is square, because it has three rows and three columns. Matrix **B** is not, because the number of rows, 3, does not equal the number of columns, 4. A square matrix **A** is said to be *symmetric* if $a_{rc} = a_{cr}$ for all pairs (r, c). Matrix **A** in Figure 2.1 is not symmetric, because $a_{12} = 4$ does not equal $a_{21} = 2$, and because $a_{32} = 6$ does not equal $a_{23} = 8$. On the other hand, matrix **A** in Figure 2.2 is symmetric. For every pair of values (r, c), $a_{rc} = a_{cr}$. As examples, $a_{12} = a_{21} = 2$, and $a_{24} = a_{42} = 4$. Only square matrices can be symmetric. Therefore, matrix **B** in Figure 2.1 can never be considered symmetric.

The *diagonal elements* of a square matrix are those elements for which the row and column numbers are identical (i.e., a_{11}, a_{22}, a_{33}, etc.). As a set, these elements are called the *diagonal* of a matrix. In Figure 2.1, matrix **A**, the diagonal elements are those printed in bold type. Those elements not on the diagonal of a square matrix are called the *off-diagonal* elements. The off-diagonal elements can be divided into two sets, the lower triangular elements and the upper triangular elements. Those elements that lie above and to the right of the diagonal are called the *upper triangular* elements. For these elements, the column number exceeds the row number. Those elements that lie below and to the left of the diagonal are called the *lower triangular* elements. For these elements, the row number exceeds the column number. In matrix **A** of Figure 2.1, the upper triangular elements have been enclosed in a solid triangle. The lower triangular elements are enclosed in a

$$A = \begin{bmatrix} 1 & 2 & 3 & 4 \\ 2 & 2 & 3 & 4 \\ 3 & 3 & 3 & 9 \\ 4 & 4 & 9 & 4 \end{bmatrix}$$

Symmetric

$$B = \begin{bmatrix} 5 & 0 & 0 & 0 \\ 0 & 2 & 0 & 0 \\ 0 & 0 & 3 & 0 \\ 0 & 0 & 0 & 4 \end{bmatrix}$$

Diagonal

$$C = \begin{bmatrix} 1 & 0 & 0 & 0 \\ 0 & 1 & 0 & 0 \\ 0 & 0 & 1 & 0 \\ 0 & 0 & 0 & 1 \end{bmatrix}$$

Identity   **Figure 2.2.** Types of square matrices.

dashed triangle. A square matrix is said to be a *diagonal matrix* if all of its off-diagonal elements equal 0. Matrices **B** and **C** in Figure 2.2 are diagonal matrices. The identity matrix is a very special and unusually important diagonal matrix. Any square, diagonal matrix is an *identity matrix* if all of its diagonal elements equal 1.0. Matrix **C** in Figure 2.2 is an identity matrix. An upper case **I** designates an identity matrix.

Whereas a matrix is a two-dimensional array of numbers, a *vector* is a one-dimensional array. A *row vector* is a $(1 \times C)$ horizontal array of numbers consisting of C elements arranged in a single row. One can think of a row vector as a matrix having only one row. Likewise, one can think of a column vector as a matrix having only one column. That is, a *column vector* is an $(R \times 1)$ vertical array of numbers arranged in a single column. Throughout this book, vectors will be designated by lower case letters set in bold type. In Figure 2.1, **a** and **b** are examples of row vectors, and **x** and **y** are examples of column vectors. Unless otherwise specified, all vectors are column vectors.

Any R by C matrix can be considered composed of R column vectors or C row vectors. Matrix **B** in Figure 2.1 can be considered composed of four column vectors. Or **B** can be considered composed of three row vectors.

Just as matrices can be broken down into vectors, vectors can be reduced to scalars. A *scalar* is a single number. Each element of a matrix or vector is a scalar. Matrices can be represented graphically. The next section of this chapter explains how.

REPRESENTING MATRICES GEOMETRICALLY

A very important matrix in MDS is the stimulus coordinate matrix. In this book, the coordinate matrix is a matrix **X** with I rows and K columns. Each row corresponds to a stimulus in the study. Each column corresponds to one dimension. The elements of **X**, x_{ik}, and x_{jk}, are the stimulus coordinates in Eq. (1.5) in the first chapter. That is, the element in row j and column k, x_{jk}, of the coordinate matrix **X**, is the coordinate of stimulus object j on dimension k.

In MDS, the coordinate matrix is typically standardized so that the mean stimulus coordinate along each dimension equals 0. This means that the sum of elements in every column of the coordinate matrix will be 0. Unless otherwise specified, the coordinate matrix will be assumed so standardized throughout this book. The stimulus coordinate matrix has a geometric interpretation that is the topic of this section. The geometric interpretation makes it possible to display an abstract coordinate matrix as a graph.

Figure 2.3 contains a coordinate matrix **X** and a graphic representation of **X**. Each coordinate axis in the graph corresponds to one column of matrix **X**. The first column, which corresponds to dimension I in the graph, contains the coordinates of the several stimuli on the first dimension. Similarly, the second column of **X** contains the coordinates of each stimulus along the second dimension.

Each row of **X** corresponds to one of the four points in the graph. For instance, the second row corresponds to stimulus b, with coordinates $(2, -1)$, and these coordinates are the elements in row 2 of **X**. In general, element x_{rc} in **X** is the coordinate of stimulus r along dimension c in the graph.

In subsequent chapters, coordinate matrices and their graphic representations will be used to describe MDS solutions. In matrix form, rows will correspond to stimuli, and columns will correspond to the stimulus attributes. When presented graphically, stimuli will be represented as points, and attributes will be presented as axes.

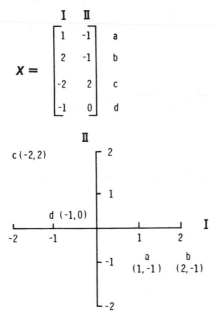

$$\mathbf{X} = \begin{bmatrix} 1 & -1 \\ 2 & -1 \\ -2 & 2 \\ -1 & 0 \end{bmatrix} \begin{matrix} a \\ b \\ c \\ d \end{matrix}$$

Dimension I vs. Dimension II

Figure 2.3. Matrix **X** and its geometric representation.

With complex stimuli, there is no guarantee that they can be represented in just two dimensions. For instance, occupations might vary along four dimensions: prestige, salary, working conditions, and educational requirements. Cities might be perceived to vary in population, average daily temperature, property tax rates, and unemployment rates. Representing solutions with more than two dimensions in matrix form presents no problem. The coordinate matrix would contain three, four, or as many columns as needed to describe all of the stimulus dimensions.

Graphically, presenting solutions with more than two or three dimensions is a problem. The printed page is two-dimensional. Hence it is ill-suited to presentation in a single graph of solutions having four or more dimensions. Although solutions of three dimensions can be presented on a two-dimensional page, nevertheless, it is difficult for most of us to visualize such a configuration.

Typically, solutions of more than two dimensions are presented as a series of two-dimensional plots, with one plot in the series for each pair of dimensions. Figure 2.4 shows the series of three two-dimensional plots needed to portray the stimulus configuration in matrix **X**.

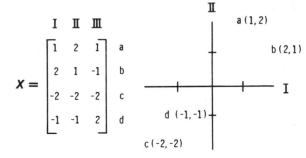

Dimension I vs. Dimension II

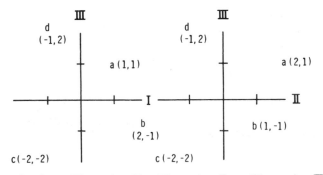

Dimension I vs. Dimension III   Dimension II vs. Dimension III

Figure 2.4. Graphs based on matrix **X**.

The arithmetic operations—addition, subtraction, multiplication, and division—are scalar operations, because they involve operations on single numbers. The next section of this chapter will introduce matrix operations: matrix addition, matrix subtraction, and so on, which correspond to the basic scalar operations. Although they are complex extensions to be sure, most matrix operations are extensions of scalar arithmetic.

MATRIX OPERATIONS

There is one operation, matrix transposition, that has no counterpart in the standard arithmetic operations. This section will begin with the operation of transposition and then move on to a discussion of addition, subtraction, multiplication, and the matrix analogue of division.

Matrix Transposition

Matrix $\mathbf{B}_{(C \times R)}$ is said to be the transpose of matrix $\mathbf{A}_{(R \times C)}$ if the column vectors in $\mathbf{A}$ are the row vectors in $\mathbf{B}$ and vice versa. As an example, consider matrix $\mathbf{B}$ in Figure 2.5, which is the transpose of matrix $\mathbf{A}$. The four elements in the first row of $\mathbf{A}$ are exactly the same as the four elements in the first column of $\mathbf{B}$. Similarly, the elements in the second row of $\mathbf{A}$ are the same as the elements in the second column of $\mathbf{B}$, and so on. In short, one can create a matrix $\mathbf{B}$, which is the transpose of $\mathbf{A}$, by taking the rows of $\mathbf{A}$ and making them the columns of $\mathbf{B}$. If $\mathbf{B}$ is the transpose of $\mathbf{A}$, then the number of rows in $\mathbf{A}$ will equal the number of columns in $\mathbf{B}$, and the number of columns in $\mathbf{A}$ will equal the number of rows in $\mathbf{B}$.

Formally, matrix $\mathbf{B}_{(C \times R)}$ is said to be the *transpose of matrix* $\mathbf{A}_{(R \times C)}$ if every element b_{cr} in $\mathbf{B}$ equals the element a_{rc} in matrix $\mathbf{A}$. In other words, the element in row c column r of matrix $\mathbf{B}$ must be the element in row r column c in matrix $\mathbf{A}$. For instance, the element in row 2 column 1 of $\mathbf{A}$ in Figure 2.3, $a_{21} = 10$, equals the element in row 1 column 2 of $\mathbf{B}$, $b_{12} = 10$. In some books the transpose of matrix $\mathbf{A}$ is designated $\mathbf{A}^T$. In this book, however, the transpose of matrix $\mathbf{A}$ will be designated $\mathbf{A}'$.

Matrix Addition and Subtraction

Two matrices can be added to each other only if they have exactly the same number of rows and the same number of columns. Likewise, one matrix can be subtracted from another only if the two matrices have exactly the same number of rows and exactly the same number of columns.

$$\mathbf{A} = \begin{bmatrix} 21 & 0 & -5 & 7 \\ 10 & 4 & 7 & -2 \\ 21 & 0 & 21 & 0 \end{bmatrix}$$

$$\mathbf{B} = \mathbf{A}' = \begin{bmatrix} 21 & 10 & 21 \\ 0 & 4 & 0 \\ -5 & 7 & 21 \\ 7 & -2 & 0 \end{bmatrix}$$

Figure 2.5. Matrix A and its transpose, $\mathbf{B} = \mathbf{A}'$.

The sum of two matrices is formed by adding corresponding elements in the two matrices. That is, if matrix $S_{(R \times C)}$ is the sum of matrices $A_{(R \times C)}$ and $B_{(R \times C)}$, then each element in S, s_{rc}, is equal to $a_{rc} + b_{rc}$. In words, the element in row r column c of matrix S is obtained by adding the element in row r column c of matrix A to the element in row r column c of matrix B. For instance, the element in row 3 column 2 of S, $s_{32} = 10$, is formed by adding the elements in row 3 column 2 of matrices A, $a_{32} = 7$, and B, $b_{32} = 3$; $s_{32} = a_{32} + b_{32} = 7 + 3 = 10$. Figure 2.6 displays the computation of matrix $S = A + B$.

Matrix subtraction is completely analogous to matrix addition. That is, the difference between two matrices is formed by subtracting corresponding elements. Formally, if matrix $D_{(R \times C)}$ is the difference between matrix $A_{(R \times C)}$ and matrix $B_{(R \times C)}$, then each element in D, d_{rc}, is formed by subtracting the element in row r column c of B from the corresponding element in A, a_{rc}. That is, $d_{rc} = a_{rc} - b_{rc}$. For instance, the element in row 3 column 2 of D, $d_{32} = 4$, is formed by subtracting the element in row 3 column 2 of B, $b_{32} = 3$, from the corresponding element in A, $a_{32} = 7$: $d_{32} = a_{32} - b_{32} = 7 - 3 = 4$.

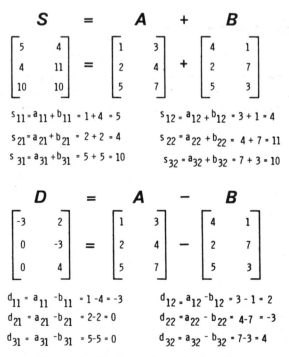

Figure 2.6. Matrix addition and subtraction.

Scalar Multiplication

Scalar multiplication involves multiplying a matrix by a scalar. That is, if we want to *scalar multiply* the matrix **A** by a scalar constant c, then we simply take every element of **A** and multiply it by c to obtain the product c**A**. Figure 2.7 shows an example of scalar multiplication.

Matrix Multiplication

There are actually two forms of matrix multiplication, premultiplication and postmultiplication. In the matrix equation $\mathbf{P}_{(R \times C)} = \mathbf{A}_{(R \times K)}\mathbf{B}_{(K \times C)}$, or

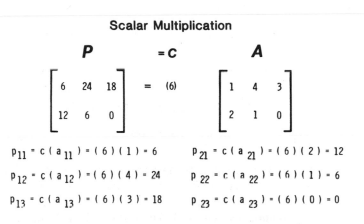

Scalar Multiplication

$$
\mathbf{P} \qquad = c \qquad \mathbf{A}
$$

$$
\begin{bmatrix} 6 & 24 & 18 \\ 12 & 6 & 0 \end{bmatrix} = (6) \begin{bmatrix} 1 & 4 & 3 \\ 2 & 1 & 0 \end{bmatrix}
$$

$$p_{11} = c\,(a_{11}) = (6)(1) = 6 \qquad p_{21} = c\,(a_{21}) = (6)(2) = 12$$
$$p_{12} = c\,(a_{12}) = (6)(4) = 24 \qquad p_{22} = c\,(a_{22}) = (6)(1) = 6$$
$$p_{13} = c\,(a_{13}) = (6)(3) = 18 \qquad p_{23} = c\,(a_{23}) = (6)(0) = 0$$

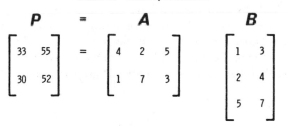

Matrix   Multiplication

$$
\mathbf{P} \qquad = \qquad \mathbf{A} \qquad \qquad \mathbf{B}
$$

$$
\begin{bmatrix} 33 & 55 \\ 30 & 52 \end{bmatrix} = \begin{bmatrix} 4 & 2 & 5 \\ 1 & 7 & 3 \end{bmatrix} \begin{bmatrix} 1 & 3 \\ 2 & 4 \\ 5 & 7 \end{bmatrix}
$$

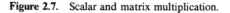

$$p_{11} = a_{11}b_{11} + a_{12}b_{21} + a_{13}b_{31} = (4)(1) + (2)(2) + (5)(5) = 33$$
$$p_{12} = a_{11}b_{12} + a_{12}b_{22} + a_{13}b_{32} = (4)(3) + (2)(4) + (5)(7) = 55$$
$$p_{21} = a_{21}b_{11} + a_{22}b_{21} + a_{23}b_{31} = (1)(1) + (7)(2) + (3)(5) = 30$$
$$p_{22} = a_{21}b_{12} + a_{22}b_{22} + a_{23}b_{32} = (1)(3) + (7)(4) + (3)(7) = 52$$

Figure 2.7. Scalar and matrix multiplication.

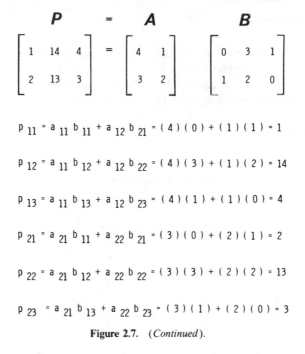

$$p_{11} = a_{11} b_{11} + a_{12} b_{21} = (4)(0) + (1)(1) = 1$$

$$p_{12} = a_{11} b_{12} + a_{12} b_{22} = (4)(3) + (1)(2) = 14$$

$$p_{13} = a_{11} b_{13} + a_{12} b_{23} = (4)(1) + (1)(0) = 4$$

$$p_{21} = a_{21} b_{11} + a_{22} b_{21} = (3)(0) + (2)(1) = 2$$

$$p_{22} = a_{21} b_{12} + a_{22} b_{22} = (3)(3) + (2)(2) = 13$$

$$p_{23} = a_{21} b_{13} + a_{22} b_{23} = (3)(1) + (2)(0) = 3$$

Figure 2.7. (*Continued*).

more simply, $\mathbf{P} = \mathbf{AB}$, matrix $\mathbf{A}$ is being postmultiplied by $\mathbf{B}$, and matrix $\mathbf{B}$ is being premultiplied by $\mathbf{A}$ to obtain the matrix product $\mathbf{P}$. The matrix product $\mathbf{P}$ will always have the same number of rows as matrix $\mathbf{A}$ and the same number of columns as matrix $\mathbf{B}$. The number of columns in $\mathbf{A}$ must equal the number of rows in $\mathbf{B}$. This means that a matrix $\mathbf{A}$ can be postmultiplied only by matrices that have the same number of rows as $\mathbf{A}$ has columns. Likewise, a matrix $\mathbf{B}$ can be premultiplied only by matrices that have the same number of columns as $\mathbf{B}$ has rows.

If matrix $\mathbf{P}$ is the product that results from *matrix multiplying* $\mathbf{A}_{(R \times K)}$ by matrix $\mathbf{B}_{(K \times C)}$, then the elements of matrix $\mathbf{P}$ are formed as follows:

$$p_{rc} = \sum_{k=1}^{K} a_{rk} b_{kc}. \tag{2.1}$$

Two examples of matrix multiplication are given in Figure 2.7. As an example of how the elements in the product $\mathbf{P}$ are formed, note that in the top portion of Figure 2.7 the element in row 1 column 2 of matrix $\mathbf{P}$,

$p_{12} = 55$, is computed as follows:

$$p_{12} = \sum_{k=1}^{3} a_{1k}b_{k2} = a_{11}b_{12} + a_{12}b_{22} + a_{13}b_{32}$$

$$= (4)(3) + (2)(4) + (5)(7) = 55. \tag{2.2}$$

The computation of the remaining elements in **P** is displayed in Figure 2.7.

There are two principles of matrix multiplication that will be used later in this book. For proofs, readers can consult a text on matrix algebra. The first principle is given in the following theorem.

Theorem 1. If matrix $\mathbf{A}_{(R \times C)}$ is postmultiplied by the identity matrix $\mathbf{I}_{(C \times C)}$, the resulting product equals **A**: **AI** = **A**. Similarly, if matrix $\mathbf{A}_{(R \times C)}$ is premultiplied by the identity matrix $\mathbf{I}_{(R \times R)}$, the resulting product is **A**: **IA** = **A**.

Readers may wish to confirm this theorem for themselves by pre- and postmultiplying matrix **A** in Figure 2.2 by $\mathbf{I}_{(4 \times 4)}$.

The second principle is given in the following theorem.

Theorem 2. If **P** = **AB**, then **P′** = **B′A′**.

In words, Theorem 2 states that if **P** is the product of two matrices, then **P′** is the product of their transposes in the reverse order. Readers can confirm this principle for themselves using the two matrix multiplication examples in Figure 2.7. By computing **B′A′**, one can show that it equals **P′** in both cases.

Matrix Analogue of Division

There is no such thing as matrix division, but there is a matrix analogue of division. In simple arithmetic, one can accomplish the same result either by dividing 12 by 6 or multiplying 12 by the inverse of 6, $1/6 = (6)^{-1}$. That is, $12 \div 6 = 12 \times 1/6 = 12 \times (6)^{-1} = 2$. Thus dividing by a number is the same as multiplying by the inverse of that number. In matrix algebra, one cannot divide one matrix by another, but one can multiply one matrix by the inverse of another. One may be able to multiply matrix **A** by the inverse of matrix **B**, designated $\mathbf{B}^{-1}$.

$\mathbf{A}^{-1}$ is defined as follows: A square matrix $\mathbf{B}_{(R \times R)}$ is said to be the inverse of the square matrix **A** if and only if

$$\mathbf{A}_{(R \times R)}\mathbf{B}_{(R \times R)} = \mathbf{B}_{(R \times R)}\mathbf{A}_{(R \times R)} = \mathbf{I}_{(R \times R)}. \tag{2.3}$$

This definition is restricted to square matrices, because only square matrices have inverses. Any text on matrix algebra (Green, 1978; Hohn, 1973) will describe methods for computing the inverse of a matrix, and many computer packages contain programs for computing matrix inverses.

There is one theorem about matrix inverses that will be used in later chapters.

Theorem 3. Let $\mathbf{P}$, $\mathbf{A}$, and $\mathbf{B}$ be square matrices with inverses $\mathbf{P}^{-1}$, $\mathbf{A}^{-1}$, and $\mathbf{B}^{-1}$ respectively. If $\mathbf{P} = \mathbf{AB}$, then $\mathbf{P}^{-1} = \mathbf{B}^{-1}\mathbf{A}^{-1}$.

In words, Theorem 3 states that if $\mathbf{P}$ is the product of two matrices, then the inverse of $\mathbf{P}$ is the product of their inverses, in the reverse order.

Solving Matrix Equations

Using matrix operations, one can solve matrix equations for unknown matrices much as one solves algebraic equations. For instance, imagine that we know the elements of matrices $\mathbf{A}$ and $\mathbf{B}$, and we wish to solve for the unknown matrix $\mathbf{X}$ in the equation $\mathbf{A} = \mathbf{B} + \mathbf{X}$. We can solve for $\mathbf{X}$ by subtracting $\mathbf{B}$ from both sides of the equation to obtain $\mathbf{A} - \mathbf{B} = \mathbf{X}$. Thus by subtracting matrix $\mathbf{B}$ from matrix $\mathbf{A}$, both of which are known, we can obtain matrix $\mathbf{X}$.

Similarly, imagine again that matrices $\mathbf{A}$ and $\mathbf{B}$ are known, and we wish to solve the following equation for the unknown matrix $\mathbf{X}$: $\mathbf{A} = \mathbf{B} - \mathbf{X}$. We can first add $\mathbf{X}$ to both sides to obtain $\mathbf{A} + \mathbf{X} = \mathbf{B}$. Then we can subtract $\mathbf{A}$ from both sides to obtain $\mathbf{X} = \mathbf{B} - \mathbf{A}$. Thus by subtracting $\mathbf{A}$ from $\mathbf{B}$, both of which are known, we can compute the unknown matrix $\mathbf{X}$.

As a third example, imagine that matrix $\mathbf{B}$ is a square symmetric matrix, whose inverse is $\mathbf{B}^{-1}$, that both matrices $\mathbf{A}$ and $\mathbf{B}^{-1}$ are known, and that we want to solve the matrix equation $\mathbf{A} = \mathbf{BX}$ for the unknown matrix $\mathbf{X}$. If we premultiply both sides of the equation by $\mathbf{B}^{-1}$, then we obtain

$$\mathbf{B}^{-1}\mathbf{A} = (\mathbf{B}^{-1}\mathbf{B})\mathbf{X}$$

$$= \mathbf{IX} \tag{2.4}$$

$$= \mathbf{X}.$$

Thus if we premultiply $\mathbf{A}$ by $\mathbf{B}^{-1}$, which one can compute from knowledge of $\mathbf{B}$, we can compute the unknown matrix $\mathbf{X}$.

Given an equation of the form $\mathbf{A} = \mathbf{XB}$, then we would simply postmultiply both sides by $\mathbf{B}^{-1}$ to obtain the result $\mathbf{AB}^{-1} = \mathbf{X}$. Thus one can compute the unknown matrix $\mathbf{X}$ by taking $\mathbf{A}$ times $\mathbf{B}^{-1}$.

If **B** is not a square matrix, then **B** does not have an inverse. In such cases, the methods of the preceding two paragraphs cannot be used to solve equations of the form $A = BX$, or $A = XB$. Under certain conditions, however, we can still solve these equations.

First, let's consider the equation $A = BX$. Even if **B** is not square, $(B'B)$ will be square. If the matrix $(B'B)$ has an inverse, then we can define a *left pseudo-inverse for* **B** as follows: $(B'B)^{-1}B'$. Then, if we premultiply both sides of the equation $A = BX$ by the left pseudo-inverse of **B**, we obtain the following result:

$$A = BX$$

$$(B'B)^{-1}B'A = (B'B)^{-1}B'BX$$

$$= IX \tag{2.5}$$

$$= X.$$

Thus by computing the quantity on the left side of Eq. (2.5), we can calculate **X**.

In a similar manner, if the matrix **BB'** has an inverse, then one can solve the matrix equation $A = XB$ by postmultiplying both sides by the *right pseudo-inverse* of **B**, which is $B'(BB')^{-1}$. Multiplying both sides by this inverse, one obtains

$$A = XB$$

$$AB'(BB')^{-1} = XBB'(BB')^{-1}$$

$$= XI \tag{2.6}$$

$$= X.$$

Thus by computing the quantity on the left side of Eq. (2.6), one can compute **X**.

A unique inverse $(B'B)^{-1}$ in Eq. (2.5) will exist only if the number of columns in **B** is as small as or smaller than the number of rows. The inverse in Eq. (2.6), $(BB')^{-1}$, will exist only if the number of rows in **B** is as small or smaller than the number of columns.

Matrix Analogue of Finding the Square Root

Technically, there is no such thing as taking the square root of a matrix. One can, however, perform operations on diagonal matrices and square symmetric matrices that are analogous to finding square roots.

$$D = \begin{bmatrix} 16 & 0 & 0 \\ 0 & 4 & 0 \\ 0 & 0 & 9 \end{bmatrix} \qquad D^{1/2} = \begin{bmatrix} 4 & 0 & 0 \\ 0 & 2 & 0 \\ 0 & 0 & 3 \end{bmatrix}$$

Figure 2.8.   A diagonal matrix and its square root.

If a matrix **D** is a diagonal matrix, then it is possible to define a second diagonal matrix $D^{1/2}$ which is analogous to the square root of **D**. The off-diagonal elements of $D^{1/2}$ all equal 0. Each diagonal element is the square root of the corresponding diagonal element in **D**. Figure 2.8 shows a matrix **D** and the corresponding matrix $D^{1/2}$.

If matrix **A** is a square symmetric matrix, then it may be possible to find a matrix **B** such that

$$A = BB'. \tag{2.7}$$

B is analogous to the square root of **A** and will have the same number of rows as **A**. The number of columns in **B** will be equal to or less than the number of columns in **A**. Interested readers should consult a text on matrix algebra (Green, 1978; Hohn, 1973) for a description of methods for computing **B** and a description of the conditions under which **A** can be expressed as the product of a matrix **B** and its transpose. For those who are familiar with factor analysis, it is possible to compute such a matrix **B** using a principal components factor analysis computer program, such as the one in Dixon and Brown (1979) or Nie et al. (1975). To compute **B**, one inputs **A** into the program as if it were a correlation matrix. From the output, one obtains a factor loading matrix, which is the desired matrix **B**.

ROTATION AND TRANSFORMATION MATRICES

In MDS a rotation is something one applies to an initial estimate of the stimulus coordinate matrix **X** to facilitate interpretation of the MDS solution. Chapter 4 illustrates how rotation can facilitate interpretation. This section simply explains the geometric concept of rotation and the matrix representation of rotation.

To begin the explanation of a rotation, consider the stimulus coordinate matrix **X** in Figure 2.9 and its graphic representation, also shown in Figure 2.9. A rotation of **X** can be obtained from the steps shown in Figure 2.10.

The first graph in Figure 2.10 (upper left corner of the figure) shows the four points in matrix **X** of Figure 2.9 and a dashed line running from its tail in the lower left to its tip in the upper right portion of the graph. The dashed line (axis 1) passes through the origin, and it lies 45° in a counterclockwise direction from dimension I and 315° from dimension II.

For points a and c in the graph, an arrow has been drawn from the point to axis 1. Each arrow, called a perpendicular, intersects the dashed line at a right (90°) angle. No perpendiculars were drawn for points b and c because they lie on the line. For each point, one could measure the distance from the origin to the intersection of the perpendicular (or the intersection of the point itself if the point lies on the line) with axis 1. This distance is the absolute value of the projection of the point onto the dashed line. The projection is negative if the intersection occurs toward the tail of the axis, and it is positive if the intersection occurs toward the tip of the axis. Column 1 of matrix **Y** in Figure 2.10 gives the projection for each point onto axis 1.

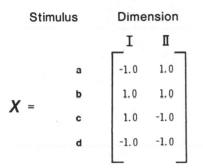

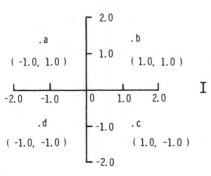

Figure 2.9. Matrix **X** and its graphic representation.

In column 1 of **Y**, points *a* and *c* have projections of 0.0, because their perpendiculars intersect the axis at the origin. Points *b* and *d* have projections of 1.4 and − 1.4. The points *b* and *d* intersect the dashed line 1.4 units from the origin. The projection for *d* is negative, because it intersects toward the tail or negative end of the axis. Point *b* intersects toward the tip, and hence its projection is positive.

Now look at the graph in the upper right corner of Figure 2.10. Like the graph we have just considered, it contains the four points from Figure 2.9. It also contains perpendiculars running from points *b* and *d* to a dashed line (axis 2). No perpendiculars were drawn for *a* and *c* because they lie on the line. Unlike axis 1 in the previous graph, axis 2 runs from a tail in the lower right portion of the graph to a tip in the upper left portion. It lies 135° from dimension I and 45° from dimension II in the counterclockwise direction. Just as dimension I is perpendicular to dimension II, axis 1 is perpendicular to axis 2.

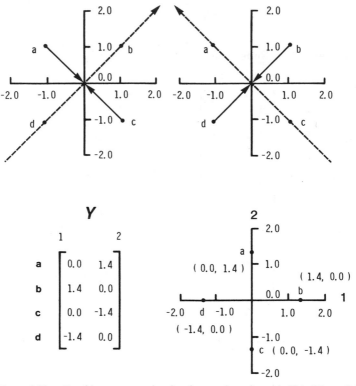

Figure 2.10.   Graphic representation for the rotation of matrix **X** in Figure 2.9.

One can compute the projections of each point onto axis 2. The absolute value of each projection will be the distance from the origin to the intersection of the corresponding perpendicular (or the intersection of the point itself, if the point lies on the line). The projection is positive if the intersection occurs toward the tip or positive end of the axis. It is negative if the intersection occurs toward the tail or negative end. Column 2 of **Y** shows the projection of the points onto axis 2.

The graph in the lower right portion of Figure 2.10 contains a plot of the coordinates in **Y**. Comparing the plot of **X** in Figure 2.9 to the plot of **Y** in Figure 2.10 will reveal that the points in **X** form a square, whereas the points in **Y** form a diamond. The diamond configuration in **Y** is the square configuration in **X** after a rotation about the origin.

The stimulus coordinates in **Y** are said to be a rotation of those in **X** because the stimulus coordinates in **Y** are projections of the points in **X** onto axes in the space defined by dimensions I and II of **X**. In general, if stimulus coordinate matrices **X** and **Y** refer to the same stimulus points, then **Y** *is a rotation of* **X** if the coordinates in **Y** are projections of the points onto axes that lie in the space defined by the dimensions of **X**. **Y** *is an orthogonal rotation of* **X** if the angles between pairs of dimensions in **Y** are the same as the angles between corresponding pairs of dimensions in **X**. In the example of Figures 2.9 and 2.10, dimensions I and II of **X** lie at right angles to each other, and dimensions 1 and 2 of **Y** lie at right angles. In other words, an orthogonal rotation preserves the angles between dimensions.

An orthogonal rotation also preserves the Euclidean distances between pairs of points. That is, if one were to compute the Euclidean distance between any pair of points, one would get the same result using the coordinates in matrix **X** or the coordinates in the rotation of it, **Y**. For instance, using the coordinates of **X** in Figure 2.9, the distance between points a and b is $d_{ab} = [(-1.0 - 1.0)^2 + (1.0 - 1.0)^2]^{1/2} = 2.0$. Using the coordinates in **Y**, $d_{ab} = [(0.0 + 1.4)^2 + (1.4 - 0.0)^2]^{1/2} = 2.0$. Whether the locations of points are expressed in the coordinates of **X** or **Y**, the Euclidean distances between locations remain the same.

The act of rotation has a matrix representation. Rotating a set of points corresponds to postmultiplying the matrix representation of those points by a transformation matrix. A transformation matrix is a square matrix with one row and column for each dimension in **X**. If one postmultiplies matrix **X** in Figure 2.9 by the transformation matrix **T** in Figure 2.11, the result is matrix **Y** in Figure 2.10.

Each element in the transformation matrix **T** of Figure 2.11 corresponds to an angle between a dimension in **X** and a dimension in **Y**. More precisely, it equals the cosine of the angle between a dimension in **X** and a dimension in **Y**. The element $t_{11} = .71$ in **T** of Figure 2.11 is the cosine of the angle between the first dimension in **X** and the first dimension in **Y**, $\cos 45° = .71$. The element $t_{12} = -.71$ is the cosine of the angle between dimension 1 in **X** and dimension 2 in **Y**, $\cos 135° = -.71$. In general, each row of **T** corresponds to a dimension of **X** and each column corresponds to a dimension of **Y**. The element t_{rc} is the cosine of the angle between dimension r in **X** and dimension c in **Y**.

T is an orthogonal transformation matrix if $T'T = TT' = I$. You may wish to satisfy yourself that **T** in Figure 2.11 is an orthogonal transformation matrix by computing the products $T'T$ and TT'. If **T** is an orthogonal transformation matrix, then the angles between dimensions in **Y** will be the same as the angles between the corresponding pairs of dimensions in **X**. Furthermore, the Euclidean distances between pairs of points will not be changed by the rotation.

If stimulus coordinate matrix **Y** is a rotation of **X**, **X** and **Y** are representations of exactly the same stimulus configuration. They simply represent different perspectives on the configuration or different frames of reference from which to view the same configuration. There are many perspectives from which to view any MDS solution **X**, each of which corresponds to a different rotation. Just as the important features of a statue can often be seen more vividly from one perspective than another, the important features of a MDS solution can often be seen more vividly in one rotation than another.

What rotation of the configuration should be used in representing the stimulus configuration? This question is the "rotation problem" or "rotation question." Further discussion of the rotation problem must wait until after our discussion of methods for data collection and methods for obtaining the initial coordinate matrix **X**. It would be putting the cart before the horse to discuss methods for finding the best rotation of a coordinate matrix **X** before discussing methods for obtaining **X** in the first place.

$$
\begin{array}{ccccc}
 & Y & = & X & T
\end{array}
$$

$$
\begin{array}{c}
a \\ b \\ c \\ d
\end{array}
\begin{bmatrix}
0.00 & 1.42 \\
1.42 & 0.00 \\
0.00 & -1.42 \\
-1.42 & 0.00
\end{bmatrix}
=
\begin{bmatrix}
-1.00 & 1.00 \\
1.00 & 1.00 \\
1.00 & -1.00 \\
-1.00 & -1.00
\end{bmatrix}
\begin{array}{c}
\text{I} \\ \text{II}
\end{array}
\begin{bmatrix}
.71 & -.71 \\
.71 & .71
\end{bmatrix}
$$

Figure 2.11. Matrix representation for the rotation of four points.

PROBLEMS

1. Compute the indicated matrix sums.

$$A = \begin{bmatrix} 1 & 3 & 5 \\ 2 & 1 & 6 \\ 7 & 9 & 4 \end{bmatrix} \quad B = \begin{bmatrix} 3 & 2 & 1 \\ 2 & 3 & 1 \\ 1 & 2 & 3 \end{bmatrix} \quad C = \begin{bmatrix} 4 & 2 & 0 \\ 5 & 3 & 1 \\ 6 & 4 & 2 \end{bmatrix}$$

a. **S = A + B**
b. **S = C + A**
c. **S = B + C**

2. Using the matrices from Problem 1 above, compute the indicated matrix differences.
a. **D = A − B**
b. **D = C − A**
c. **D = B − C**

3. Using the matrices in Problem 1 above, compute the following.
a. **A′**
b. **B′**
c. **C′**

4. Using the matrices **A**, **B**, and **C** from Problem 1 above, solve the following matrix equations for the unknown matrix **X**.
a. **B′ = A + X**
b. **A = B + X**
c. **B′ = A − X**
d. **B = X − A**

5. Using the matrices in Problem 1, perform the indicated scalar multiplications.
a. **(2)A = P**
b. **(− 1)C = P**
c. **(.2)B = P**

6. Using the matrices from Problem 1, compute the following matrix products.
a. **P = AB**
b. **P = B′C**
c. **P = A′C′**

7. Answer questions a–g below using the following matrices.

$$\mathbf{a} = (1, 2, 3) \qquad \mathbf{b} = \begin{pmatrix} 1 \\ 2 \\ 3 \end{pmatrix} \qquad \mathbf{C} = \begin{bmatrix} 1 & 2 & 3 \\ 4 & 5 & 6 \end{bmatrix}$$

$$\mathbf{D} = \begin{bmatrix} 1 & 2 & 3 \\ 2 & 4 & 5 \\ 3 & 5 & 6 \end{bmatrix} \quad \mathbf{E} = \begin{bmatrix} 1 & 0 & 0 \\ 0 & 1 & 0 \\ 0 & 0 & 1 \end{bmatrix} \quad \mathbf{F} = \begin{bmatrix} 1 & 2 & 3 \\ 4 & 5 & 6 \\ 7 & 8 & 9 \end{bmatrix}$$

$$\mathbf{G} = \begin{bmatrix} 1 & .5 & .7 \\ .5 & 2 & .6 \\ .3 & .4 & 3 \end{bmatrix} \quad \mathbf{H} = \begin{bmatrix} 2 & 0 & 0 \\ 0 & -5 & 0 \\ 0 & 0 & 1 \end{bmatrix}$$

a. Which are column vectors?
b. Which are identity matrices?
c. Which are diagonal matrices?
d. Which are row vectors?
e. Which are square matrices?
f. Which are nonsquare rectangular matrices?
g. Which are symmetric matrices?

8. Demonstrate that matrix **B** below is the inverse of matrix **A**, but that matrix **C** is not the inverse of matrix **A**.

$$\mathbf{A} = \begin{bmatrix} 3 & 1 & 0 \\ 1 & 1 & 0 \\ 0 & 0 & 2 \end{bmatrix} \quad \mathbf{B} = \begin{bmatrix} .5 & -.5 & .0 \\ -.5 & 1.5 & .0 \\ .0 & .0 & .5 \end{bmatrix} \quad \mathbf{C} = \begin{bmatrix} .5 & -.5 & .5 \\ .5 & 1.5 & -.5 \\ 0 & 0 & .5 \end{bmatrix}$$

9. Using matrices **A**, **B**, and **C** in Problem 8, solve the matrix equation **C** = **XA** for the unknown matrix **X**.

10. Demonstrate that matrix **B** in Problem 8 is the inverse of the matrix **DD'**, where

$$\mathbf{D} = \begin{bmatrix} 1 & 1 & 1 \\ 0 & 0 & 1 \\ -1 & 1 & 0 \end{bmatrix}$$

11. Use the right pseudo-inverse of **D** to solve the matrix equation **C** = **XD**, where **C** refers to matrix **C** in Problem 8.

12. Use the left pseudo-inverse of **D'** to solve the matrix equation **C** = **D'X**, where **C** refers to matrix **C** in Problem 8.

13. Use matrix **A** to answer questions a–d below:

$$
\mathbf{A} = \begin{bmatrix} 1 & 5 & 6 & 7 \\ 10 & 2 & 7 & 8 \\ 11 & 12 & 3 & 9 \\ 13 & 14 & 15 & 4 \end{bmatrix}
$$

    a. What are the diagonal elements of **A**?

    b. What are the off-diagonal elements of **A**?

    c. What are the lower triangular elements of **A**?

    d. What are the upper triangular elements of **A**?

14. Use coordinate matrices **X** and **Y** below to answer the following questions.

$$
\mathbf{X} = \begin{array}{c} a \\ b \\ c \\ d \end{array}
\begin{bmatrix} -1.5 & -1.0 \\ -0.5 & 1.0 \\ 0.5 & -1.0 \\ 1.5 & 1.0 \end{bmatrix}
\qquad
\mathbf{Y} = \begin{array}{c} a \\ b \\ c \\ d \end{array}
\begin{bmatrix} -1.0 & -1.5 & -1.0 \\ 1.0 & -0.5 & 0.5 \\ -1.5 & 1.0 & 1.5 \\ 1.5 & 1.0 & -1.0 \end{bmatrix}
$$

with column headers I, II for **X** and I, II, III for **Y**.

    a. Graph coordinate matrix **X**.

    b. Graph coordinate matrix **Y** as a series of two-dimensional plots.

15. What is the matrix form of the two-dimensional plot in Figure 2.12?

16. What is the matrix representation of the three coordinate dimensions displayed in the two-dimensional plots in Figure 2.13?

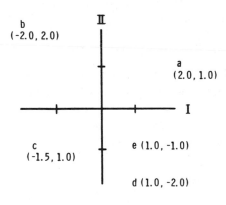

b
(-2.0, 2.0)

a
(2.0, 1.0)

c
(-1.5, 1.0)

e (1.0, -1.0)

d (1.0, -2.0)

Figure 2.12. Two-dimensional plot for Problem 15.

17. Use matrices **X** and **T** to answer the following questions.

$$\mathbf{X} = \begin{bmatrix} -1.0 & -1.0 \\ -0.5 & 0.5 \\ 1.0 & -1.0 \\ -0.5 & -0.5 \end{bmatrix} \quad \mathbf{T} = \begin{bmatrix} .50 & -.87 \\ .87 & .50 \end{bmatrix}$$

a. Use matrix **T** to obtain the rotation of **X**, **Y** = **XT**
b. What is the cosine of the angle between dimension I in **X** and dimension I in **Y**,
c. What is the angle between dimension I in **X** and dimension II in **Y**
d. Show that **T** is an orthogonal transformation matrix.

18. Use vectors $\mathbf{t}_1, \mathbf{t}_2, \mathbf{t}_3$, and matrix **X** to answer the following questions.

$$\mathbf{t}_1 = \begin{pmatrix} .80 \\ .60 \\ .60 \end{pmatrix} \quad \mathbf{t}_2 = \begin{pmatrix} -.60 \\ .80 \\ .60 \end{pmatrix} \quad \mathbf{t}_3 = \begin{pmatrix} -.60 \\ .60 \\ .80 \end{pmatrix}$$

$$\mathbf{X} = \begin{bmatrix} 1.00 & 0.00 & 1.00 \\ 1.00 & 1.00 & 1.00 \\ 1.00 & 0.00 & 0.00 \\ 0.00 & 1.00 & 1.00 \end{bmatrix}$$

a. What is the transformation matrix **T** formed by assembling the column vectors $\mathbf{t}_1, \mathbf{t}_2$, and $\mathbf{t}_3$?
b. Use **T** to obtain the rotation **Y**, **Y** = **XT**.
c. What is the angle between dimension II in **X** and dimension II in **Y**?
d. Is **T** orthogonal? Defend your answer.

19. The coordinates shown in Figure 2.14 are the coordinates of the points along dimensions I and II. Assume the coordinates are accurate to 2 decimal points.

a. What is the angle between dimensions I and 2?
b. What is the angle between dimensions II and 1?
c. Assemble matrix **X**, containing the stimulus coordinates along dimensions I and II.
d. What is the transformation matrix **T** that can be used to map the coordinates in **X** onto dimensions 1 and 2 above?
e. Compute **Y** = **XT**.
f. Is **T** orthogonal? Defend your answer.

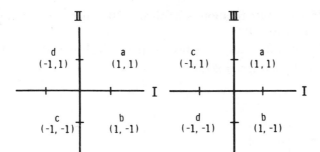

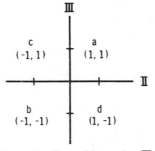

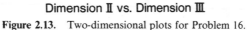

Dimension II vs. Dimension III

Figure 2.13. Two-dimensional plots for Problem 16.

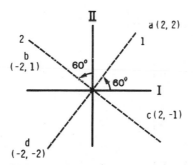

Figure 2.14. Two-dimensional plot for Problem 19.

20. Use a principal components factor program to answer the following questions:

a. What is matrix $\mathbf{B}_{(3 \times 3)}$ such that $\mathbf{BB'}$ equals $\mathbf{C}$?

$$\mathbf{C} = \begin{bmatrix} 3.00 & -1.00 & -1.00 \\ -1.00 & 1.00 & 1.00 \\ -1.00 & 1.00 & 3.00 \end{bmatrix}$$

    b. If a varimax rotation is applied to **B**, what is the rotated coordinate matrix **B***?

    c. What is the transformation matrix **T** such that $\mathbf{B}^* = \mathbf{BT}$?

    d. Verify that $\mathbf{B}^* = \mathbf{BT}$.

Answers

1. a. $\mathbf{S} = \begin{bmatrix} 4 & 5 & 6 \\ 4 & 4 & 7 \\ 8 & 11 & 77 \end{bmatrix}$

    b. $\mathbf{S} = \begin{bmatrix} 5 & 5 & 5 \\ 7 & 4 & 7 \\ 13 & 13 & 6 \end{bmatrix}$

    c. $\mathbf{S} = \begin{bmatrix} 7 & 4 & 1 \\ 7 & 6 & 2 \\ 7 & 6 & 5 \end{bmatrix}$

2. a. $\mathbf{D} = \begin{bmatrix} -2 & 1 & 4 \\ 0 & -2 & 5 \\ 6 & 7 & 1 \end{bmatrix}$

    b. $\mathbf{D} = \begin{bmatrix} 3 & -1 & -5 \\ 3 & 2 & -5 \\ -1 & -5 & -2 \end{bmatrix}$

    c. $\mathbf{D} = \begin{bmatrix} -1 & 0 & 1 \\ -3 & 0 & 0 \\ -5 & -2 & 1 \end{bmatrix}$

3. a. $\mathbf{A}' = \begin{bmatrix} 1 & 2 & 7 \\ 3 & 1 & 9 \\ 5 & 6 & 4 \end{bmatrix}$

    b. $\mathbf{B}' = \begin{bmatrix} 3 & 2 & 1 \\ 2 & 3 & 2 \\ 1 & 1 & 3 \end{bmatrix}$

    c. $\mathbf{C}' = \begin{bmatrix} 4 & 5 & 6 \\ 2 & 3 & 4 \\ 0 & 1 & 2 \end{bmatrix}$

4. a. $\mathbf{X} = \begin{bmatrix} 2 & -1 & -4 \\ 0 & 2 & -4 \\ -6 & -8 & -1 \end{bmatrix}$

    b. $\mathbf{X} = \begin{bmatrix} -2 & 1 & 4 \\ 0 & -2 & 5 \\ 6 & 7 & 1 \end{bmatrix}$

c. $\mathbf{X} = \begin{bmatrix} -2 & 1 & 4 \\ 0 & -2 & 4 \\ 6 & 8 & 1 \end{bmatrix}$

d. $\mathbf{X} = \begin{bmatrix} 4 & 5 & 6 \\ 4 & 4 & 7 \\ 8 & 11 & 7 \end{bmatrix}$

5. a. $\mathbf{P} = \begin{bmatrix} 2 & 6 & 10 \\ 4 & 2 & 12 \\ 14 & 18 & 8 \end{bmatrix}$

b. $\mathbf{P} = \begin{bmatrix} -4 & -2 & 0 \\ -5 & -3 & -1 \\ -6 & -4 & -2 \end{bmatrix}$

c. $\mathbf{P} = \begin{bmatrix} .6 & .4 & .2 \\ .4 & .6 & .2 \\ .2 & .4 & .6 \end{bmatrix}$

6. a. $\mathbf{P} = \begin{bmatrix} 14 & 21 & 19 \\ 14 & 19 & 21 \\ 43 & 49 & 28 \end{bmatrix}$

b. $\mathbf{P} = \begin{bmatrix} 28 & 16 & 4 \\ 35 & 21 & 7 \\ 27 & 17 & 7 \end{bmatrix}$

c. $\mathbf{P} = \begin{bmatrix} 8 & 18 & 28 \\ 14 & 27 & 40 \\ 32 & 47 & 62 \end{bmatrix}$

7. a. **b**
   b. **E**
   c. **E, H**
   d. **a**
   e. **D, E, F, G, H**
   f. **A, B, C**
   g. **D, E, H**

8. a. $\mathbf{AB} = \mathbf{BA} = \begin{bmatrix} 1 & 0 & 0 \\ 0 & 1 & 0 \\ 0 & 0 & 1 \end{bmatrix} = \mathbf{I}$

   b. $\mathbf{AC} = \begin{bmatrix} 2 & 0 & 1 \\ 1 & 1 & 0 \\ 0 & 0 & 1 \end{bmatrix} \neq \mathbf{I}$

or

$$CA = \begin{bmatrix} 1 & 0 & 1 \\ 3 & 2 & -1 \\ 0 & 0 & 1 \end{bmatrix} \neq I$$

9. $X = CA^{-1} = CB = \begin{bmatrix} .50 & -1.00 & .25 \\ -.50 & 2.00 & -.25 \\ .00 & .00 & .25 \end{bmatrix}$

10. $DD' = \begin{bmatrix} 3 & 1 & 0 \\ 1 & 1 & 0 \\ 0 & 0 & 2 \end{bmatrix} = A$ from Problem 8.

$$AB = I = \begin{bmatrix} 1 & 0 & 0 \\ 0 & 1 & 0 \\ 0 & 0 & 1 \end{bmatrix}$$

11. $X = CD'(DD')^{-1} = CD'B = \begin{bmatrix} .0 & .5 & -.5 \\ 1.0 & -1.5 & .5 \\ .0 & .5 & .0 \end{bmatrix}$

$$D'(DD')^{-1} = D'B = \begin{bmatrix} .5 & -.5 & -.5 \\ .5 & -.5 & .5 \\ .0 & 1.0 & .0 \end{bmatrix}$$

12. $X = (DD')^{-1}DC = BDC = \begin{bmatrix} .5 & .5 & .0 \\ -.5 & -.5 & .5 \\ .0 & 1.0 & -.5 \end{bmatrix}$

$$(DD')^{-1}D = BD = \begin{bmatrix} .5 & .5 & .0 \\ -.5 & -.5 & 1.0 \\ -.5 & .5 & .0 \end{bmatrix}$$

13. a. $a_{11} = 1, a_{22} = 2, a_{33} = 3, a_{44} = 4.$

    b. $a_{21} = 10, a_{31} = 11, a_{41} = 13, a_{12} = 5, a_{32} = 12, a_{42} = 14.$
       $a_{13} = 6, a_{23} = 7, a_{43} = 15, a_{14} = 7, a_{24} = 8, a_{34} = 9.$

    c. $a_{21} = 10, a_{31} = 11, a_{41} = 13, a_{32} = 12, a_{42} = 14, a_{43} = 15.$

    d. $a_{12} = 5, a_{13} = 6, a_{14} = 7, a_{23} = 7, a_{24} = 8, a_{34} = 9.$

14. a.

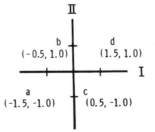

Dimension I vs. Dimension II

Figure 2.15. Two-dimensional plot for Answer 14a.

b.

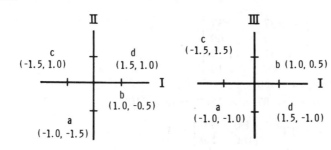

Dimension I vs. Dimension II   Dimension I vs. Dimension III

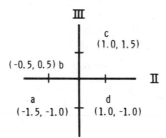

Dimension II vs. Dimension III

Figure 2.16. Two-dimensional plots for Answer 14b.

15.

$$\mathbf{X} = \begin{array}{c} a \\ b \\ c \\ d \\ e \end{array} \begin{bmatrix} 2.0 & 1.0 \\ -2.0 & 2.0 \\ -1.5 & 1.0 \\ 1.0 & -2.0 \\ 1.0 & -1.0 \end{bmatrix} \begin{array}{cc} \mathrm{I} & \mathrm{II} \end{array}$$

16.

$$\mathbf{X} = \begin{array}{c} a \\ b \\ c \\ d \end{array} \begin{bmatrix} 1 & 1 & 1 \\ 1 & -1 & -1 \\ -1 & -1 & 1 \\ -1 & 1 & -1 \end{bmatrix} \begin{array}{ccc} \mathrm{I} & \mathrm{II} & \mathrm{III} \end{array}$$

17. a. $\mathbf{Y} = \begin{bmatrix} -1.37 & .37 \\ .19 & .69 \\ -.37 & -1.37 \\ -.69 & .19 \end{bmatrix}$

     b. cosine $\alpha = .50$

     c. cosine $\alpha = .87$, $\alpha = 150°$ or $\alpha = 210°$

     d. $\mathbf{T'T} = \mathbf{TT'} = \begin{bmatrix} 1.0 & 0.0 \\ 0.0 & 1.0 \end{bmatrix} = \mathbf{I}$

18. a. $\mathbf{T} = \begin{bmatrix} .80 & -.60 & -.60 \\ .60 & .80 & .60 \\ .60 & .60 & .80 \end{bmatrix}$

     b. $\mathbf{Y} = \begin{bmatrix} 1.40 & 0.00 & 0.20 \\ 2.00 & 0.80 & 0.80 \\ 0.80 & -0.60 & -0.60 \\ 1.20 & 1.40 & 1.40 \end{bmatrix}$

     c. cosine $\alpha = .80$, $\alpha = 37°$ or $\alpha = 323°$

     d. No, because $\mathbf{T'T} = \begin{bmatrix} 1.36 & 0.36 & 0.36 \\ 0.36 & 1.36 & 1.32 \\ 0.36 & 1.32 & 1.36 \end{bmatrix} \neq \mathbf{I}$

         or because

         $\mathbf{TT'} = \begin{bmatrix} 1.36 & 0.36 & 0.36 \\ 0.36 & 1.36 & 1.32 \\ 0.36 & 1.32 & 1.36 \end{bmatrix} \neq \mathbf{I}$

19. a. $\alpha = 150°$

     b. $\alpha = 330°$

     c.

	I	II
a	2.00	2.00
b	-2.00	1.00
c	2.00	-1.00
d	-2.00	-2.00

$\mathbf{X} =$

     d.

	1	2
I	.50	-.87
II	.87	.50

$\mathbf{T} =$

e.

$$
\begin{array}{c c}
 & 1 \qquad\quad 2 \\
\begin{array}{c} a \\ b \\ c \\ d \end{array}
\left[
\begin{array}{rr}
2.74 & -0.74 \\
-0.13 & 2.24 \\
0.13 & -2.24 \\
-2.74 & 0.74
\end{array}
\right]
\end{array}
$$

f.   Yes, $\mathbf{T'T = TT'} = \begin{bmatrix} 1 & 0 \\ 0 & 1 \end{bmatrix} = \mathbf{I}$

20.   a. $\mathbf{B} = \begin{bmatrix} -1.40 & 1.00 & 0.17 \\ 0.79 & 0.00 & 0.62 \\ 1.40 & 1.00 & -0.17 \end{bmatrix}$

b. $\mathbf{B^*} = \begin{bmatrix} -0.24 & 1.65 & -0.46 \\ 0.31 & -0.31 & 0.90 \\ 1.65 & -0.24 & 0.46 \end{bmatrix}$

c. $\mathbf{T} = \begin{bmatrix} 0.63 & -0.63 & 0.44 \\ 0.71 & 0.71 & 0.00 \\ -0.31 & 0.31 & 0.90 \end{bmatrix}$

d. $\mathbf{BT = B^*} = \begin{bmatrix} -0.24 & 1.65 & -0.46 \\ 0.31 & -0.31 & 0.90 \\ 1.65 & -0.24 & 0.46 \end{bmatrix}$

CHAPTER 3

Proximity Measures

In most MDS studies, the data matrix is a square symmetric proximity matrix with one row and one column for each stimulus. The element δ_{ij} in row i column j of the proximity matrix is a measure of the proximity between stimuli i and j. Unless otherwise specified, the reader should assume that δ_{ij} is a measure of dissimilarity, rather than similarity, on the stimulus pair (i, j). The estimates of the stimulus coordinates x_{ik} and x_{jk} are then obtained from the data in the proximity matrix. But how does one obtain a measure of proximity on a pair of stimuli, and how does one design a study to collect such measurements? These are the questions addressed in this chapter. Specifically, this chapter explains four classes of proximity measures: direct dissimilarity judgments, conditional probabilities, joint probabilities, and indices of profile dissimilarity. Since most MDS studies employ direct dissimilarity judgments as measures of dissimilarity, the discussion will begin by outlining issues that must be addressed in designing a study to collect such judgments.

DIRECT DISSIMILARITY JUDGMENTS

In designing a study to collect dissimilarity judgments about pairs of stimuli, three issues must be considered: the sampling of stimuli and subjects, the choice of a judgment task, and the design of the instrument for presenting the task to subjects. This section considers each of these issues in turn.

The first step in obtaining direct dissimilarity judgments is to define as precisely as possible the population of people whose judgments are to be sampled and the population of stimuli that is to be sampled. Once the population of stimuli has been defined, researchers should attempt to draw a random sample or a stratified random sample of stimuli. If some of the stimuli in the population would be unfamiliar to many subjects, then the user might be forced to narrow the sampled population of stimuli to those that are familiar. Subjects can give informed judgments only about stimuli with which they are well acquainted.

In sampling stimuli, existing taxonomies can be very helpful in stratifying the sample and ensuring that the resultant sample is representative of the stimulus population. For example, the classification system employed by the *United States Employment Service Dictionary of Occupational Titles* (1977) can be used in selecting occupations for a study of occupational perceptions. If the stimuli were educational objectives in a particular subject field, one might stratify on the basis of topic areas corresponding to major chapter headings in textbooks on the subject. As a rule, the sample should contain five or more stimuli for each dimension expected to emerge in the resultant solution.

With the exception of Coxon and Jones (1974), little attention has been given to the importance of stimulus sampling. One suspects that the stimulus selection process can have a major influence on the obtained solution. For instance, imagine a study of occupations. If only white collar occupations were included in the sample, one would not expect a dimension to emerge that reflected the safety associated with each occupation, because most white collar jobs are safe. On the other hand, if the sample also included blue collar occupations with more risk, such as coal miner and iron worker, then a dimension of occupational safety might emerge, because the jobs in this sample vary considerably in safety.

The definition of the subject population and the sampling from that population are also important steps in any MDS study. If some segments of the population are unfamiliar with the type of stimulus being researched, the investigator may be forced to limit the population to those who can give informed judgments. Stratification of the population by variables such as age, sex, or level of education can be useful means of ensuring a representative sample.

As a rule of thumb, when the dissimilarity of an object pair is estimated by averaging the judgments of several people, the number of judgments M averaged for each pair should be at least $M = 40K^*/(I - 1)$, where I is the number of stimuli and K^* is the anticipated number of dimensions. If one considers each judgment about a pair to be a data point, then this rule ensures that there will be 20 data points for each estimated parameter x_{jk}, if the number of dimensions equals the anticipated number.

Judgment Task

Having selected a sample of stimuli and a sample of subjects, the user must then decide which type of dissimilarity judgment task to require of the subjects. There are several possibilities suggested in the literature. Four such tasks are described here: magnitude estimation, category rating, graphic rating, and category sorting.

In Stevens' (1971) *magnitude estimation* task, one stimulus pair is chosen as a standard. Each of the remaining pairs, called the judged stimulus pairs, are compared to the standard. The subject is to assign a number to each judged stimulus pair that indicates how dissimilar the judged pair is relative to the standard pair. For instance, if the subject thought a judged pair was twice as dissimilar as the standard pair, then the subject would assign a "2" to the judged pair. Or if the subject thought the judged pair were two thirds as dissimilar as the standard pair, then the subject would assign the number "2/3" to the judged pair.

For any judged pair, the estimated dissimilarity is taken to be the geometric mean (or less frequently the median) of the numbers assigned it. The standard pair should be neither extremely high nor extremely low in dissimilarity as compared to the other stimulus pairs. Although the magnitude estimation task can be difficult to communicate to unsophisticated subjects, it has generally worked quite well in psychophysics and other areas (Bass et al., 1974).

The *category rating* technique is the most common method of obtaining direct dissimilarity judgments. Here the subject is presented a stimulus pair of the following form:

	Highly Similar			√			Highly Dissimilar
Harvard : Yale	—	—	—	—	—	—	—
	(0) (1) (2) (3) (4) (5) (6) (7)						

The subject's task is to indicate how similar or dissimilar she or he thinks the two stimuli are by checking the appropriate category along the rating scale. Often a scale containing six to nine categories will work quite well.

Typically, each category is assigned an integer, and a subject's response is given a score corresponding to the integer associated with the category checked. In the example above, the categories might be assigned the integers shown in parentheses below the rating scale. The response shown in that example would receive a score of "4." For a given pair, its dissimilarity is taken to be the arithmetic mean of the scores assigned to it by all subjects.

The *graphic rating* scale method is a slight variation of the category rating method. In this approach, the subject is presented something of the form:

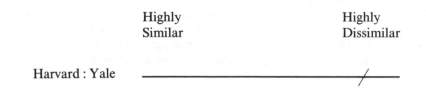

| Highly | Highly |
| Similar | Dissimilar |

Harvard : Yale

The subject is to place a hash mark across the rating scale like the one shown above so that the distance from the leftmost edge of the scale to the hash mark corresponds to the dissimilarity between the two stimuli. In the example above, the distance is 6 mm. If responses for several subjects are to be combined, the arithmetic mean (or less frequently the median) can be used as the measure of dissimilarity for a stimulus pair. Having to measure each subject's responses with a ruler is highly inconvenient.

A second variation of the category rating technique is the *category sorting* method. In this procedure, each pair of stimuli is written on a separate card. The subject places each pair into one of several ordered categories. The subject is to arrange the stimulus pairs that are highly similar in the lowest category. The highest category contains pairs that are highly dissimilar. To prevent subjects from placing too many pairs in any one pile and hence not discriminating in their judgments, the researcher may specify how many categories the subject is to use (often six to nine categories) and what proportion of the stimulus pairs are to be placed in each category.

Category sorting judgments are scored like category rating data. Each category is assigned an integer, and a subject's judgment is given a score corresponding to the category in which the pair was placed. For a given pair, its dissimilarity is taken to be the arithmetic mean of the scores assigned to it.

To sum up, in obtaining direct similarity judgments, the researcher can choose from among at least four judgment tasks: magnitude estimation, category rating, graphic rating, and category sorting. One can choose among the methods by considering the practical problems each poses and by considering the subject's ability and willingness to perform the various tasks. A small pilot study is often needed to assess these factors.

Instrument Design

Having decided on the judgment task, the researcher must then decide how to present the task to subjects. The stimulus pairs to be judged must be arranged in some logical fashion. The subjects must receive some directions. Further, the researcher must decide whether to use a complete design, in which each subject judges every possible stimulus pair, or whether to use an incomplete design, in which each subject judges only one subset of the stimulus pairs. This section reviews psychological research with implications for these instrument design issues: the arrangement of stimulus pairs, the preparation of directions, and the use of incomplete designs.

Arrangement of Stimulus Pairs

Psychological research suggests that there are two phenomena that can influence subjects' judgments and that need to be considered in choosing a logical arrangement of the stimulus pairs. The order in which two stimuli in a pair are presented (i.e., "Harvard : Yale" versus "Yale : Harvard") does clearly influence subjects' judgments about the similarity of these two stimuli (Tversky, 1977; Zinnes and Wolff, 1977). This influence will be called the *space effect*. Space effects are said to be balanced for a given stimulus if that stimulus appears as the first member in one half of the pairs in which it appears, and it is the second member in one half of the pairs in which it appears. The stimulus pairs should be presented so that space effects are balanced for every stimulus to be judged.

Time effects are those effects associated with the ordering of the stimulus pairs in the list of pairs to be judged. Time effects are said to be balanced for a given stimulus if the pairs in which that stimulus appears are equally spaced throughout the list. Ideally, time effects will be balanced for every stimulus.

Ross (1934) describes a method for deriving an ordering and arrangement of the pairs so that both time and space effects are balanced. This is called a *Ross ordering*. Cohen and Davison (1973) have written a computer program that uses Ross' method to determine the optimal ordering and arrangement of stimulus pairs. The program will print a questionnaire that presents all possible pairs in the optimal order and asks for a category rating of each one. Users who want the details of Ross' method must consult his original paper.

Figure 3.1 shows a Ross ordering for all possible pairs of seven colleges: Harvard, Yale, Antioch College, the University of California, the University of Michigan, the Massachusetts Institute of Technology, and the Georgia Institute of Technology. Appearances of the stimulus "Harvard" have been circled. Notice how the appearances of "Harvard" are regularly spaced throughout the 21 pairs. Note also that "Harvard" appears as the left member of exactly four pairs in which it appears, and it appears as the right member in exactly the same number of pairs. Time and space effects are optimally balanced.

An alternative to the Ross ordering is a *random ordering*. Here the stimulus pairs are presented in a random order. For each pair, the user decides which of the two stimuli will appear first by some random process, such as a coin flip. In this procedure, deciding the arrangement of stimuli involves two steps, randomly ordering the pairs and randomly selecting the first member of each pair. Randomly arranging the pairs does not guarantee that time and space effects are balanced.

A third method, the *rotating standard* method, is very easy to derive. If there are I stimuli, numbered $1, \ldots i, \ldots I$, then the arrangement of pairs is divided into $(I - 1)$ sections. In the ith section, stimulus i serves as a standard. The subject's task in the ith section is to judge the similarity between the standard and each of the stimuli numbered $(i + 1)$ to I.

	Highly Similar						Highly Dissimilar
(Harvard): Yale	—	—	—	—	—	—	—
Georgia T. : Antioch	—	—	—	—	—	—	—
M. I. T. : California	—	—	—	—	—	—	—
Michigan : (Harvard)	—	—	—	—	—	—	—
Antioch : Yale	—	—	—	—	—	—	—
California : Georgia T.	—	—	—	—	—	—	—
Michigan : M. I. T.	—	—	—	—	—	—	—
(Harvard): Antioch	—	—	—	—	—	—	—
Yale · California	—	—	—	—	—	—	—
Georgia T. : Michigan	—	—	—	—	—	—	—
M. I. T. : (Harvard)	—	—	—	—	—	—	—
California : Antioch	—	—	—	—	—	—	—
Michigan : Yale	—	—	—	—	—	—	—
M. I. T. : Georgia T.	—	—	—	—	—	—	—
(Harvard): California	—	—	—	—	—	—	—
Antioch : Michigan	—	—	—	—	—	—	—
Yale : M. I. T.	—	—	—	—	—	—	—
Georgia T. : (Harvard)	—	—	—	—	—	—	—
California : Michigan	—	—	—	—	—	—	—
Antioch : M. I. T.	—	—	—	—	—	—	—
Yale : Georgia T.	—	—	—	—	—	—	—

Figure 3.1. Ross ordering of stimulus pairs.

Figure 3.2 shows two pages from a questionnaire that employs the rotating standard method. Normally, the section numbers would not appear in the questionnaire. They are included here only to aid the discussion. The stimuli are numbered as shown at the top of the figure. Notice that in the first section, stimulus 1, Harvard is compared to each of the remaining six stimuli. In Section II, the second stimulus, Yale, is compared to all but the first stimulus. There is no need to compare Yale to the first stimulus since this comparison was made in Section I. In Section III, the third stimulus, Antioch College, is compared to stimuli 4 through 7. There is no need to compare Antioch to either of the first two stimuli, because these comparisons were included in Sections I and II. With this method, neither time nor space effects are balanced.

Since a Ross arrangement balances time and space effects, it is the best design. The random arrangement is a close second. Unless the user knows

1. Harvard   5. University of Michigan
2. Yale   6. Massachusetts Institute of Technology
3. Antioch College   7. Georgia Institute of Technology
4. University of California

	Section I	Page 1
Harvard:	Highly Similar	Highly Dissimilar
Yale	—— —— —— —— —— ——	
Antioch	—— —— —— —— —— ——	
U. of Calif.	—— —— —— —— —— ——	
U. of Mich.	—— —— —— —— —— ——	
M.I.T.	—— —— —— —— —— ——	
Georgia Tech.	—— —— —— —— —— ——	

	Section II	
Yale:	Highly Similar	Highly Dissimilar
Antioch	—— —— —— —— —— ——	
U. of Calif.	—— —— —— —— —— ——	
U. of Mich.	—— —— —— —— —— ——	
M.I.T.	—— —— —— —— —— ——	
Georgia Tech.	—— —— —— —— —— ——	

Figure 3.2. Rotating standard arrangement of pairs.

Section III						Page 2
Antioch: Highly Similar						Highly Dissimilar
U. of Calif.	___	___	___	___	___	___
U. of Mich.	___	___	___	___	___	___
M.I.T.	___	___	___	___	___	___
Georgia Tech.	___	___	___	___	___	___

Section IV						
U. of Calif: Highly Similar						Highly Dissimilar
U. of Mich.	___	___	___	___	___	___
M.I.T.	___	___	___	___	___	___
Georgia Tech.	___	___	___	___	___	___

Section V						
U. of Mich: Highly Similar						Highly Dissimilar
M.I.T.	___	___	___	___	___	___
Georgia Tech.	___	___	___	___	___	___

Section VI						
M.I.T.: Highly Similar						Highly Dissimilar
Georgia Tech.	___	___	___	___	___	___

Figure 3.2. (*Continued*)

that time and space effects will be minimal, the rotating standard method above has only expediency to recommend it.

Directions

Psychological research suggests that a subject's judgments can change depending on what he or she expects to be included in the stimulus set. The directions can be used to standardize this expectation for each subject by asking subjects to read through a complete list of the stimuli after reading the directions, but before making any judgments. If reading through a complete list is too inconvenient, then subjects can read through a representative list to establish a context for their judgments.

The directions can constrain what the user considers in making judgments. Subjects can be asked to disregard irrelevant cues, such as the length of stimulus words. Some dimensions of stimulus variation might be irrelevant to the researchers' purposes. Subjects might be asked to judge colleges under the assumption that they would be admitted to each college and that they would receive full financial aid to each one. The assumption embodied in the instructions effectively tells subjects to ignore two possible dimensions along which the schools differ: the difficulty of getting in and the difficulty of raising the tuition. A researcher may wish to specify in some way the dimensions that should be considered. For instance, subjects judging colleges might be asked to consider only those college characteristics that would influence their decision to attend one college rather than another.

Incomplete Designs

As the number of stimuli I increases, the number of possible pairs, $\frac{1}{2}I(I-1)$, increases rapidly. With 10 stimuli, the number of pairs is 45. Doubling the number of stimuli to 20 increases the number of pairs by almost a factor of 4 to 190 pairs. Often the number of stimuli is so large that no one subject can be expected to judge them all. In such cases, the researcher must employ an incomplete design in which each pair of stimuli is judged by some, but not all, subjects. In an incomplete design, the pairs are divided into subsets, and each subject judges the pairs in only one subest. An equal number of subjects judge each subset.

How can one divide the pairs into subsets? The work of MacCallum (1979) and Spence and Domoney (1974) suggests that randomly dividing the possible pairs into subsets works as well as anything. Each pair should appear in an equal number of subsets. If possible, each stimulus should appear in at least one pair of every subset. Partially overlapping subsets work well, but are not necessary. The estimates of the stimulus coordinates should be adequate as long as each pair is judged by at least $M = 40K^*/(I-1)$ people (MacCallum, 1979; Spence and Domoney, 1974).

Summary

Anyone who wishes to use dissimilarity judgments in an MDS study must consider the following issues in the design of their research. First, one must define the population of stimuli and the population of subjects and devise a plan for adequately sampling both. Second, a judgment task must be selected. Magnitude estimation, category rating, graphic rating, and category sorting methods all work well. Third, the researcher must devise an instrument for presenting the task to subjects. In devising such an instrument, the researcher should arrange the stimulus pairs so that time and space effects are as nearly balanced as possible. Directions should standardize subjects' expectations about the stimuli to be judged. If necessary, the directions should instruct the subjects to ignore irrelevant features of the stimuli. Should the number of stimuli be large, the researcher will need to devise an incomplete design in which each subject judges only a small subset of the stimulus pairs.

CONDITIONAL AND JOINT PROBABILITIES

Various kinds of conditional and joint probability matrices have been used as measures of stimulus similarity. In studies that employ conditional probabilities, the probability that stimulus (or event) j occurs given stimulus (or event) i has been taken to be a measure of the similarity between stimuli (or events) i and j. In studies that employ joint probabilities, the probability that stimuli (or events) i and j occur together has been taken as a measure of the similarity between stimuli (or events) i and j. Readers should note that such probabilities are treated as measures of similarity, not dissimilarity. The following section describes several kinds of studies that generate probability matrices suitable for MDS analysis. It begins with a description of studies that generate conditional probabilities.

Conditional Probabilities

Recognition studies and transition studies, both defined below, can be used to generate conditional probability matrices in MDS research. The purpose of recognition studies is to understand what kinds of errors people make in identifying or classifying objects. MDS has been used to study the dimensions of similarity that account for the confusion of one stimulus with another and hence to errors of identification. A recognition study contains a large number of trials. On each trial, the experimenter presents a stimulus visually or orally and asks the subject to label it. For each pair (i, j), the experimenter can then compute the proportion of trials in which the researcher presented stimulus i and the subject responded with label j. The conditional probability, the probability that label j was the response given that i was the presented stimulus, can be taken as a measure of the similarity between stimulus i and stimulus j. An error occurs when the label j does not match the stimulus i. These errors are the focus of a recognition study.

In the probability matrix derived from a recognition experiment, the rows correspond to stimuli. The columns correspond to responses. The entry in row i column j of the matrix p_{ij} is the proportion of experimental trials in which response j occurred given that stimulus i was the presented stimulus.

Diagonal entries in the matrix correspond to trials in which the correct response was given. The off-diagonal elements correspond to trials in which an error was made; that is, trials for which $i \neq j$, and hence the stimulus and response did not match. Only the off-diagonal elements are analyzed.

It is assumed in such an analysis that the more similar two stimuli are, the more likely they are to be confused. Consequently, p_{ij}, the probability that response j occurred given that stimulus i was presented, can be taken as a measure of the similarity between i and j. In general, such matrices will not be symmetric. That is, $p_{ij} \neq p_{ji}$. The easiest way to make a symmetric proximity matrix is to create a new measure of similarity by taking the sum of the two values p_{ij} and p_{ji}: $\delta_{ji} = p_{ij} + p_{ji}$.

Figure 3.3 shows what such a matrix might look like. These are hypothetical data from an experiment in which children were shown a letter in written form and asked to name it. Rows correspond to the presented letters, and columns represent the names given in response. Each element in **P** is the proportion of times the row letter was presented and the column letter was named. For instance, the element in row 4 column 3 indicates that in 40% of the trials in which stimulus E was presented, F was named as the response. Matrix Δ in Figure 3.3 is a similarity matrix derived from the confusion matrix **P**. Each element of Δ, δ_{ij}, was computed as follows:
$\delta_{ij} = \delta_{ji} = p_{ij} + p_{ji}$.

Transition probability matrices are another form of conditional probability matrix that can be analyzed in MDS. In such matrices, the rows correspond to states at some initial time. The column elements correspond

		Response			
		C	G	F	E
	C	.60	.40	.00	.00
P = Stimulus	G	.25	.75	.00	.00
	F	.00	.00	.50	.50
	E	.00	.00	.40	.60

		C	G	F	E
	C	--	.65	.00	.00
Δ =	G	.65	--	.00	.00
	F	.00	.00	--	.90
	E	.00	.00	.90	--

Figure 3.3. Hypothetical confusion matrix **P** and a similarity matrix Δ derived from it.

to states at some terminal time. Each element of the matrix p_{ij} designates the proportion of observations in state i at the initial time that appeared in state j at the terminal time. The presumption here is that the more similar two states, the more likely an observation is to move between them. The purpose of the MDS would be to recover the dimensions of similarity associated with the transitions.

Transition matrices are not symmetric. Again, the easiest way to form a symmetric proximity matrix is to create a new matrix with elements of the form $\delta_{ij} = \delta_{ji} = p_{ij} + p_{ji}$.

Figure 3.4 shows a hypothetical transition matrix and the similarity matrix derived from it. The row states correspond to college majors declared by freshmen, and the column states are majors of those same people at time of graduation. Each element p_{ij} is the proportion of people in major i as a freshman who later declared major j. For instance, the element in row 2 column 4 indicates that 40% of the people in biology as freshmen graduated with a major in education. Diagonal elements in both **P** and Δ would be ignored in the analysis. Δ is the matrix of similarities formed of entries $\delta_{ij} = \delta_{ji} = p_{ij} + p_{ji}$.

Studies of social interaction can also provide conditional probability matrices. The rows and columns represent people or social organizations. Element p_{ij} in the conditional interaction matrix is the proportion of interactions initiated by person i (or organization i) with person (or organization) j. Typically, such a matrix will be asymmetric. Again, the simplest way to form a symmetric proximity matrix Δ would be to create elements

Graduation Major

		PM	Bi	Bu	E
P =	Pre-Med. (PM)	.30	.20	.40	.10
	Biology (Bi)	.20	.30	.10	.40
	Business (Bu)	.05	.10	.70	.15
	Education (E)	.02	.08	.30	.60

(Freshman Major)

		PM	Bi	Bu	E
Δ =	PM	--	.40	.45	.12
	Bi	.40	--	.20	.48
	Bu	.45	.20	--	.45
	E	.12	.48	.45	--

Figure 3.4. Transition matrix **P** and the similarity matrix Δ derived from it.

$\delta_{ij} = p_{ij} + p_{ji}$. The assumption in such a study is that stimulus i is more likely to initiate interactions with stimuli that are similar to itself. Therefore, p_{ij} and δ_{ij} reflect the similarity between interacting parties i and j.

Other kinds of conditional probability matrices might also be used to form similarity matrices for input into MDS if those conditional probabilities can be construed as reflecting the degree of similarity between objects. Since conditional probability matrices are seldom if ever symmetric, the researcher must devise some method for deriving a symmetric matrix of proximities from the asymmetric, conditional probability matrix.

In deriving a symmetric matrix from asymmetric conditional probabilities, however, important information can be lost. The asymmetries may arise because there is something fundamentally asymmetric about the relationship between the two objects. In forming the symmetric matrix, the researcher may lose the information contained in the probabilities about the nonreciprocal nature of the object relationships, and hence the resulting MDS solution would not reflect those asymmetries. As an example, matrix **P** in Figure 3.4 shows that the probability of shifting from medicine to business is .40, but the probability of going from business to medicine is much smaller, .05. This asymmetry is not reflected in Δ and would not be reflected in the distance between medicine and business in a MDS of the four majors. If a symmetric similarity matrix is derived from conditional probabilities, the resulting MDS can reveal many important stimulus features, but not those features associated with the asymmetries.

Joint Probabilities

Joint probabilities of various kinds can also be indicators of the similarity between pairs of objects. Since joint probability matrices are by definition symmetric, they always satisfy at least one requirement of a MDS data matrix.

Just as studies of social interaction patterns can be used to derive asymmetric, conditional probability matrices, they can also be used to derive symmetric, joint probability matrices. The rows and columns in a joint interaction matrix represent interacting parties. Element p_{ij} in the joint interaction matrix is the proportion of interactions that involved parties i and j. Since the matrix is symmetric, it can be used directly as a matrix of similarities in a MDS analysis. The assumption is that if parties i and j are highly similar, they are more likely to interact. Such joint interaction matrices represent only one possible type of joint probability matrix suitable for a MDS analysis.

A study (Adkins, 1973) by the American Psychological Association (APA) is another example of a joint probability matrix suitable for MDS.

Although to my knowledge the data were not submitted to a MDS analysis, the APA once counted up the number of its members who held simultaneous membership in each pair of its divisions. The study resulted in a large joint probability matrix **P** with one element for each pair of divisions. An element p_{ij} represented the proportion of members who held membership simultaneously in divisions i and j. This joint probability matrix could readily have been submitted to a MDS analysis to yield a dimensional representation of the APA division structure. Such a matrix is called a *co-occurrence matrix* because each cell corresponds to the co-occurrence of two events, membership of the same person in two divisions.

The joint probabilities in the APA study were computed from the association's records. Co-occurrence matrices can be derived in other ways, however. Rosenberg and his coworkers (1968) have derived a joint probability matrix for trait adjectives by asking subjects to think of several acquaintances. Then subjects are given a list of trait names. Subjects must assign each trait to the person on their list of acquaintances whom it best describes. A similarity measure can be obtained for traits i and j by counting up the total number (or proportion) of acquaintances who are assigned both traits. For instance, if subjects had named a total of 100 acquaintances, 47 of whom were said to be both shrewd and intelligent, then the similarity between traits shrewd and intelligent could be the number 47 or the corresponding proportion .47.

Rosenberg's method involves having subjects sort traits into categories where each category corresponds to one of the subjects' acquaintances. Category sorting can be applied in any stimulus domain. That is, one can have subjects sort a set of stimuli into nominal categories so that the stimuli in any category are all like each other in some respects and different from the stimuli in all other categories in those same respects. Subjects may be left free to choose how many categories they will use, or the experimenter may wish to restrict the number. Often 5 to 10 categories per subject work well. As in the case of direct similarity judgments, directions should give subjects the response set desired by the experimenter.

For any pair of stimuli, the similarity measure becomes the number (or proportion) of subjects who put the two stimuli in the same category. Because the categorization task requires the subject to make judgments about single stimuli, not pairs of stimuli, it can be used as a basis for scaling large numbers (up to 200) of stimuli without overtaxing subjects.

Rosenberg's sorting task, here called the *stimulus sorting task*, differs in two major respects from the category sorting task described in the section on direct similarity judgments. First, in the category sorting method, the subject must assign pairs of stimuli, not single stimuli, to categories. Second, in the category sorting method, the categories are ordered from highest to lowest in terms of similarity. In the stimulus sorting method, the categories are purely nominal. Although category and stimulus sorting are superficially quite similar in that both involve sorting, they are, in fact, quite different and should not be confused. Davison (1972) and Rosenberg and Kim (1975) discuss methodological issues in stimulus sorting.

In summary then, various kinds of probability matrices provide an alternative to direct dissimilarity judgments in MDS studies. Conditional probability matrices are one such alternative, including matrices derived from recognition or transition studies. Because such conditional probability matrices are asymmetric, the user must derive a symmetric proximity matrix from the conditional probability matrix before the MDS analysis. Some information about the asymmetric relationship between objects may be lost in the process. Joint probability matrices offer another alternative to direct similarity judgments. Rosenberg's stimulus sorting technique is one method of obtaining joint probabilities in MDS studies. The stimulus sorting method can be used to scale a large number of stimuli without overtaxing subjects.

PROFILE DISSIMILARITY MEASURES

Once a profile of scores has been obtained on a set of objects, these scores can be used to compute measures of profile dissimilarity. A profile is simply a set of quantitative observations on an object. If the object were a person, the set of quantitative observations might consist of his or her scores on the subscales of a test battery. Or if the objects were cities, the profile for each might consist of temperatures recorded at 10 different times throughout the year.

Table 3.1 shows the percentage of workers who were unemployed in five different industries during five different years. Each row of the table

Table 3.1. **Percentages of Workers Unemployed in Five Labor Force Segments During Five Different Years.**

Occupation	Year				
	1	2	3	4	5
Private wage/salary workers	5.7	4.3	4.8	4.8	5.7
Mining	9.7	5.4	3.1	2.9	2.9
Manufacturing	6.2	4.0	5.6	4.3	5.7
Construction	13.5	10.1	9.7	8.8	10.6
Finance, insurance, real estate	2.4	2.3	2.8	2.7	3.1

constitutes a profile of scores on the corresponding industry. Throughout this section it will be assumed that the score profiles for the objects are arrayed in a matrix, such as that in Table 3.1, in which rows correspond to objects and columns correspond to observations. Thus if Matrix V is the matrix containing the profiles, then v_{ik} refers to the kth observation on object i.

Numerous measures of profile similarity have been proposed (Arabie and Boorman, 1973; Rosenberg and Jones, 1972; Sneath and Sokal, 1973), but the most common one is the distance measure:

$$\delta_{ij} = \left[\sum_k (v_{ik} - v_{jk})^2 \right]^{1/2}. \tag{3.1}$$

In some cases, the dissimilarity is defined as the square of this quantity:

$$\delta_{ij}^2 = \sum_k (v_{ik} - v_{jk})^2. \tag{3.2}$$

In these equations, v_{ik} and v_{jk} represent the kth observations on objects i and j in their respective profiles. The profile dissimilarity measure for objects i and j is δ_{ij} (or δ_{ij}^2).

In Eq. (3.1), the sum is obtained by adding squared differences between corresponding elements in rows i and j of the data matrix V. For instance, the measure of dissimilarity for the first two objects (private wage and mining) in Table 3.1 would be

$$\delta_{ij} = \left[\sum_k (v_{1k} - v_{2k})^2 \right]^{1/2}$$

$$= \left[(5.7 - 9.7)^2 + (4.3 - 5.4)^2 + (4.8 - 3.1)^2 \right. \tag{3.3}$$

$$\left. + (4.8 - 2.9)^2 + (5.7 - 2.9)^2 \right]^{1/2}$$

$$= 5.62.$$

To obtain a full dissimilarities matrix, one computes the quantity δ_{ij} for each pair of objects.

Researchers have applied the distance measure of profile similarity in different ways. Sometimes the elements of V are transformed to column-standardized form before the dissimilarity measures are computed. A data matrix is *column-standardized* if the mean of the elements in each column equals 0.0 and the variance of the elements in each column equals 1.00. If the researcher believes that column means and variances are substantively unimportant, then a new matrix $\mathbf{Z}$ would be created in which each element of $\mathbf{Z}$ would be of the form $z_{ik} = (1/s_k)(v_{ik} - v_{.k})$. Here $v_{.k}$ and s_k are the mean and standard deviation of elements in column k. The dissimilarities would then be computed over the elements in the column standardized matrix $\mathbf{Z}$ rather than $\mathbf{V}$. The means and variances of subjective rating scales and of many psychological tests are often considered arbitrary. If the profiles consisted of such variables, then column standardization of the data matrix would be considered appropriate.

In psychological research, the data are sometimes row-centered or row-standardized. A data matrix is *row-centered* if the mean of the elements in each row equals 0.00. It is said to be *row-standardized* if the mean of the elements in each row equals 0.00 and the variance of the elements in each row equals 1.00. The rationale for doing so stems from work by Cronbach (1955). Cronbach distinguished three aspects of a profile: level, scatter, and shape. *Level* is simply the mean of the scores in a profile $v_{i.}$. *Scatter* is the spread of scores in a profile about their mean. The standard deviation of scores in a profile s_i can be used to quantify its scatter. Roughly speaking, *shape* is the rank order of the scores in a profile.

The scores in a profile can be row-centered by creating a matrix $\tilde{\mathbf{V}}$ with elements $\tilde{v}_{ik} = v_{ik} - v_{i.}$; that is, by subtracting the row mean from every element of $\mathbf{V}$. $\mathbf{V}$ can be row-standardized by creating a matrix $\mathbf{Z}$ with elements $z_{ik} = (1/s_i)(v_{ik} - v_{i.})$, where $v_{i.}$ and s_i are the mean and standard deviation of elements in profile i.

If the dissimilarities δ_{ij} are computed from the original matrix $\mathbf{V}$, then those dissimilarities will reflect the level, shape, and scatter similarities of profiles i and j. If, however, the row-centered data matrix $\tilde{\mathbf{V}}$ is used, the dissimilarities will reflect only the scatter and shape of the profiles. Any differences in level between profiles will not be expressed by δ_{ij}. If the row-standardized matrix $\mathbf{Z}$ is employed, then δ_{ij} will reflect only differences in shape. Any differences in level or scatter would not be expressed in δ_{ij}. Whether $\mathbf{V}$ should be row-centered or row-standardized depends entirely on which aspects of the profiles—level, shape, and scatter—are important to the researcher.

When δ_{ij} is computed on a row-standardized matrix $\mathbf{Z}$, then δ_{ij}^2 is within a linear transformation of r_{ij}, the correlation between the elements in rows i and j of the original data matrix $\mathbf{V}$. More precisely, $\delta_{ij}^2 = 2K - 2Kr_{ij}$. This means that many MDS procedures will yield the same result no matter whether one inputs a similarity matrix $\mathbf{R}$ with elements $(r_{ij})^{1/2}$ or a dissimilarity matrix Δ composed of elements δ_{ij} computed from the row standardized profiles in $\mathbf{Z}$.

The profile dissimilarity measure in Eq. (3.1) can be used with virtually any kind of quantitative profile data. In order to develop a profile of scores for each stimulus, however, the researcher must know the important attributes of the stimuli. Further, the researcher must be able to develop a measure of each important attribute so that the measure can be included in the profile. On the other hand, in order to use either direct dissimilarity judgments or probability measures of proximity, the researcher need not be able to define the important attributes or develop a measure of each. Hence direct dissimilarity judgments and probability measures may be preferable to profile dissimilarity measures when the important stimulus attributes are poorly understood or when it is difficult to obtain independent measures of each separate attribute (Shepard, 1980).[†]

SUMMARY

A great variety of experimental methods can be used to collect data for an MDS study. Whichever method is chosen, however, the user must first select a sample of stimuli and a set of observations on those stimuli. It is best to have three or more stimuli for each dimension expected to emerge in the analysis.

The most common experimental method involves having subjects make direct dissimilarity judgments about all possible pairs of stimuli. In collecting direct dissimilarity judgments, the user can employ a category rating task, a graphic rating task, a category sorting task, or a magnitude estimation task. Researchers need to design the task so as to minimize time and space effects on subject judgments.

Conditional and joint probability matrices also can be used as input in MDS studies. S. Rosenberg et al. (1968) have devised a sorting task that can be used to generate co-occurrence data even when the number of stimuli is large. Since conditional probability (frequency) data are not symmetric, the researcher must devise some method of generating a symmetric similarity matrix from the asymmetric conditional probability matrix.

Profile dissimilarity indices can also be used to generate a dissimilarity matrix for pairs of stimuli. The most common profile dissimilarity measure is the distance index of Eq. (3.1). Before using this measure, however, the researcher must decide whether to use raw scores, column-standardized scores, row-centered scores, or row-standardized scores in computing profile dissimilarities. The decision depends solely on substantive considerations unique to each field of application.

[†] It is possible to create a column-centered data matrix by transforming raw scores so that the mean score in each column is zero. Likewise, it is possible to construct a double-centered data matrix by transforming the raw data so that the mean of each row and each column is zero. There is no need to consider these data transformations separately. The profile dissimilarity matrix Δ defined over the column-centered data matrix will be equal to the profile dissimilarity matrix defined over the raw scores. Similarly, the profile dissimilarity matrix Δ defined over the double-centered data matrix will be equal to the profile dissimilarity matrix defined over the row-centered data matrix.

PROBLEMS

1. Read Ross's (1934) article on optimal orderings of paired comparisons. Then determine an optimal ordering for the following eight stimuli. Balance the pairs for space effects.
   a. J. Anderson
   b. R. Reagan
   c. J. Carter
   d. W. Mondale
   e. G. Bush
   f. P. Lucey
   g. T. O'Neil
   h. H. Baker

2. Construct the complete profile dissimilarity matrix for the data in Table 3.1 using raw scores.

3. Using the data in Table 3.1, compute the following.
   a. Grand mean
   b. Mean for each row
   c. Mean for each column
   d. Standard deviation for each row
   e. Standard deviation for each column

4. Convert the data in Table 3.1 to the following forms.
   a. Row-centered
   b. Row-standardized
   c. Column-standardized

5. Convert the following asymmetric interaction frequency matrix into symmetric form.

Table 3.2. Frequency With Which Each Row Stimulus Initiated an Interaction With the Column Stimulus.

	Bill	Mary	Pete	Cathy
Bill	—	3	3	7
Mary	4	—	3	8
Pete	4	4	—	7
Cathy	2	3	2	—

Answers

1. a. J. Anderson : R. Reagan   o. J. Anderson : W. Mondale
   b. H. Baker : W. Mondale   p. J. Carter : G. Bush
   c. T. O'Neil : G. Bush   q. R. Reagan : P. Lucey
   d. P. Lucey : J. Anderson   r. H. Baker : J. Anderson
   e. J. Carter : R. Reagan   s. G. Bush : W. Mondale
   f. G. Bush : H. Baker   t. P. Lucey : J. Carter
   g. P. Lucey : T. O'Neil   u. T. O'Neil : R. Reagan
   h. J. Anderson : J. Carter   v. J. Anderson : G. Bush
   i. R. Reagan : W. Mondale   w. W. Mondale : P. Lucey
   j. H. Baker : P. Lucey   x. J. Carter : T. O'Neil
   k. T. O'Neil : J. Anderson   y. R. Reagan : H. Baker
   l. W. Mondale : J. Carter   z. G. Bush : P. Lucey
   m. G. Bush : R. Reagan   aa. W. Mondale : T. O'Neil
   n. T. O'Neil : H. Baker   bb. J. Carter : H. Baker

2.

	Private	Mining	Manu-facturing	Con-struction	Finance
Private	—				
Mining	5.62	—			
Manufacturing	1.11	5.50	—		
Construction	12.59	13.20	12.31	—	
Finance	5.48	7.94	5.87	18.03	—

3. a. $v_{..} = 5.64$
   b. $v_{1.} = 5.06$, $v_{2.} = 4.80$, $v_{3.} = 5.16$, $v_{4.} = 10.54$, $v_{5.} = 2.66$
   c. $v_{.1} = 7.50$, $v_{.2} = 5.22$, $v_{.3} = 5.20$, $v_{.4} = 4.70$, $v_{.5} = 5.60$
   d. $s_1 = .55$, $s_2 = 2.63$, $s_3 = .85$, $s_4 = 1.59$, $s_5 = .29$
   e. $s_1 = 3.79$, $s_2 = 2.63$, $s_3 = 2.48$, $s_4 = 2.20$, $s_5 = 2.78$

4. a.

P	0.64	−0.76	−0.26	−0.26	0.64
Mi	4.90	0.60	−1.70	−1.90	−1.90
Ma	1.04	−1.16	0.44	−0.86	0.54
Con	2.96	−0.44	−0.84	−1.74	0.06
Fi	−0.26	−0.36	0.14	0.04	0.44

b. P   1.16   − 1.38   − 0.47   − 0.47   1.16
    Mi   1.86   0.23   − 0.65   − 0.72   − 0.72
    Ma   1.22   − 1.36   0.52   − 1.01   0.64
    Con   1.86   − 0.28   − 0.53   − 1.09   0.04
    Fi   − 0.90   − 1.24   0.48   0.14   1.52

c. P   − 0.48   − 0.35   − 0.16   0.05   0.04
    Mi   0.58   0.07   − 0.85   − 0.82   − 0.97
    Ma   − 0.34   − 0.46   0.16   − 0.18   0.04
    Con   1.58   1.86   1.81   1.86   1.80
    Fi   − 1.35   − 1.11   − 0.97   − 0.91   − 0.90

5.

	B	M	P	C
B	—			
M	7	—		
P	7	7	—	
C	9	11	9	—

Torgerson's Metric Group Method

Greatly assisted by Ledyard Tucker and building on work by Young and Householder (1938, 1941), Torgerson (1952, 1958) proposed one of the first MDS algorithms. Gower (1966, 1982) discusses and extends Torgerson's (1952) results. The assumptions of Torgerson's (1952) algorithm are much more restrictive than those of recent methods. Consequently, his approach is seldom used in its original form. Various features of his method have been incorporated into the algorithms described in Chapters 5 and 6 and, therefore, the Torgerson method will be described in some detail.

At this point, a few words are in order about the first example in this chapter. Table 4.1 shows a hypothetical dissimilarity matrix for six sports. The dissimilarity matrix was constructed to reflect two dimensions along which these sports differ: the speed of the games and the degree of contact between players. Hockey and football are two fast contact sports. Tennis and basketball are two fast noncontact sports. Golf and croquet are slow noncontact sports. The data in Table 4.1 will be used to illustrate how Torgerson's method can be employed to recover the two-dimensional configuration of stimuli underlying the data matrix in Table 4.1. The illustration will constitute a dimensional application of MDS.

TORGERSON'S MODEL

In Torgerson's model, the dissimilarity estimates comprising the data are assumed equal to distances in a Euclidean multidimensional space. Again let δ_{ij} be the dissimilarity between objects i and j. Let x_{ik} and x_{jk} ($i = 1, \ldots, I$; $j = 1, \ldots, J$; $I = J$; $k = 1, \ldots, K$) be the coordinates of stimuli i and j

61

Table 4.1. The Dissimilarity Matrix Δ for Five Sports and the Scalar Product Matrix Δ* Derived from It.

	Dissimilarity Matrix Δ						
	H	F	B	T	G	C	$\delta_{i.}^2$
Hockey	0.00	0.71	1.41	1.73	2.00	2.00	2.25
Football	0.71	0.00	1.41	1.73	2.00	2.00	2.25
Basketball	1.41	1.41	0.00	1.00	1.41	1.41	1.50
Tennis	1.73	1.73	1.00	0.00	1.00	1.00	1.50
Golf	2.00	2.00	1.41	1.00	0.00	0.71	1.92
Croquet	2.00	2.00	1.41	1.00	0.71	0.00	1.92
$\delta_{.j}^2$	2.25	2.25	1.50	1.50	1.92	1.92	

$$\delta_{..}^2 = 1.89$$

Scalar Product Matrix Δ*

	H	F	B	T	G	C
Hockey	1.31	1.06	−0.07	−0.57	−0.86	−0.86
Football	1.06	1.31	−0.07	−0.57	−0.86	−0.86
Basketball	−0.07	−0.07	0.56	0.06	−0.24	−0.24
Tennis	−0.57	−0.57	0.06	0.56	0.27	0.27
Golf	−0.86	−0.86	−0.24	0.27	0.98	0.73
Croquet	−0.86	−0.86	−0.24	0.27	0.73	0.98

along dimension k. Note that the number of rows in the dissimilarity matrix I will equal the number of columns J because the rows and columns correspond to the same stimuli. Torgerson's fundamental assumption is:

$$\delta_{ij} = d_{ij} = \left[\sum_k (x_{ik} - x_{jk})^2 \right]^{1/2}. \qquad (4.1)$$

Without loss of generality, it can be assumed that the mean coordinate along each stimulus dimension equals zero:

$$\sum_i x_{ik} = \sum_j x_{jk} = 0.0. \qquad (4.2)$$

Torgerson began by constructing a double-centered matrix Δ* with elements δ_{ij}^* computed directly from the data matrix. A double-centered matrix is one in which the mean of the elements in each row and the mean of the elements in each column equals 0.0. Each element of the new matrix Δ^* is of the form:

$$\delta_{ij}^* = -\tfrac{1}{2}\left(\delta_{ij}^2 - \delta_{i.}^2 - \delta_{.j}^2 + \delta_{..}^2\right). \tag{4.3}$$

Here $\delta_{i.}^2$, $\delta_{.j}^2$, and δ^2 are defined as follows:

$$\delta_{i.}^2 = \frac{1}{J}\sum_j \delta_{ij}^2$$

$$\delta_{.j}^2 = \frac{1}{I}\sum_i \delta_{ij}^2 \tag{4.4}$$

$$\delta_{..}^2 = \frac{1}{IJ}\sum_i \sum_j \delta_{ij}^2.$$

The matrix Δ^* computed from matrix Δ is also shown in Table 4.1. The element in row 2 and column 3 of Δ^*, $\delta_{23}^* = -0.07$, was obtained by taking $\delta_{23}^2 = (1.41)^2 = 2.00$, subtracting the mean of squared elements in row 2, $\delta_{2.}^2 = 2.25$, subtracting the mean of squared elements in column 3, $\delta_{.3}^2 = 1.50$, adding the grand mean squared element, $\delta_{..}^2 = 1.89$, and multiplying the result by -0.50:

$$\delta_{23}^* = -\tfrac{1}{2}\left(\delta_{23}^2 - \delta_{2.}^2 - \delta_{.3}^2 + \delta_{..}^2\right)$$

$$= -\tfrac{1}{2}(2.00 - 2.25 - 1.50 + 1.89) = -0.07. \tag{4.5}$$

The element in row 4 column 5 of Δ^* was computed as follows:

$$\delta_{45}^* = -\tfrac{1}{2}\left(\delta_{45}^2 - \delta_{4.}^2 - \delta_{.5}^2 + \delta_{..}^2\right)$$

$$= -\tfrac{1}{2}(1.00 - 1.50 - 1.92 + 1.89) = 0.27, \tag{4.6}$$

and so forth.

Torgerson showed that if the data satisfy Eq. (4.1), then each element in the new matrix Δ^* would be of the form

$$\delta_{ij}^* = \sum_k x_{ik}x_{jk}. \tag{4.7}$$

For the interested reader, a proof is given later in this chapter. Equation (4.7) is the fundamental theorem around which Torgerson designed his algorithm. Matrix Δ^* is often called a *scalar product matrix* because, as Eq. (4.7) shows, each of its elements is the sum of products between scalars x_{ik} and x_{jk}.

The matrix form of Eq. (4.7) is as follows:

$$\Delta^* = XX' \tag{4.8}$$

where X is the $(I \times K)$ matrix of stimulus coordinates. As described in Chapter 2, a principal components factor program can be used to find a matrix X satisfying Eq. (4.8) so long as such a matrix exists. Interested readers can consult a text on matrix algebra (Green, 1978; Hohn, 1973) for a description of methods for computing X and of the conditions under which such a matrix X will exist.

Figure 4.1 shows the matrix X obtained by extracting the first two principal components from the scalar product matrix Δ^* in Table 4.1.

ROTATION

The matrix X obtained from the principal components analysis is a solution of Eq. (4.8) but not the only solution. To see why it is not the only solution, imagine a $(K \times K)$ orthogonal transformation matrix T. If X satisfies Eq. (4.8), then any matrix $X^* = XT$ will also satisfy Eq. (4.8). That is, if

$$\Delta^* = XX', \tag{4.9}$$

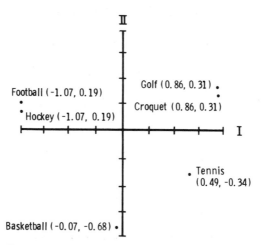

Figure 4.1.   Unrotated metric scaling of sports data.

then

$$\Delta^* = \mathbf{X}^*\mathbf{X}^{*\prime}. \tag{4.10}$$

Since **T** is orthogonal, $\mathbf{TT}' = \mathbf{I}$ (see the definition of orthogonal transformation matrix in Chapter 2). Hence

$$\mathbf{X}^*\mathbf{X}^{*\prime} = (\mathbf{XT})(\mathbf{XT})' \tag{4.11}$$

Theorem 2 of Chapter 2 tells us that $(\mathbf{XT})'$ in Eq. (4.11) equals $\mathbf{T}'\mathbf{X}'$. Inserting this result into Eq. (4.11) yields

$$\mathbf{X}^*\mathbf{X}^{*\prime} = (\mathbf{XT})(\mathbf{T}'\mathbf{X}')$$

$$= \mathbf{X}(\mathbf{TT}')\mathbf{X}'$$

$$= \mathbf{XIX}' \tag{4.12}$$

$$= \mathbf{XX}'$$

$$= \Delta^*.$$

As the proof in Eq. (4.12) shows, if **X** is a solution to Eq. (4.8), then so is any matrix $\mathbf{X}^*$. If there are several rotations of **X** that can reproduce Δ^* equally well, then which rotation should one prefer?

The above question is usually a moot issue in data reduction or configural applications of MDS as long as K does not exceed two dimensions. In such a small number of dimensions, the important features of the configuration should be visually recognizable irrespective of rotation. In dimensional applications, however, it is not a moot issue. If the dimensions are not rotated to a suitable orientation, the coordinates will not correspond to meaningful stimulus attributes, and it will be difficult to interpret the dimensions. The phrase "meaningful stimulus attributes" will be explained below.

The configuration in Figure 4.1 illustrates the kind of interpretational problem that can occur. Dimension I has the slow noncontact games at one end, the fast contact games at the other, and fast noncontact sports in the middle. The scale represented by this dimension cannot, therefore, be interpreted as representing the speed of each game or the degree of contact. It is a confound of the two. Dimension II is also a confound of the two stimulus attributes, speed and contact. It has fast noncontact sports at the positive end. Slow noncontact and fast contact sports are found at the other end.

In deciding on a rotation for the solution, there are three basic options. If the unrotated solution is interpretable, one need not rotate the solution at all. Such is not the case for the data in Figure 4.1. Consequently, either an objective rotation or a hand rotation must be employed to obtain an interpretable representation of the configuration. It is to these latter options, objective and hand rotations, to which our attention now turns.

Objective Rotations

An objective rotation is a mathematical algorithm for finding an interpretable rotation of a solution. Since objective rotations were designed primarily for use in factor analysis and are used only occasionally in MDS, they will be mentioned briefly in this book. Interested readers can consult a text on factor analysis (Harman, 1976) for a detailed description of such rotations. The objective rotations commonly available were designed for rotating a factor analytic configuration of tests so the configuration conforms as closely as possible to the criterion of simple structure (Thurstone, 1947; Tucker, 1967). Stated simply, a MDS solution would satisfy the criterion of simple structure if each stimulus had a nonzero scale value on one or, at most, a few stimulus attributes. Such rotations are seldom used in MDS because, to this author's knowledge, there is no reason to believe that naturally occurring stimuli would satisfy this criterion. Nor is there any reason to believe that rotation to such a criterion will yield a more interpretable solution. In some applications, an objective rotation to simple structure, such as varimax (Kaiser, 1958) or equimax (Saunders, 1960), will yield a highly interpretable solution. Users should not, however, assume that such an objective rotational algorithm will automatically produce the most interpretable possible solution.

Figure 4.2 gives the varimax rotation of the original solution matrix in Figure 4.1. The varimax solution is little different from the unrotated solution, and hence shares its interpretational problems. For this particular example, the varimax dimensions are no easier to interpret than are the unrotated dimensions in Figure 4.1.

Hand Rotations

Computers perform objective rotations. People perform hand rotations. A hand rotation is one performed by the experimenter and chosen on the basis of her or his visual inspection of the unrotated configuration. In practice, one can sometimes see by inspection what rotation of the solution would yield interpretable dimensions. If dimension I in Figure 4.1 were rotated 45°, as shown in Figure 4.3, then all of the fast sports would fall at the

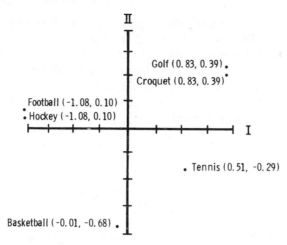

Figure 4.2. Varimax rotation of metric sports dimensions.

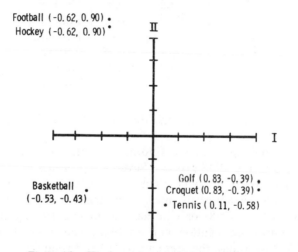

Figure 4.3. Hand rotation of metric sports data.

positive end. Slow sports would fall at the negative end. Scale values along the resulting dimension could be said to reflect the speed of the various sports. Rotating dimension II 45°, as shown in Figure 4.3, would yield an axis with contact sports at one end and noncontact sports at the other. The resulting dimension could be said to reflect the degree of contact in each game.

One can quickly compute the angles between dimensions I and II in Figure 4.2 and dimensions 1 and 2 in Figure 4.3. The angle between dimensions I and 1 would be 45°; the angle between dimensions II and 1 would be 315°; the angle between dimensions I and 2 would be 135°; the angle between dimensions II and 2 would be 45°. The corresponding cosines would be .71, .71, −.71, and .71. Assembling these cosines yields the orthogonal transformation matrix

$$
\mathbf{T} = \begin{array}{c} \\ \text{I} \\ \\ \text{II} \end{array} \begin{array}{cc} 1 & 2 \\ \left[\begin{array}{cc} .71 & -.71 \\ \\ .71 & .71 \end{array} \right] \end{array} \tag{4.13}
$$

Postmultiplying the unrotated scale values **X** in Figure 4.1 by **T** yields the rotated coordinate matrix plotted in Figure 4.3. The resulting dimensions

$$
\mathbf{X^*} = \begin{array}{c} \left[\begin{array}{cc} -0.62 & 0.90 \\ -0.62 & 0.90 \\ -0.53 & -0.43 \\ 0.11 & -0.58 \\ 0.83 & -0.39 \\ 0.83 & -0.39 \end{array} \right] \end{array} \begin{array}{l} \text{Hockey} \\ \text{Football} \\ \text{Basketball} \\ \text{Tennis} \\ \text{Golf} \\ \text{Croquet} \end{array} \tag{4.14}
$$

can be interpreted as reflecting the degree of contact in and the speed of each sport.

In dimensional applications, finding an interpretable rotation is an important step in the MDS process. Several approaches are possible. If the original solution is interpretable, then the user need not rotate at all. If the unrotated solution is not easily interpreted, then an objective rotation such as varimax (Kaiser, 1958) or equimax (Saunders, 1960) can be tried. If neither the unrotated solution nor an objectively rotated solution yield interpretable dimensions, the user can try a hand rotation.

DIMENSIONALITY

To this point, the discussion of Torgerson's method has proceeded as if the number of dimensions K were known. In practice, however, it is not known and must be estimated in the analysis. In most MDS methods, the user must obtain several solutions in different dimensionalities and choose between them on the basis of three criteria: interpretability, fit to the data, and reproducibility. Torgerson's algorithm minimizes the following measure of fit: $F = \sum_{(i,j)} (\delta_{ij}^* - \sum_k \hat{x}_{ik} \hat{x}_{jk})^2$, where $\hat{x}_{ik}$ and $\hat{x}_{jk}$ are the estimates of coordinates for stimuli i and j along dimension k. That is, the algorithm minimizes the sum of squared discrepancies between the predicted, $\hat{\delta}_{ij}^* = \sum_k \hat{x}_{ik} \hat{x}_{jk}$, and actual scalar products, δ_{ij}^*.

Torgerson's method is one of two methods discussed in this book in which the fit measure plays little or no role in deciding how many dimensions are required to adequately reproduce the data. There is, however, a series of eigenvalues (also called characteristic roots or eigen roots) that do play a role in the dimensionality decision. Each eigenvalue is associated with one dimension in the solution. For our purposes, the eigenvalue associated with a given dimension is simply the sum of squared stimulus scale values along that dimension. That is, if we let $\hat{x}_{ik}$ refer to the estimated scale value for stimulus i along dimension k, then the kth eigenvalue is

$$\lambda_k = \sum_i \hat{x}_{ik}^2. \tag{4.15}$$

If one takes stimulus 1 to be hockey, stimulus 2 to be football, 3 to be basketball, 4 to be tennis, 5 to be golf, and 6 to be croquet, then in the solution of Figure 4.1, the second eigenvalue is simply

$$\lambda_2 = \sum \hat{x}_{i2}^2 = \hat{x}_{12}^2 + \hat{x}_{22}^2 + \hat{x}_{32}^2 + \hat{x}_{42}^2 + \hat{x}_{52}^2 + \hat{x}_{62}^2$$

$$= (.19)^2 + (.19)^2 + (-.68)^2 + (-.34)^2 + (.31)^2 \tag{4.16}$$

$$+ (.31)^2 = .84.$$

A plot like the one in Figure 4.4 can be useful in determining dimensionality. The vertical axis represents eigenvalues for the *unrotated* solution, and the horizontal axis corresponds to dimensions. The graph is constructed by plotting one point for each dimension at a height corresponding to the eigenvalue associated with that dimension. For instance, the point corresponding to the second dimension indicates that the eigenvalue associated with the second dimension of the unrotated solution was 0.84.

If the data conform exactly to the model of Eq. (4.1), then the plot should level off at exactly $(K + 1)$ dimensions, just as the plot in Figure 4.4 levels off at 3 dimensions. In other words, there should be an "elbow" in the graph one dimension beyond K, the correct number of dimensions. In real data that do not conform exactly to the model or in which there is a large amount of measurement and sampling error, an elbow may be difficult to discern. Indeed, the elbow is difficult to discern in Figure 4.4. In such cases, a plot of the eigenvalues may not suffice to determine the correct number of

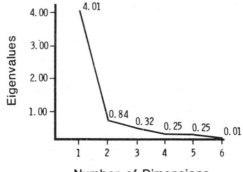

Number of Dimensions

Figure 4.4.   Eigenvalues plotted against dimensions for the unrotated scaling of sports.

dimensions. Interpretation and reproducibility of dimensions must also be considered.

Reproducibility can be used as a criterion only when there are two or more subsamples. The basic idea is that one should retain as many dimensions in the final solution as emerge consistently in the separate subsamples. If one derives separate solutions for each subsample, and there are K dimensions that appear consistently in all of the subsamples, then the final solution should contain exactly K dimensions. Each of the subsamples should come from the same population.

Interpretability as a criterion requires some subjective judgment on the user's part. The basic idea, however, is that a higher dimensional solution is preferred over a lower dimensional solution if there are important stimulus features that appear in the higher dimensional solution but fail to appear in the lower dimensional solution. Conversely, the lower dimensional solution is preferred if there are no important stimulus features that fail to appear in the lower dimensional solution.

In our example, neither stimulus feature, degree of contact, nor speed of game can be distinctly discerned in the one-dimensional solution, which consists solely of the first dimension plotted in Figure 4.1. Both features are confounded in the lone dimension of the one-dimensional solution. Only after the extraction of two dimensions can the solution be rotated so that each stimulus feature corresponds to a unique dimension as in Figure 4.3. Because it is more readily interpreted, the two-dimensional solution is preferred.

INTERPRETATION

Interpretability was discussed above in the section on deciding dimensionality, but a few more comments need to be made about interpreting solutions.

EXAMPLE   71

Particularly, the phrase "meaningful stimulus features" from the prior discussion needs clarification. Such features are typically either orderings or groupings of stimuli.

A substantively meaningful grouping of stimuli is a set of stimuli that cluster together in a region of the multidimensional solution space and that possess some common attribute. For instance, in a study of occupations, sales jobs may cluster together to form a meaningful grouping. Women's magazines (*MS.*, *Ladies Home Journal*, *Vogue*, etc.) may group together in a study of popular periodicals.

A meaningful ordering of stimuli is an ordering that corresponds to the arrangement of stimuli along an important stimulus attribute. For instance, the ordering of the stimuli along dimension I in Figure 4.3 corresponds to their ordering by degree of contact. The ordering along dimension II corresponds to the ordering of the games by speed. Both of these dimensions represent meaningful orderings because they correspond to important attributes of games, speed, and contact. Ideally, the dimensions will be rotated so that each represents one of the meaningful orderings.

Interpreting a solution involves identifying the important groupings and orderings of stimuli. For groupings, one must identify the feature or features that the members of each cluster share in common. For orderings, one must identify the attribute corresponding to the ordering. One way to interpret a solution is by simple inspection of the configuration. More formal methods are considered in Chapter 8.

EXAMPLE

Smith and Siegel (1967) use MDS to derive dimensions of job tasks for the position Office of Civil Defense (OCD) director. In three successive stages, they identify 34 job functions which, in their opinion, are representative of the total tasks performed by OCD directors. Thirty-five supervisory level OCD personnel then rate the dissimilarity of each pair of tasks on an 11-point scale. For each job task pair, the dissimilarity judgments of the 35 subjects are pooled to obtain a dissimilarity matrix.

Torgerson's algorithm was used to obtain a four-dimensional solution. Smith and Siegel use an objective rotation called equimax (Saunders, 1960). For each of the four dimensions, Table 4.2 shows the functions that have the highest positive scale values and the lowest negative scale values. The authors summarize their interpretations of the dimensions in the labels they assign to each: internal versus external system maintenance (dimension I), routine versus emergency programming (dimension II), resource use versus resource evaluation (dimension III), and emergency system integration (dimension IV).

Table 4.2. Dimensions of Civil Defense Director Job Tasks.

Scale Value	Job Task
	Dimension I: Internal vs. External System Maintenance
3.43	Issuing necessary emergency orders and instructions to the public
4.21	Prescribing information channels
4.70	Relaying information from higher-level CD organizations
5.66	Informing public and private groups of CD activities
−3.19	Assisting in legal actions arising from CD activities
−3.96	Accounting for CD funds and property
−4.94	Assuring the preservation of essential CD records
	Dimension II: Routine vs. Emergency Programming
3.58	Administering the protected facilities program
4.46	Preparing and presenting a CD budget
4.82	Inspecting and reporting on installations assigned to or related to CD
6.39	Accounting for CD funds and property
−2.16	Prescribing mobilization procedures
−2.24	Evaluating potential emergencies
−3.00	Programming the continuity of government
−4.88	Establishing the order of succession within the CD system
	Dimension III: Resource Use vs. Resource Evaluation
2.81	Accounting for CD funds and property
4.27	Advising on needed CD legislation
6.33	Assisting on legal actions arising from CD activities
−3.20	Conducting required research
−3.68	Determining the availability of human and material resources
−3.94	Assuring the proficiency of CD workers
−4.65	Conducting and evaluating CD tests
	Dimension IV: Emergency System Integration
3.79	Advising on needed CD legislation
4.14	Preparing and presenting a CD budget
4.26	Appointing CD technical advisory committees
4.91	Conducting required research
−2.11	Prescribing information channels
−2.49	Relaying information from higher-level CD organizations
−3.26	Maintaining liaison with federal and state military groups
−3.35	Issuing necessary emergency orders and instructions to the public
−4.90	Alerting and mobilizing the CD system

Source: Smith and Siegel (1967). Copyright 1967 by the American Psychological Association. Adapted by permission of the publisher and author.

The authors suggest that the obtained dimensions could be used as a basis for developing unidimensional, employee evaluation scales. For instance, since resource evaluation tasks emerged at one pole of dimension III, one may wish to develop a corresponding employee evaluation scale. The authors go on to suggest that employee selection measures and training programs might be planned around the obtained dimensions.

PROOF: TORGERSON'S FUNDAMENTAL THEOREM[†]

Torgerson's method rests on his proof that if one starts from a data matrix Δ with elements of the form

$$\delta_{ij} = d_{ij} = \left[\sum_k (x_{ik} - x_{jk})^2 \right]^{1/2}, \tag{4.17}$$

and one applies the following transformation to those elements

$$\delta_{ij}^* = -\tfrac{1}{2}\left(\delta_{ij}^2 - \delta_{i.}^2 - \delta_{.j}^2 + \delta_{..}^2 \right), \tag{4.18}$$

then one obtains quantities of the form

$$\delta_{ij}^* = \sum_k x_{ik} x_{jk}. \tag{4.19}$$

Although Torgerson did not do so, one can assume without loss of generality that

$$\sum_i x_{ik} = \sum_j x_{jk} = 0 \qquad \text{for all } k. \tag{4.20}$$

As preliminary steps in the proof, it is necessary to derive expressions for $\delta_{i.}^2$, $\delta_{.j}^2$, and δ^2 in terms of the stimulus coordinates x_{ik} and x_{jk}. The re-expression of $\delta_{i.}^2$ in terms of stimulus coordinates will be sought first.

Squaring and expanding the term on the right side of Eq. (4.17) yields

$$\delta_{ij}^2 = \sum_k x_{ik}^2 + \sum_k x_{jk}^2 - 2\sum_k x_{ik} x_{jk}. \tag{4.21}$$

Squaring and taking the average over j of the quantity on the left side of Eq.

[†] Throughout this book, an asterisk designates a more technical section containing a proof or a description of an algorithm. Readers can omit such sections without loss of continuity.

(4.17) yields

$$\delta_{i.}^2 = \frac{1}{J} \sum_j \delta_{ij}^2.$$ (4.22)

Substituting the quantity on the right side of Eq. (4.21) for the expression on the right side of Eq. (4.22) yields

$$\delta_{i.}^2 = \frac{1}{J} \sum_j \left(\sum_k x_{ik}^2 + \sum_k x_{jk}^2 - 2\sum_k x_{ik}x_{jk} \right)$$

$$= \frac{1}{J} \sum_j \sum_k x_{ik}^2 + \frac{1}{J} \sum_j \sum_k x_{jk}^2 - 2\frac{1}{J} \sum_j \sum_k x_{ik}x_{jk}.$$ (4.23)

Consider the third term on the right side of Eq. (4.23), $-2(1/J)\sum_j\sum_k x_{ik}x_{jk}$. Since x_{ik} does not depend on j, this term can be rewritten as $-2(1/J)\sum_k x_{ik}(\sum_j x_{jk})$. According to Eq. (4.20), $\sum_j x_{jk} = 0$, and hence $-2(1/J)\sum_k x_{ik}(\sum_j x_{jk}) = 0$. Consequently, Eq. (4.23) can be rewritten as

$$\delta_{i.}^2 = \sum_k x_{ik}^2 + \sum_k x_{.k}^2,$$ (4.24)

where $x_{.k}^2 = (1/J)\sum_j x_{jk}^2$. Equation (4.24) states that $\delta_{i.}^2$ can be expressed as the sum of squared coordinates for stimulus i plus the sum of the average squared coordinates. Both of these sums are taken across the K dimensions. Equation (4.24) provides the desired re-expression of $\delta_{i.}^2$ in terms of stimulus coordinates. Let's turn our attention now to a similar re-expression of $\delta_{.j}^2$.

Squaring and taking the average over i of the quantity on the left side of Eq. (4.17) yields

$$\delta_{.j}^2 = \frac{1}{I} \sum_i \delta_{ij}^2.$$ (4.25)

Substituting the quantity on the right side of Eq. (4.21) for the expression on the right side of Eq. (4.25) yields

$$\delta_{.j}^2 = \frac{1}{I} \sum_i \left(\sum_k x_{ik}^2 + \sum_k x_{jk}^2 - 2\sum_k x_{ik}x_{jk} \right)$$

$$= \frac{1}{I} \sum_i \sum_k x_{ik}^2 + \frac{1}{I} \sum_i \sum_k x_{jk}^2$$ (4.26)

$$- 2\frac{1}{I} \sum_i \sum_k x_{ik}x_{jk}.$$

Consider the third term on the right side of Eq. (4.26). Since x_{jk} does not depend on i, the term can be rewritten as $-2(1/I)\Sigma_k x_{jk}(\Sigma_i x_{ik})$. According to Eq. (4.20), $\Sigma_i x_{ik} = 0$, and hence $-2(1/I)\Sigma_k x_{jk}(\Sigma_i x_{ik}) = 0$. Consequently, Eq. (4.26) can be written as

$$\delta_{\cdot j}^2 = \sum_k x_{\cdot k}^2 + \sum_k x_{jk}^2, \qquad (4.27)$$

where

$$x_{\cdot k}^2 = \frac{1}{I}\sum_i x_{ik}^2 = \frac{1}{J}\sum_j x_{jk}^2.$$

Equation (4.27) expresses $\delta_{\cdot j}^2$ in a form directly analogous to the expression for $\delta_{i\cdot}^2$ in Eq. (4.24), and it provides the desired re-expression of $\delta_{\cdot j}^2$ in terms of stimulus coordinates. Before beginning the proof of Torgerson's fundamental theorem, Eq. (4.19), we need only re-express δ^2 in terms of stimulus coordinates.

Squaring and taking the average over j and i of the quantity on the left side of Eq. (4.17) yields

$$\delta^2 = \frac{1}{IJ}\sum_i \sum_j \delta_{ij}^2. \qquad (4.28)$$

Substituting the quantity on the right side of Eq. (4.21) for the expression on the right side of Eq. (4.28) yields

$$\delta^2 = \frac{1}{IJ}\sum_i \sum_j \left(\sum_k x_{ik}^2 + \sum_k x_{jk}^2 - 2\sum_k x_{ik}x_{jk}\right)$$

$$= \frac{1}{IJ}\sum_i \sum_j \sum_k x_{ik}^2 + \frac{1}{IJ}\sum_i \sum_j \sum_k x_{jk}^2 \qquad (4.29)$$

$$- 2\frac{1}{IJ}\sum_i \sum_j \sum_k x_{ik}x_{jk}.$$

Consider the third term on the right side of Eq. (4.29). According to Eq. (4.20), $\Sigma_i x_{ik} = \Sigma_j x_{jk} = 0$, and hence $-2(1/IJ)\Sigma_i\Sigma_j\Sigma_k x_{ik}x_{jk} = -2(1/IJ)\Sigma_k(\Sigma_i x_{ik})(\Sigma_j x_{jk}) = 0$. Consequently, Eq. (4.29) can be rewritten as

$$\delta^2 = \sum_k x_{\cdot k}^2 + \sum_k x_{\cdot k}^2 = 2\sum_k x_{\cdot k}^2. \qquad (4.30)$$

To prove Torgerson's theorem in Eq. (4.19), we need only combine the results in Eqs. (4.24), (4.27), and (4.30) with the expression in Eqs. (4.18) and (4.21).

For the four terms on the right side of Eq. (4.18): δ_{ij}^2, $\delta_{i.}^2$, $\delta_{.j}^2$, and $\delta_{..}^2$, it is necessary to substitute the corresponding expressions on the right sides of Eqs. (4.21), (4.24), (4.27), and (4.30). These substitutions yield

$$
\delta_{ij}^* = -\tfrac{1}{2}\left[\left(\sum_k x_{ik}^2 + \sum_k x_{jk}^2 - 2\sum_k x_{ik}x_{jk}\right) - \left(\sum_k x_{ik}^2 + \sum_k x_{.k}^2\right) \right.
$$

$$
\left. - \left(\sum_k x_{.k}^2 + \sum_k x_{jk}^2\right) + 2\sum_k x_{.k}^2\right]. \tag{4.31}
$$

Combining terms and multiplying through by $(-\tfrac{1}{2})$ yields the desired result.

$$
\delta_{ij}^* = \sum_k x_{ik}x_{jk}. \tag{4.32}
$$

Thus one arrives at Torgerson's fundamental theorem expressed originally in this chapter by Eq. (4.7).

OTHER METRIC MODELS

Torgerson's (1952, 1958) algorithm makes very restrictive assumptions. A slightly less restrictive model is the following:

$$
\delta_{ij} = d_{ij} + c. \tag{4.33}
$$

where c is an additive constant. One way to analyze such proximity data would be to first estimate c, subtract the estimate of c from each proximity δ_{ij}, and then analyze the new data points $(\delta_{ij} - \hat{c})$ via Torgerson's algorithm. The problem of first estimating c is often called the *additive constant problem* in MDS (Cooper, 1972).

One can set the estimate of c equal to the following:

$$
\hat{c} = (-1) \max_{(h,i,j)} \left(\delta_{hj} - \delta_{hi} - \delta_{ij}\right). \tag{4.34}
$$

If one generates new proximities γ_{ij} such that

$$\gamma_{ij} = 0 \qquad \text{if } i = j \qquad\qquad (4.35)$$

$$\gamma_{ij} = \delta_{ij} - c \qquad \text{if } i \neq j,$$

then the proximities γ_{ij} will satisfy the triangular inequality of Eq. (1.4). The additive constant estimate $\hat{c}$ is the smallest value one can subtract from each proximity δ_{ij} ($i \neq j$) that will ensure that the transformed data satisfy the triangular inequality (Carroll and Wish, 1974a).

Ramsey (1978, 1980) developed maximum likelihood estimates for the stimulus coordinates. He proposed two models. The first assumes that each proximity δ_{ij} is a normally distributed random variable with unknown mean $\mu_{ij} = d_{ij}$ and variance σ^2. The other model assumes that the natural logarithms of the data $\ln(\delta_{ij})$ are normally distributed random variables with unknown means $\mu_{ij} = d_{ij}$ and variance σ^2. The maximum likelihood theory on which these algorithms are based makes it possible to develop a fit measure that is approximately distributed as a chi square variable under the null hypothesis represented by the scaling model. Early versions of Ramsey's algorithm required so much computer time that they were practical only for small data sets. If the computational problems can be overcome, the maximum likelihood approach may enable researchers to examine the fit of the model to their data more rigorously than has been possible with other approaches.

SUMMARY

Torgerson (1952) assumed that dissimilarities were equal to distances in a Euclidean space. From this assumption, he derived one of the first multidimensional scaling algorithms. Using data that satisfy Torgerson's metric assumption, one can solve for the coordinate dimensions by applying a principal components analysis to the scalar product matrix Δ^*.

One can decide upon the number of dimensions by considering the replicability of dimensions across subsamples, the interpretability of solutions with varying numbers of dimensions, and a dimensions-by-eigenvalues plot. The solution can be left unrotated, it can be rotated by hand, or it can be rotated by some objective algorithm such as varimax (Kaiser, 1958) or equimax (Saunders, 1960). Of these three rotation options, the one that gives the most interpretable orientation of the axes is preferred. Interpreting the solution involves identifying groupings of stimuli or orderings of stimuli that correspond to meaningful stimulus attributes.

Smith and Siegel (1967) use Torgerson's algorithm to derive dimensions of job task performance. They conclude that the dimensions could be used as a basis for developing unidimensional employee evaluation scales and for planning employee training programs.

PROBLEMS

1. Imagine that matrix Δ below contains dissimilarity data for all possible pairs of eight countries. Compute the scalar product matrix Δ^* from the matrix of dissimilarities.

	An	Ar	Au	Ch	Cu	J	US	Z
Angola	0.00	1.41	1.00	1.00	1.41	1.41	1.73	0.71
Argentina	1.41	0.00	1.00	1.73	1.41	1.41	1.00	1.41
Australia	1.00	1.00	0.00	1.41	1.73	1.00	1.41	1.00
China	1.00	1.73	1.41	0.00	1.00	1.00	1.41	1.00
$\Delta =$ Cuba	1.41	1.41	1.73	1.00	0.00	1.41	1.00	1.41
Japan	1.41	1.41	1.00	1.00	1.41	0.00	1.00	1.41
United States	1.73	1.00	1.41	1.41	1.00	1.00	0.00	1.73
Zimbabwe	0.71	1.41	1.00	1.00	1.41	1.41	1.73	0.00

2. Use a principal components analysis to extract three components from the scalar product matrix computed in Problem 1. Be sure to have all eight eigenvalues printed. Also, print both the unrotated and varimax rotated solutions in three dimensions. Then answer each of the following questions.

    a. What are the scale values along the first three unrotated dimensions? Can you interpret these dimensions?

    b. What are the scale values along the first three varimax rotated dimensions? Can you interpret these dimensions?

    c. What are the eight eigenvalues?

3. Construct a dimensions-by-eigenvalues plot. How many dimensions does this plot suggest should be retained?

4. Apply the transformation below to the varimax rotated dimensions? What are the obtained scale values? Interpret each of the dimensions.

$$T = \begin{bmatrix} .63 & .53 & -.63 \\ .55 & -.63 & .59 \\ -.59 & -.63 & -.55 \end{bmatrix}$$

Answers

1.

	An	Ar	Au	Ch	Cu	J	US	Z
An	.70	−.21	.17	.17	−.21	−.34	−.71	.45
Ar	−.21	.89	.26	−.74	−.12	−.24	.39	−.21
Au	.17	.26	.64	−.37	−.74	.14	−.24	.17
Δ = Ch	.17	−.74	−.37	.64	.26	.14	−.24	.17
Cu	−.21	−.12	−.74	.26	.89	−.24	.39	−.21
J	−.34	−.24	.14	.14	−.24	.64	.26	−.34
US	−.71	.39	−.24	−.24	.39	.26	.89	−.71
Z	.45	−.21	.17	.17	−.21	−.34	−.71	.70

2. a.

		I	II	III
	An	−.73	.00	−.21
	Ar	.42	.71	−.45
	Au	−.28	.71	.26
	Ch	−.28	−.71	.26
X −	Cu	.42	−.71	−.45
	J	.24	.00	.77
	US	.95	.00	.04
	Z	−.73	.00	−.21

These dimensions are difficult, if not impossible, to interpret.

b.

		I	II	II
	An	−.75	.10	.10
	Ar	.18	−.92	.08
	Au	−.14	−.25	.75
	Ch	−.14	.75	−.25
X =	Cu	.18	.08	−.92
	J	.56	.41	.41
	US	.87	−.27	−.27
	Z	−.75	.10	.10

These dimensions are difficult, if not impossible, to interpret.

c.

Dimension	I	II	III	IV	V	VI	VII	VIII
Eigenvalue	2.55	2.01	1.22	.25	.02	.01	$-.00$	$-.07$

3. Figure 4.5 suggests that $K = 3$ because there is an elbow above the fourth dimension.

4.

		I	II	III
	An	$-.48$	$-.53$	.48
	Ar	$-.45$	.63	$-.70$
	Au	$-.67$	$-.39$	$-.48$
	Ch	.48	$-.39$	.67
$\mathbf{X} =$	Cu	.70	.63	.45
	J	.34	$-.22$	$-.34$
	US	.56	.80	$-.56$
	Z	$-.48$	$-.53$	.48

Along the first dimension, stimuli are roughly arrayed along an axis running from north to south. The countries in the southern hemisphere—Angola, Argentina, Australia, and Zimbabwe—fall at the negative end of this axis. Countries in the northern hemisphere—China, Cuba, Japan, and the United States—fall at the positive end of this dimension. The arrangement from north to south is not perfect, how-

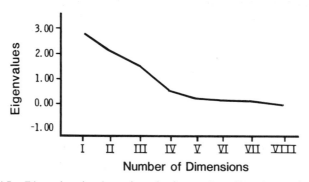

Figure 4.5. Dimensions-by-eigenvalues plot for metric scaling of countries' data.

ever; note, for instance, that Cuba has a higher scale value than the United States, even though Cuba is farther south. Nevertheless, dimension I can be interpreted as roughly reflecting the locations of the countries on a north–south axis.

Dimension II seems to be an east–west axis. The countries in the western hemisphere—Argentina, Cuba, and the United States—are located at the positive end of this dimension. Countries in the eastern hemisphere—Angola, Australia, China, Japan, and Zimbabwe—are found at the negative end.

Dimension III appears to be a Marxist–capitalist dimension. Countries headed by Marxist governments (in 1980)—Angola, China, Cuba, and Zimbabwe—appear at the positive end of this dimension. At the negative end, one will find the capitalist countries—Argentina, Australia, Japan, and the United States.

CHAPTER 5

Nonmetric Group Solutions

Shepard (1962) proposed a method for estimating stimulus coordinates under less restrictive assumptions than those of Torgerson (1952). Whereas Torgerson's model requires that the data be proportional to distances, Shepard's requires only that the data be monotonically related to distances. Specifically, his algorithm assumes that were it not for measurement and sampling error, the dissimilarity data would have the following form:

$$\delta_{ij} = f(d_{ij}) = f\left[\sum_k (x_{ik} - x_{jk})^2\right]^{1/2}.$$ (5.1)

Here f is a monotone function such that

$$d_{ij} < d_{i'j'} \Rightarrow f(d_{ij}) < f(d_{i'j'}) \qquad \text{for all } i, i', j, \text{ and } j'.$$ (5.2)

Examples of such functions include linear, power, exponential, and logarithmic functions. Any algorithm for estimating stimulus coordinates under the assumption that the data are related to distances in space by an unknown monotone function f satisfying Expression (5.2) is said to be a *nonmetric multidimensional scaling algorithm*. Nonmetric MDS algorithms compute stimulus coordinate estimates $\hat{x}_{ik}$ in a prespecified number of dimensions K so that when distance estimates $\hat{d}_{ij}$ are computed from those coordinate estimates, the rank order of the distance estimates agrees with the rank order of the original data δ_{ij} as closely as possible.

Shortly after Shepard's (1962) work, Kruskal (1964) described another algorithm for fitting data of an even more general form, data that are monotonically related to distances in a general Minkowski space. Before describing his algorithm, it will be necessary to explain Minkowski distance functions.

82

MINKOWSKI DISTANCE FUNCTIONS

The Euclidean distance function of Eq. (1.5) is a special case of the more general *Minkowski distance function*:

$$d_{ij} = \left(\sum |x_{ik} - x_{jk}|^p \right)^{1/p}. \qquad (5.3)$$

Several special cases of this function are of particular interest, and each case corresponds to a different value of p. First, if $p = 2$, then Eq. (5.3) reduces to the standard Euclidean distance function of Eq. (1.5).

As p approaches ∞, Eq. (5.3) approaches the *dominance metric* in which the distance between stimuli i and j is determined by the difference between coordinates along only one dimension, that dimension for which the value $|x_{ik} - x_{jk}|$ is greatest. That is,

$$d_{ij} = \max_k |x_{ik} - x_{jk}|. \qquad (5.4)$$

In general, the one dimension determining the distance d_{ij} will vary from one stimulus pair to another.

The third special case of interest is the *city-block metric* in which $p = 1$ (Attneave, 1950). In the city-block model,

$$d_{ij} = \sum_k |x_{ik} - x_{jk}|. \qquad (5.5)$$

It is called the city-block metric because, in two dimensions, the distance between points i and j corresponds to the distance one would travel in going from the point corresponding to stimulus i to the point corresponding to stimulus j along city streets running parallel to the coordinate axes.

If the stimulus space is unidimensional for a given set of stimuli, d_{ij} will be the same no matter what value of p is employed in the Minkowski distance function. In more than two dimensions, exactly the same coordinates will yield different distances depending on whether those distances are based on the Euclidean model of Eq. (1.5), the dominance model of Eq. (5.4), or the city-block model of Eq. (5.5). For example, consider stimuli B and C in Figure 5.1. The Euclidean distance ($p = 2$) between them is simply

$$d_{BC} = \left[\sum_k (x_{Bk} - x_{Ck})^2 \right]^{1/2}$$

$$= \{[2 - (-2)]^2 + [1 - (-1)]^2\}^{1/2} = (20)^{1/2} = 4.47. \qquad (5.6)$$

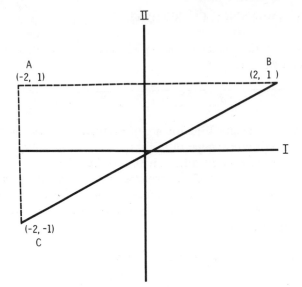

Figure 5.1. Euclidean, dominance, and city-block distances between stimuli B and C.

According to the dominance metric, the distance between B and C is the absolute value of the difference between their coordinates along dimension I, the dimension along which the two stimuli differ most:

$$d_{BC} = \max_k |x_{Bk} - x_{Ck}|$$

$$= |2 - (-2)| \qquad (5.7)$$

$$= 4.00.$$

The dominance metric gives a smaller distance between points B and C than does the Euclidean model. The city-block metric gives the largest distance. The city-block distance between B and C is

$$d_{BC} = \sum_k |x_{Bk} - x_{Ck}|$$

$$= |2 - (-2)| + |1 - (-1)| \qquad (5.8)$$

$$= 6.00.$$

Another way to represent the difference between the metrics is in terms of the line lengths in Figure 5.1. The length of the solid line connecting points B and C corresponds to their Euclidean distance. The dominance metric distance is the length of the dashed line connecting points A and B. The city-block distance corresponds to the combined lengths of the dashed lines connecting stimulus pairs (A, B) and (A, C).

Kruskal's (1964) algorithm allows the user to estimate stimulus coordinates from data that, were it not for measurement and sampling error, would have the form:

$$\delta_{ij} = f(d_{ij}) = f\left[\left(\sum_k |x_{ik} - x_{jk}|^p\right)^{1/p}\right] \qquad (5.9)$$

where f is again any monotone function satisfying Expression (5.2). The value of p is not estimated by the algorithm and must be specified by the user.

What value of p should users specify? Some researchers have used fit measures to guide their choice of p (Arnold, 1971; Wiener–Ehrlich, 1978). These authors each fitted several Minkowski distance models to their data, differing only in the value of p, and they decided in favor of the model (p value) that provided the best fit to the data. Sherman's (1972) work indicates that this approach must be used with care. When the dimensionality K is known, then the fit measure can be used to indicate the best value of p. In the Wiener–Ehrlich (1978) study, for instance, the stimuli had been chosen to vary along two dimensions. If K is unknown, however, Sherman's (1972) work suggests that the fit measure can be a misleading indicator of the best value for p.

The nonmetric MDS computer programs generally require a larger amount of computer time to fit a nonEuclidean model ($p \neq 2$) than to fit the Euclidean model ($p = 2$). Furthermore, several computational problems described below are more commonly encountered when fitting a non-Euclidean model. When the dimensionality is unknown, as is usually the case, researchers have overwhelmingly set $p = 2$ for the Euclidean model. Unless the user has some strong theoretical reason for preferring a non-Euclidean model or unless the dimensionality is known, computational considerations argue for a Euclidean model.

FIT MEASURES

One important feature of Kruskal's algorithm is the fit measure he proposed for assessing the degree to which the stimulus coordinate estimates $\hat{x}_{ik}$ and

$\hat{x}_{jk}$ reproduce the rank order of the data δ_{ij}. All major nonmetric algorithms, including Kruskal's, compute three sets of parameters on which the fit measure is based. The first and most important set contains the coordinate estimates $\hat{x}_{ik}$. The second set contains distance estimates computed from the coordinate estimates as follows:

$$\hat{d}_{ij} = \left(\sum_k |\hat{x}_{ik} - \hat{x}_{jk}|^p \right)^{1/p}. \tag{5.10}$$

The third set contains dummy parameters that Guttman (1968) calls the *rank images* of the data, and that others call *disparities*. Guttman's phrase, rank images, more accurately describes these dummy parameters because, as shown below, these parameters mirror the rank order of the data points. Hereafter, however, this book will employ the more common term, disparities. The *disparities* $\hat{\delta}_{ij}$ are values computed to be as nearly equal to the distance estimates $\hat{d}_{ij}$ as possible subject to the constraint that they be monotonically related to the original data. That is, they must match the distance estimates as closely as possible subject to the following monotonicity constraint:

$$\delta_{ij} < \delta_{i'j'} \Rightarrow \hat{\delta}_{ij} \leqslant \hat{\delta}_{i'j'} \qquad \text{for all } i, i', j, j'. \tag{5.11}$$

It is these disparities and the distance estimates that figure most prominently in the definitions of fit measures.

Ties

Expression (5.11) says nothing about the relationship between the disparities $\hat{\delta}_{ij}$ and $\hat{\delta}_{i'j'}$, when the corresponding data values are tied: $\delta_{ij} = \delta_{i'j'}$. There are two different approaches to the treatment of ties in the data, the primary (or untied) and the secondary (or tied). In the *primary approach to ties*, the monotone function relating the original data to the disparities is constrained to satisfy only the condition stated in Expression (5.11). No constraint is placed on the relationship between $\hat{\delta}_{ij}$ and $\hat{\delta}_{i'j'}$ when corresponding data points are tied. The computed disparity estimate $\hat{\delta}_{ij}$ may equal $\hat{\delta}_{i'j'}$, it may be greater than $\hat{\delta}_{i'j'}$, or it may be smaller than $\hat{\delta}_{i'j'}$.

In the *secondary approach*, the disparities are computed so as to satisfy the condition in Expression (5.11) and one additional condition stated in Expression (5.12):

$$\delta_{ij} = \delta_{i'j'} \Rightarrow \hat{\delta}_{ij} = \hat{\delta}_{i'j'} \qquad \text{for all } i, i', j, j'. \tag{5.12}$$

Most authors recommend the primary approach over the secondary approach, because it results in a better fit to the data. Whether the disparities are computed according to the primary or secondary approach to ties, they play a prominent role in the definition of all three fit measures employed by the major nonmetric MDS algorithms. Those fit measures are called STRESS, S-STRESS, and the coefficient of alienation.

STRESS

Kruskal used the disparities and distances to define a fit measure that he called STRESS but that is often called STRESS formula one (S_1) to distinguish it from a variation of that same measure called STRESS formula two (S_2):

$$
S_1 = \left[\frac{\Sigma_{(i,\,j)}\left(\hat{\delta}_{ij} - \hat{d}_{ij}\right)^2}{\Sigma_{(i,\,j)}\hat{d}_{ij}^2} \right]^{1/2}.
\tag{5.13}
$$

STRESS formula two is defined as follows:

$$
S_2 = \left[\frac{\Sigma_{(i,\,j)}\left(\hat{\delta}_{ij} - \hat{d}_{ij}\right)^2}{\Sigma_{(i,\,j)}\left(\hat{d}_{ij} - \hat{d}_{..}\right)^2} \right]^{1/2}.
\tag{5.14}
$$

In Eq. (5.14)

$$
\hat{d}_{..} = \frac{1}{IJ} \sum_{(i,\,j)} \hat{d}_{ij}.
\tag{5.15}
$$

In words, $\hat{d}_{..}$ is the arithmetic mean of the estimated distances. S_1 and S_2 differ only in the normalizing constant for the denominator of the fraction under the square root sign. As a normalizing constant, S_1 uses the sum of squared distance estimates. S_2 uses a quantity proportional to the variance of the distance estimates, the sum of squared deviations about the mean distance estimate.

Three of the major nonmetric MDS programs—M-D-SCAL (Kruskal and Carmone, undated), TORSCA (Young and Torgerson, 1967), and KYST (Kruskal et al., 1973)—yield coordinate estimates that minimize STRESS. KYST, the most recent of these three, incorporates the best features of both M-D-SCAL and TORSCA; hence KYST is superior to both of them. One advantage of KYST is that it gives users a choice between STRESS formulas one and two as the function to be minimized by the coordinate estimates. Several authors (Kruskal and Carroll, 1969; Roskam, 1969; Takane et al., 1977) have concluded that when data matrix is a symmetric matrix of dissimilarities (or similarities), then the various computational problems discussed below can be reduced by employing formula one. On the other hand, if the data are preferences, then formula two should lead to fewer problems.

S-STRESS

Young's (Takane et al., 1977; Young and Lewyckyj, 1979) ALSCAL algorithm employs a fit measure called S-STRESS. Like STRESS, S-STRESS has two variations called formulas one and two. S-STRESS formula one is defined as follows:

$$SS_1 = \left[\frac{\Sigma_{(i,j)}\left(\hat{\delta}_{ij}^2 - \hat{d}_{ij}^2\right)^2}{\Sigma_{(i,j)}\left(\hat{d}_{ij}^2\right)^2} \right]^{1/2}. \tag{5.16}$$

S-STRESS formula one and STRESS formula one differ only in that SS_1, Eq. (5.16), is defined in terms of squared distances and squared disparities. S_1 in Eq. (5.13), on the other hand, is defined in terms of distances and disparities.

S-STRESS formula two is defined as:

$$SS_2 = \left[\frac{\Sigma_{(i,j)}\left(\hat{\delta}_{ij}^2 - \hat{d}_{ij}^2\right)^2}{\Sigma_{(i,j)}\left(\hat{d}_{ij}^2 - \hat{d}_{..}^2\right)^2} \right]^{1/2}. \tag{5.17}$$

In Eq. (5.17),

$$\hat{d}_{..}^2 = \frac{1}{IJ} \sum_{(i,j)} \hat{d}_{ij}^2. \tag{5.18}$$

It is the mean squared distance estimate. The definition of S-STRESS formula two, Eq. (5.17), parallels that for STRESS formula two, Eq. (5.14). The former, however, is defined in terms of squared, rather than unsquared, distances and disparities.

ALSCAL allows the user to choose either S-STRESS formula one or two as the function minimized by the coordinate estimates. Formula one is recommended when the data are dissimilarities (or similarities) but not when they are preference responses. For the user who cannot afford the luxury of two separate programs, one for nonmetric and one for individual differences analyses of dissimilarity data (Chapter 6), ALSCAL has much to offer. It can be used to perform the nonmetric analyses described in this chapter and some of the individual differences analyses described in Chapter 6. Because the SAS computer package contains a version of ALSCAL, the program is available to anyone with access to this system (Young et al., 1980).

The Coefficient of Alienation

Guttman (1968) proposed a third measure of fit for nonmetric analyses, the coefficient of alienation. In order to define the coefficient of alienation, he first defines a coefficient of monotonicity,

$$\mu = \frac{\Sigma_{(i,j)} \hat{\delta}_{ij} \hat{d}_{ij}}{\left[\left(\Sigma_{(i,j)} \hat{\delta}_{ij}^2 \right) \left(\Sigma_{(i,j)} \hat{d}_{ij}^2 \right) \right]^{1/2}} \tag{5.19}$$

Essentially, μ is a rank order measure of agreement indexing the degree of ordinal association between the original data and the distance estimates. The coefficient of alienation is a goodness-of-fit measure; the better the fit of the nonmetric model to the data, the higher μ will be.

The *coefficient of alienation* is defined in terms of μ as follows:

$$\kappa = \left(1 - \mu^2 \right)^{1/2}. \tag{5.20}$$

The better the fit of the nonmetric model to the data, the lower κ will be; hence κ is a badness-of-fit measure. Lingoes' (1973) Smallest Space Analysis (SSA) programs yield coordinate estimates that maximize the coefficient of monotonicity and minimize the coefficient of alienation.

DIMENSIONALITY, ROTATION, AND INTERPRETATION

The core of the input to any nonmetric MDS program is a dissimilarity matrix. The output contains the following key elements: first, a measure of fit, either STRESS, S-STRESS, or the coefficient of alienation, and second, an $I \times K$ matrix $\hat{X}$ of stimulus coordinate estimates. Decisions about dimensionality, rotation, and interpretation are based primarily on these two elements. Before discussing dimensionality, rotation, and interpretation, a few words need to be said about the data used to illustrate these issues.

Table 5.1. Intercorrelations of the *Vocational Preference Inventory* Scales for a Sample of 1234 Men.

	R	I	A	S	E	C
Realistic	1.00	.46	.16	.21	.30	.36
Investigative	.46	1.00	.34	.30	.16	.16
Artistic	.16	.34	1.00	.42	.35	.11
Social	.21	.30	.42	1.00	.54	.38
Enterprising	.30	.16	.35	.54	1.00	.68
Conventional	.36	.16	.11	.38	.68	1.00

Source: Holland, Whitney, Cole, and Richards 1969. Copyright 1969 by the American College Testing Program. Reprinted with permission.

Example

The data in Table 5.1 come from a study by Rounds et al. (1979). This table shows the intercorrelations among the six scales of the *Vocational Preference Inventory* (Holland, 1965) in a sample of 1234 men. Each scale corresponds to one of six occupational types in Holland's (1973) theory of career choice. Holland has a model of occupational types often represented as a hexagon pictured in Figure 5.2. According to this theory, the interests of people in occupational types adjacent to each other along the hexagon are more similar than the interests of people in occupational types more distant from each other. Occupational types opposite each other along the hexagon are least similar.

Because a hexagon is a two-dimensional figure, Holland's theory led Rounds et al. to the hypothesis that the correlations could be represented in two dimensions and that the stimuli, the six *Vocational Preference Inventory* scales, would array themselves in a roughly hexagonal shape; the ordering of the points along the hexagon would correspond to their ordering in

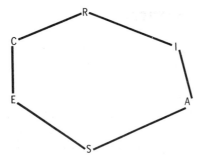

Figure 5.2. Holland's hexagonal model for six occupational types. R = Realistic, I = Investigative, A = Artistic, S = Social, E = Enterprising, and C = Conventional type.

Holland's theory (Figure 5.2). The original authors applied TORSCA (Young and Torgerson, 1967) to their data, but the results reported here are based on a KYST reanalysis (Kruskal et al., 1973).

The Rounds et al. (1979) study is a configural application of MDS, an application designed to explore an hypothesis that specifies the number of dimensions and the configuration that should be formed by the points. The KYST analysis of the data in Table 5.1 will be used to illustrate how a user can decide the issues of dimensionality and interpretation in a nonmetric MDS.

Dimensionality

Following the pattern set in Chapter 4, the discussion to this point has proceeded as if the dimensionality K were known. In practice, the dimensionality must often be determined in the MDS analysis. To decide upon K in such cases, one must obtain solutions in several different dimensionalities. If K^* is the user's best a priori guess as to the dimensionality, one can proceed by obtaining solutions in every dimensionality from $K^* - 3$ to $K^* + 3$. If $K^* \leqslant 3$, making $(K^* - 3) < 1$, then one would obtain solutions in 1 to $K^* + 3$ dimensions.

Having obtained solutions in several dimensionalities, the user must choose among them. Again, the criteria of interpretability, reproducibility, and fit provide the basis for the choice. The interpretability criterion dictates that the number of dimensions be the smallest dimensionality in which all of the important stimulus features (stimulus orderings or groupings) appear. Reproducibility dictates that the solution be composed of dimensions that emerge consistently across subgroups.

One way to evaluate fit is to obtain a dimensions-by-fit-measure plot, such as the one in Figure 5.3. Such a plot is analogous to the dimensions-by-eigenvalues plot discussed in Chapter 4 (see Figure 4.4). There is, however, one essential difference. In a fit-by-dimensions plot, the elbow should occur directly over the appropriate dimensionality K whereas the elbow should occur over the $(K + 1)$st dimension in an eigenvalue-by-dimension plot. In Figure 5.3, the plot begins to level off at two dimensions, suggesting that the appropriate solution may be the two-dimensional configuration.

Kruskal and Wish (1978, p. 56) caution against accepting solutions with STRESS values above .10, unless it is a one-dimensional solution. If the data contain high levels of measurement or sampling error, however, one may accept a STRESS above .10. A STRESS of .15 or less in one dimension usually represents a good fit to the data. Further, Kruskal and Wish (1978) conclude that it is seldom necessary to add dimensions beyond the number

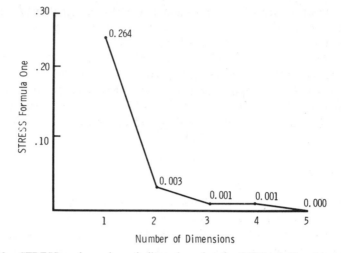

Figure 5.3. STRESS and number of dimensions for the MDS of *Vocational Preference Inventory* scale intercorrelations.

needed to reduce STRESS below .05. For our example, the Kruskal–Wish guidelines clearly suggest two dimensions. Retaining less than two dimensions yields a solution with a STRESS value above .10. No more than two dimensions are needed to reduce STRESS below .05.

In some cases, there can be one other indication of dimensionality. A one-dimensional set of stimuli often form a very distinctive C or U shape when scaled in two dimensions. The ordering of the stimuli along the C or U should correspond to their ordering along the one dimension. Some two-dimensional stimulus sets may also form a C or U. Nevertheless, if the two-dimensional configuration is a C or U *shape*, the researcher should seriously consider a one-dimensional solution.

Rotation

If some nonEuclidean metric has been employed, then there is no rotation problem. If $\hat{\mathbf{X}}$ is a solution, then in general $\hat{\mathbf{X}}^* = \hat{\mathbf{X}}\mathbf{T}$ will *not* also be a solution.[†] If, on the other hand, a Euclidean solution has been employed, $\hat{\mathbf{X}}^* = \hat{\mathbf{X}}\mathbf{T}$ will be another solution.

Even when a Euclidean metric has been employed, the rotation problem is not a serious issue in configural or data reduction applications when the

---

[†]$\hat{\mathbf{X}}^* = \hat{\mathbf{X}}\mathbf{T}$ will be a solution only if $\mathbf{T}$ is a diagonal matrix, and every diagonal element in $\mathbf{T}$ equals either 1.00 or -1.00.

solution contains only two dimensions; the important stimulus features should be identifiable irrespective of rotation.

Rotation is an issue, however, for dimensional applications when the Euclidean metric has been employed. As in the case of a metric solution, if the unrotated dimensions correspond to interpretable stimulus orderings, then a rotation is unnecessary. If not, some objective rotation can be tried. If this too fails to yield an interpretable solution, then the user will be forced to rotate the solution by hand.

In the example of Table 5.1, the application is a configural one in only two dimensions. The hexagonal configuration, if it emerges, should be easy to visualize irrespective of rotation. Hence rotation is not an important issue in this example.

Interpretation

In nonmetric MDS, interpretation of the solution proceeds in the same manner as in metric MDS. It consists largely of identifying important stimulus groupings or orderings. Furthermore, one must label or describe the stimulus attribute corresponding to each ordering, and one must describe the feature shared in common by each stimulus grouping.

For the example of Table 5.1, the two-dimensional coordinates are shown in Table 5.2. These coordinates are plotted in Figure 5.4. Inspection of Figure 5.4 shows that the points do fall in a roughly hexagonal pattern, although not all sides of the hexagon are equal in length. If one starts in the upper right corner of the figure and proceeds clockwise around the hexagon, the stimuli fall in the order suggested by Holland's theory depicted in Figure 5.2. Both the dimensionality of the obtained solution and the configuration of points support the hexagonal hypothesis.

Table 5.2. Two-Dimensional Coordinates of the
***Vocational Preference Inventory* Scales.**

	Dimension I	Dimension II
Realistic	0.62	0.83
Investigative	1.15	0.10
Artistic	0.22	− 1.17
Social	− 0.40	− 0.50
Enterprising	− 0.83	0.03
Conventional	− 0.77	0.70

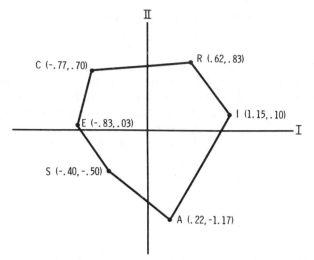

Figure 5.4. Two-dimensional plot of the *Vocational Preference Inventory* scales. R = Realistic, I = Investigative, A = Artistic, S = Social, E = Enterprising, and C = Conventional.

Summary

Dimensionality, rotation, and interpretation are decided in much the same way for either a metric or nonmetric scaling. To decide on the dimensionality, several solutions of different dimensionalities must be obtained. The choice between the several solutions must be made on the basis of interpretability, reproducibility, and fit. A dimensions-by-fit-measure plot, guidelines provided by Kruskal and Wish (1978), and the shape of the two-dimensional configuration are all useful indicators of dimensionality.

Rotation is a serious issue only when the Euclidean metric has been employed. Rotation is a more difficult problem in dimensional applications than in configural or data reduction applications. Since the important stimulus features usually stand out in two dimensions irrespective of rotation, rotation becomes more of a problem when the solution contains three or more dimensions. Objective and hand rotations can be used as needed to obtain an interpretable solution. Interpretation consists largely of identifying the important stimulus orderings and groupings.

SCATTER PLOTS

The results in Table 5.3 come from the analysis of the *Vocational Preference Inventory* scale intercorrelations. Columns one and two indicate which pair of scales corresponds to each row of Table 5.3. Columns 3–5, respectively, give the similarity data, disparity estimates, and distance estimates for each pair of scales. As an example, the first element under the heading "Similarity" is the correlation between the Investigative and Realistic scales. This same correlation, .46, is also shown in row 2 column 1 of Table 5.1. As another example, the ninth element in the column labeled "Similarity" is the correlation, .35, between the Enterprising and Artistic scales, also shown in row 5 column 3 of Table 5.1.

The distance estimates in the last column of Table 5.3 were constructed from the coordinate estimates in Table 5.2. For instance, the first element in this column, .90, is the estimated distance between the second stimulus (Investigative) and the first stimulus (Realistic). Letting $\hat{d}_{IR}$ represent the estimated distance between these two stimuli, and letting $\hat{x}_{Ik}$ and $\hat{x}_{Rk}$ be their coordinates estimates in Table 5.2, then

$$\hat{d}_{IR} = \left[\sum_k (\hat{x}_{Ik} - \hat{x}_{Rk})^2 \right]^{1/2} = \left[(1.15 - 0.62)^2 + (0.10 - 0.83)^2 \right]^{1/2}$$

$$= .90. \qquad (5.21)$$

Table 5.3. Similarity Data, Disparity Estimates, and Estimated Distances for the Two-Dimensional MDS of the *Vocational Preference Inventory* Scale Intercorrelations.[a]

Row	Column	Similarity	Disparity	Distance Estimate
I	R	.46	.90	.90
A	R	.16	2.04	2.04
A	I	.34	1.59	1.57
S	R	.21	1.67	1.67
S	I	.30	1.66	1.66
S	A	.42	.92	.92
E	R	.30	1.66	1.66
E	I	.16	1.98	1.98
E	A	.35	1.59	1.59
E	S	.54	.68	.68
C	R	.36	1.40	1.40
C	I	.16	2.01	2.01
C	A	.11	2.12	2.12
C	S	.38	1.25	1.25
C	E	.68	.67	.67

[a] R = Realistic, I = Investigative, A = Artistic, S = Social, E = Enterprising, and C = Conventional.

As a second example, $\hat{d}_{EA}$, the ninth element in the last column of Table 5.3, can be computed from the coordinate estimates in Table 5.2 as follows:

$$\hat{d}_{EA} = \left[\sum_k (\hat{x}_{Ek} - \hat{x}_{Ak})^2\right]^{1/2} = \{[-0.83 - 0.22]^2 + [0.03 - (-1.17)]^2\}^{1/2}$$

$$= 1.59, \tag{5.22}$$

and so forth.

Three scatter plots are sometimes discussed in the MDS literature. One is what Guttman (1968) calls an *image diagram*. The distance estimates are plotted along one axis and the disparities along the other. Figure 5.5 shows such a plot based on the data in Table 5.3. There is one point in an image diagram for each pair of stimuli. (This graph appears to contain only 14 points, even though there are 15 pairs of scales. This is because two pairs have exactly the same disparities and data values, 1.66, and hence fall at exactly the same point on the graph.) The height of each point corresponds to its disparity in column 4 of Table 5.3. Its position along the horizontal axis corresponds to the associated distance in column 5 of Table 5.3.

If the data satisfy the model perfectly, in which case the fit measure will be zero, these points will fall along a straight line extending from the origin

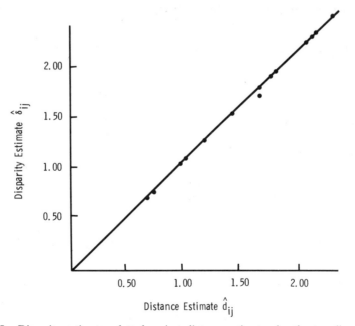

Figure 5.5. Disparity estimates plotted against distance estimates for the two-dimensional MDS of the *Vocational Preference Inventory* scale intercorrelations.

at a 45° angle to the horizontal axis. The points in Figure 5.5 deviate only slightly from this line. The more the points deviate from this line, the worse the fit of the model to the data. The points that deviate most markedly from this line, the outliers, are the ones that satisfy the nonmetric distance model least well. A careful inspection of the outliers may lead to the discovery of theoretically important deviations from the model.

The second scatter diagram of interest is a plot of the disparities against the original data. Figure 5.6 shows the disparities plotted against the similarities data. Again there is one point for each pair of stimuli. (And again this graph appears to contain only 14 points, even though there are 15 pairs of scales. This is because two pairs have exactly the same data value,

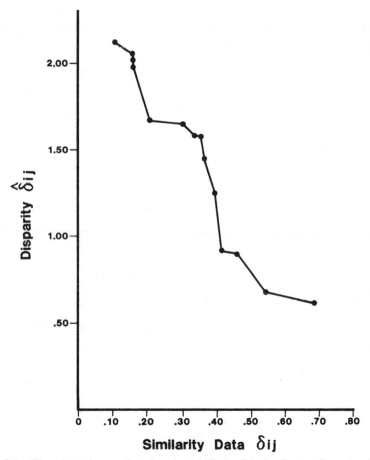

Figure 5.6. Disparity estimates plotted against similarity data for the two-dimensional MDS of the *Vocational Preference Inventory* scale intercorrelations.

.30, and the same disparity, 1.66, and hence fall at exactly the same point on the graph.) The vertical axis represents the disparity estimate and the horizontal axis represents the data value associated with each stimulus pair. This diagram gives a pictorial representation of the function f in Eq. (5.1) or (5.9), the monotone function relating the data to the distances on the right side of these equations.

Although the third type of scatter diagram is not shown, one can also plot the estimated distances ($\hat{d}_{ij}$) against the original data (δ_{ij}). Such a plot provides another way to represent the monotone function f in Eqs. (5.1) and (5.9). These two pictorial representations of the monotone function, the plot of distance estimates against the original data and the plot of the disparities against the original data, are called *Shepard diagrams*.

As an aside, STRESS formula one can be computed from the values in the image diagram of Figure 5.5. These values also appear in columns 4 and 5 of Table 5.3. The denominator of the fraction under the square root sign in STRESS formula 1, Eq. (5.13), is

$$\sum_{(i,j)} \hat{d}_{ij}^2 = (.90)^2 + (2.04)^2 + (1.57)^2 + (1.67)^2$$
$$+ (1.66)^2 + (.92)^2 + (1.66)^2 + (1.98)^2$$
$$+ (1.59)^2 + (.68)^2 + (1.40)^2 + (2.01)^2 \qquad (5.23)$$
$$+ (2.12)^2 + (1.25)^2 + (.67)^2$$
$$= 36.00.$$

The numerator of the fraction under the square root sign in Eq. (5.13) is

$$\sum_{(i,j)} \left(\delta_{ij} - \hat{d}_{ij}\right)^2 = (.90 - .90)^2 + (2.04 - 2.04)^2$$
$$+ (1.59 - 1.57)^2 + (1.67 - 1.67)^2$$
$$+ (1.66 - 1.66)^2 + (.92 - .92)^2$$
$$+ (1.66 - 1.66)^2 + (1.98 - 1.98)^2$$
$$+ (1.59 - 1.59)^2 + (.68 - .68)^2 \qquad (5.24)$$
$$+ (1.40 - 1.40)^2 + (2.01 - 2.01)^2$$
$$+ (2.12 - 2.12)^2 + (1.25 - 1.25)^2$$
$$+ (.67 - .67)^2$$
$$= .0004.$$

Combining the results from Eqs. (5.23) and (5.24) gives

$$S_1 = \left(\frac{.0004}{36.00} \right)^{1/2} = .003. \tag{5.25}$$

COMPUTATIONAL PROBLEMS

Whichever fit measure is employed, there exists a set of equations such that the disparities $\hat{\delta}_{ij}$ and coordinate estimates $\hat{x}_{ik}$, $\hat{x}_{jk}$ that minimize the fit measure satisfy those equations. These equations will be called the solution equations. The object of any algorithm is to find disparities and coordinate estimates that satisfy those equations. The solution equations are always complex, and often they cannot be solved by standard algebraic techniques. Instead, they must be solved using numerical analytic techniques called gradient methods.

The first step in any gradient method is to obtain an initial matrix of stimulus coordinates $\hat{X}^o_{(I \times K)}$ called the *starting configuration*. The starting configuration is an initial guess about the coordinates. Each succeeding step in the algorithm is called an iteration. In each iteration, the stimulus coordinate estimates $\hat{X}$ are adjusted so they more closely approximate the coordinates that satisfy the solution equations. Furthermore, new estimates of disparities are calculated in each iteration. If all goes well, iteration continues until a set of coordinate estimates and disparities have been found that satisfy the solution equations.

Unfortunately, there are several things that can go wrong in the iterative process. These potential problems are called the local minima problem, the problem of degenerate solutions, and the convergence problem. Each problem will be treated in turn.

Local Minima

As a rule, there are several sets of parameters (coordinate estimates and disparities) that satisfy the solution equations. The fit statistics corresponding to each such set of solution parameters are not all equal. Of these several sets of solution parameters, the one that corresponds to the lowest value of the fit measure (STRESS, S-STRESS, or alienation) is said to constitute the *global minimum*. All other sets of parameters that satisfy the solution equations are said to constitute *local minima*.

The desired solution is the set of parameter estimates that gives a global minimum for the fit measure. The algorithms yield parameters that satisfy the solution equations, but not necessarily those parameter estimates corresponding to the global minimum. The local minima problem is the problem of ensuring that the user's solution corresponds to the global minimum of the fit measure, not some local minimum.

The best way to ensure that the obtained solution is a global and not a local minimum, is to use a good starting configuration. Variations on Torgerson's metric scaling method (Chapter 4) provide the best methods for obtaining a single starting configuration. ALSCAL (Young and Lewyckyj, 1979), KYST (Kruskal et al., 1973), SSA (Lingoes, 1973), and TORSCA (Young and Torgerson, 1976) all allow the user to employ Torgerson's (1958) metric MDS algorithm in deriving the starting configuration. Although the programs use different transformations, they begin by applying some monotone transformation to the dissimilarity (or similarity) data. They then apply Torgerson's (1952) analysis to obtain coordinate estimates in K dimensions. These coordinate estimates become the starting configuration $\hat{X}^\circ$ for the K-dimensional nonmetric MDS solution.

Starting configurations generated via some variation of Torgerson's (1952) algorithm are called *rational starting configurations*. Algorithms that use rational starting configurations appear less prone to local minima problems than algorithms that employ a single nonrational start (Arabie, 1978; Clark, 1976; Lingoes and Roskam, 1973; Spence, 1972, 1974; Spence and Young, 1978). M-D-SCAL (Kruskal and Carmone, undated), which does not use a rational start, is more prone to local minima problems than its successor KYST (Kruskal et al., 1973).

Arabie (1973, 1978) has proposed an extremely conservative approach to the local minima problem. Specifically, he argues that one should generate up to 20 different solutions, each beginning from a different starting configuration, and choose that solution that provides the best fit from among twenty or so solutions obtained. Arabie's conclusion may be premature. As Spence and Young (1978) cogently argue in response to Arabie, Arabie's conclusion was reached without making any systematic comparison between his multiple start approach and the rational start approach employed by most programs. At this time, the multiple start approach seems expensive, time consuming, and largely untested in any systematic way. However, with particularly difficult kinds of data, it may be a prudent approach.

Degenerate Solutions

A solution is said to be degenerate when the number of distinct points in the solution configuration is small compared to the number of stimulus points. Figure 5.7 shows a degenerate two-dimensional solution. Notice that stimuli A, B, and C have the same coordinates on both dimensions; hence in the

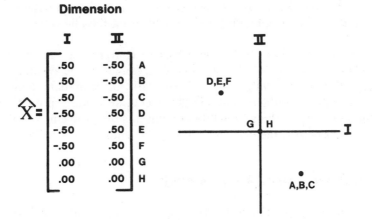

Figure 5.7. A degenerate solution for eight points in two dimensions.

graph they collapse onto a single point. Similarly, D, E, and F collapse onto a single point because they have exactly the same coordinates. The last two stimuli, G and H, also collapse onto a single point. Consequently, there are only three distinct points in the graph even though there are eight stimuli. The solution is degenerate because the number of distinct points (three) is small compared to the number of stimuli (eight).

Users should. always inspect their solutions for degeneracy, particularly solutions in one or two dimensions. Shepard (1974) states that solutions with STRESS values near zero are often degenerate, so users should make a special effort to inspect those solutions with suspiciously low fit statistics. When a degenerate solution is encountered, it should be discarded. Sometimes, a degenerate solution means that the solution should be sought in a higher dimensionality.

Lack of Convergence

Of the three problems discussed in this section—local minima, degeneracies, and lack of convergence—lack of convergence is the easiest to solve but probably the most frequent. A user must specify the maximum number of iterations he or she will allow in solving for the parameters (stimulus scale value estimates and disparities). In some cases, the number of iterations required to achieve the solution will exceed the maximum number specified by the user. Most computer programs print some message, such as "MAXIMUM NUMBER OF ITERATIONS EXCEEDED" to indicate that the desired solution was not achieved in the allowed number of iterations.

Usually this message appears near the fit statistic in the computer print-out. The problem can be circumvented by increasing the allowable number of iterations.

Local minima, degeneracies, and lack of convergence may seem like a formidable triad of problems. Local minima can largely be avoided by using a rational starting configuration. Particularly difficult data may require multiple starting configurations. Degeneracies are readily spotted. Often a solution in a higher dimensionality circumvents the problem. When lack of convergence occurs, the user can solve again using more iterations.

CONSONANT PHONEME EXAMPLE

A study by Shepard (1972b, 1974) illustrates an application of MDS that is quite different from the ones described previously. In his data reduction application, Shepard uses MDS to obtain a two-dimensional representation of the stimuli, a representation that could readily be displayed graphically. As shown below, the two-dimensional graph provided a way to visually portray stimulus groupings which are the real focus of his study. Shepard's (1972b, 1974) stimuli are the 16 consonant phonemes shown in Figure 5.8. The data are taken from an earlier study by Miller and Nicely (1955). In the original Miller and Nicely study, a speaker pronounces each phoneme to a listener who then writes down the phoneme he or she understands to have been spoken. The purpose of the study is to identify those features of the phonemes that lead to confusions between them.

According to Miller and Nicely, these 16 phonemes were chosen because they "make up almost three quarters of the consonants we utter in normal speech and about 40% of all phonemes, vowels included" (p. 338). Four of the symbols in Figure 5.8 are probably unfamiliar to most readers and will be explained here. /ʃ/ designates the "sh" sound in "ship," /θ/ the "th" sound in "thumb," /ð/ the "th" sound in "though," and /ʒ/ the "s" sound in "treasure."

The basic matrix derived from the Miller–Nicely study was a confusion matrix in which each cell contained the number of trials on which the row phoneme was pronounced by the speaker and the column phoneme was written by the listener. Presumably, the more similar the sound of two phonemes, the more likely their confusion.

After converting the confusion matrix to a symmetric form, Shepard (1974) scales the stimuli in two dimensions. Figure 5.8 shows his two-dimensional solution. The scaling can be interpreted in terms of phonetic groups. Specifically, the phonemes seem to group themselves on the basis of several features: whether they are stops or fricatives, whether they are nasal,

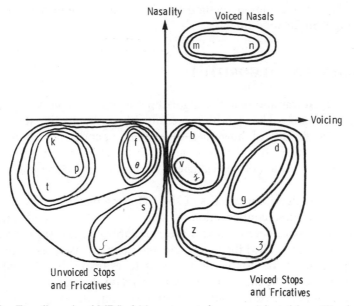

Figure 5.8. Two-dimensional MDS of 16 consonant phonemes. Adapted from "Psychological Representation of Speech Sounds" by R. N. Shepard. Copyright 1972 by McGraw-Hill. Used with the permission of the McGraw Hill Book Company.

whether they are voiced, and whether they are pronounced in the front, back, or middle of the mouth.

Beginning at the top right and moving clockwise, the major groupings are as follows. First, there are the voiced nasals {m, n}. Second, there is the large group of voiced fricatives and stops {b, v, ð, d, g, z, ʒ}. This group of seven stimuli can be broken into the middle voiced fricatives {z, ʒ}, the voiced stops {d, g}, and the front voiced consonants {b, v, ð}. Within this latter group of three, there are the two voiced fricatives {v, ð}.

The third major grouping contains the six unvoiced phonemes {k, p, t, f, θ, s, ʃ}. This large set can be broken down into the unvoiced stops {k, p, t}, the front unvoiced fricatives {f, θ}, and the middle unvoiced fricatives {s, ʃ}. Voiced phonemes lie to the right of the configuration and unvoiced phonemes lie to the left. Hence the horizontal dimension seems to reflect voicing. The two nasal phonemes lie at the top of the configuration, suggesting that the vertical dimension reflects nasality.

Shepard's application of MDS belongs in the data reduction category. The scaling serves to reduce the structure of the confusion data to a two-dimensional plot in which the stimulus clusters can be readily displayed. Figure 5.8 not only illustrates a data reduction application of MDS, it also shows a common method of designating stimulus groupings by enclosing them in solid lines.

*ILLUSTRATIVE ALGORITHM

There is great variation in the algorithms actually employed to perform nonmetric scalings. The algorithm presented here should give the interested reader a rough idea of how such algorithms operate. For more detailed descriptions, the reader should consult Guttman (1968), Kruskal (1964), Lingoes and Roskam (1973), Takane et al. (1977), or Young and Lewyckyj (1979).

Each major algorithm consists of the following major phases. In the first phase, the starting configuration is derived. In the second phase, the distance and coordinate estimates are standardized. The third and fourth phases will here be called the nonmetric and metric phases, respectively. The major purpose of the nonmetric phase is to estimate the disparities. The major purpose of the metric phase is to estimate the stimulus coordinates. After the initial starting configuration has been derived, each iteration consists of one standardization, one nonmetric phase, and one metric phase. Iteration continues until the change in the fit measure from one iteration to the next falls below some suitably small figure such as .001. Figure 5.9 diagrams the major steps in a nonmetric algorithm.

Each of the next four sections discusses one of the steps in a nonmetric algorithm: obtaining a starting configuration, standardizing the distance and coordinate estimates, the nonmetric phase, and the metric phase.

In the following discussion, it will be assumed that the fit measure is STRESS formula one, the primary approach to ties has been selected, and a Euclidean solution in two dimensions is desired. The correlations between *Vocational Preference Inventory* scales in Table 5.1 will be used to illustrate the analysis. Since the analysis described here applies to dissimilarities, rather than similarities, the correlations in Table 5.1 were first converted

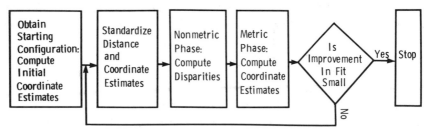

Figure 5.9.   Flow chart of a nonmetric algorithm.

into dissimilarities using the following transformation:

$$\delta_{ij} = \left(1 - r_{ij}\right)^{1/2}. \tag{5.26}$$

Any transformation that reverses the rank order of the data could have been used in place of the one in Eq. (5.26). Table 5.4 shows the dissimilarity matrix so derived.

Starting Configuration

Any nonmetric MDS algorithm begins with the derivation of a starting configuration, a step performed only once. Rational approaches, the best methods for obtaining a single starting configuration, all employ Torgerson's (1952) metric algorithm in some fashion. To derive the starting configuration for this example, Torgerson's (1952) algorithm was applied directly to the dissimilarity data in Table 5.4. The top of Table 5.5 shows the raw scale value estimates obtained using the *Statistical Package for the Social Sciences* (Nie et al., 1975) to extract two principal components from the scalar product matrix. In general, the first K principal components of the scalar product matrix constitute the starting configuration for a K-dimensional solution. The matrix labeled "Unstandardized Distance Estimates" in Table 5.4 shows the Euclidean distance estimates computed from the unstandardized coordinate estimates of Table 5.5. These distance estimates were computed in the usual manner:

$$\hat{d}_{ij}^{\circ} = \left[\sum_{k} \left(\hat{x}_{ik}^{\circ} - \hat{x}_{jk}^{\circ} \right)^2 \right]^{1/2}. \tag{5.27}$$

In Eq. (5.27) $\hat{x}_{ik}^{\circ}$ and $\hat{x}_{jk}^{\circ}$ refer to initial coordinate estimates in the starting configuration, and $\hat{d}_{ij}^{\circ}$ refers to an initial distance estimate.

Standardizing Distance and Coordinate Estimates

After the starting configuration has been obtained, the first iteration begins. At the beginning of each iteration, many algorithms employ some standardization of the current distance ($\hat{d}_{ij}$) and coordinate estimates ($\hat{x}_{ik}$). Beginning the first iteration, the current estimates are those obtained from the starting configuration. For each iteration after the first, the current estimates are those obtained in the metric phase of the previous iteration.

Table 5.4. Dissimilarities, Scalar Products, and Initial Distance Estimates from a Nonmetric Scaling of *Vocational Preference Inventory* Scales.

Dissimilarities

	R	I	A	S	E	C	
Realistic	.00						
Investigative	.73	.00					
Artistic	.92	.82	.00				
Social	.89	.84	.76	.00			$= \Delta$
Enterprising	.84	.92	.81	.68	.00		
Conventional	.80	.92	.94	.79	.57	.00	

Scalar Products

	R	I	A	S	E	C	
Realistic	.31						
Investigative	.05	.32					
Artistic	−.11	−.01	.32				
Social	−.12	−.07	−.01	.25			$= \Delta^*$
Enterprising	−.09	−.15	−.06	.01	.22		
Conventional	−.03	−.13	−.15	−.05	.09	.27	

Unstandardized Distance Estimates

	R	I	A	S	E	C
Realistic	.000					
Investigative	.404	.000				
Artistic	.859	.591	.000			
Social	.761	.681	.373	.000		
Enterprising	.732	.828	.698	.332	.000	
Conventional	.628	.848	.885	.550	.255	.000

Standardized Distance Estimates $\hat{d}_{ij}^{\,o}$

	R	I	A	S	E	C
Realistic	.000					
Investigative	.158	.000				
Artistic	.337	.232	.000			
Social	.298	.267	.146	.000		
Enterprising	.287	.324	.273	.130	.000	
Conventional	.246	.332	.347	.215	.100	.000

Experience has indicated that this standardization of the distances reduces the likelihood of encountering a degenerate solution. If STRESS formula one is used, it is convenient to standardize the distances so that their sum of squares equals 1.00: $\Sigma_{(i,\,j)}\hat{d}_{ij}^2 = 1.00$. When the distances are so standardized, then S_1 reduces to:

$$S_1 = \left[\sum_{(i,\,j)} \left(\hat{\delta}_{ij} - \hat{d}_{ij} \right)^2 \right]^{1/2}. \tag{5.28}$$

Hence minimizing S_1 becomes equivalent to minimizing F:

$$F = \sum_{(i,\,j)} \left(\hat{\delta}_{ij} - \hat{d}_{ij} \right)^2. \tag{5.29}$$

The algorithm described below presumes that the distance estimates are standardized so their sum of squares equals 1.00. This standardization can be accomplished by multiplying each unstandardized distance estimate $\hat{d}_{ij}$ by a constant so that their sum of squares equals 1.00. For the coordinate

Table 5.5. Starting Configuration for a
Nonmetric Scaling of the *Vocational Preference Inventory* Scales.

	Unstandardized Coordinate Estimates	
	I	II
Realistic	−.224	.416
Investigative	−.456	.085
Artistic	−.189	−.442
Social	.134	−.256
Enterprising	.366	−.018
Conventional	.378	.237

	Standardized Coordinate Estimates		
	I	II	
Realistic	−.088	.163	
Investigative	−.179	.033	
Artistic	−.074	−.173	
Social	.052	−.100	$= \hat{\mathbf{X}}^\circ$
Enterprising	.143	−.007	
Conventional	.148	.093	

estimates to be expressed on the same scale as the distances, each coordinate estimate must be multiplied by the same constant. Typically, this standardization would occur once in each iteration just prior to the nonmetric phase.

The bottom of Table 5.4 shows the standardized distance estimates obtained by multiplying each unstandardized distance estimate in Table 5.4 by a constant so that the sum of squared distance estimates will equal 1.00. Multiplying each unstandardized coordinate estimate in Table 5.5 by the same constant yielded the standardized coordinate estimates at the bottom of Table 5.5. Since the nonmetric and metric phases operate solely on standardized coordinate and distance estimates, the terms "distance estimate" and "coordinate estimate" in the ensuing discussion refer to standardized values.

Nonmetric Phase

The nonmetric phase uses the dissimilarity data and the standardized distances from the previous iteration (or the starting configuration) to compute disparities. A series of passes through the data (described below) constitutes the major portion of the nonmetric phase for a single iteration. Before beginning the passes, however, the data points δ_{ij} must be sorted into ascending order. This section begins by describing the arrangement of data points into ascending order, and then it proceeds to a description of the passes. Readers should note that *each* iteration contains a complete series of these passes. The nonmetric phase does *not* adjust the stimulus coordinate estimates or the distance estimates. Only the disparities $\hat{\delta}_{ij}$ change in the nonmetric phase. Before describing the nonmetric phase itself, some notation must be defined.

Let $\hat{\delta}_{ij}^{(c+1)}$ be the disparity for stimulus pair (i, j) to be derived in this, the $(c + 1)$st, iteration. Let $\hat{x}_{ik}^c$ be the coordinate estimate from iteration c ($c = 0, \ldots, C$), the iteration just completed. If $c = 0$, then these coordinate estimates constitute the starting configuration. Finally, let $\hat{d}_{ij}^c$ be a distance estimate from the cth iteration:

$$\hat{d}_{ij}^c = \left[\sum_k \left(\hat{x}_{ik}^c - \hat{x}_{jk}^c \right)^2 \right]^{1/2}. \tag{5.30}$$

In the most common nonmetric phase (Kruskal, 1964), disparities $\hat{\delta}_{ij}^{(c+1)}$ are calculated so that they constitute a monotone transformation of the original dissimilarity data δ_{ij}. That is, the disparities satisfy expression (5.11). The algorithm does *not* simply find some well-known continuous monotone function (such as a log or power function) and apply it to the data. Rather, the nonmetric phase consists of steps in which each disparity $\hat{\delta}_{ij}^{(c+1)}$ is set equal to the corresponding distance estimate $\hat{d}_{ij}^c$, or is set equal to the average of several distance estimates. DeLeeuw (1977) shows that when the disparities are calculated in this way, they minimize the following sum of squared discrepancies: $\Sigma_{(i,j)}(\hat{\delta}_{ij}^{(c+1)} - \hat{d}_{ij}^c)^2$.

The distance estimates from iteration c become the initial disparity estimates for iteration $(c + 1)$. In our example, the disparity estimates for the first iteration of the nonmetric phase are the standardized distance estimates at the bottom of Table 5.4. Column 4 of Table 5.6 contains the distance estimate $\hat{d}_{ij}^o$ corresponding to each data point δ_{ij}.

The first step in the nonmetric phase is to arrange the dissimilarity data into a single column so that the data in the column are in ascending order. Column 3 of Table 5.6 contains the dissimilarity data from Table 5.4 arranged from smallest to largest as one moves down the column. For instance, the smallest data point, $\delta_{CE} = .57$, is the first element of column 3, Table 5.6. The next smallest data point, $\delta_{E3} = .68$, is the second smallest dissimilarity in Table 5.4, and so forth. The last dissimilarity in Table 5.6 is the largest value in Table 5.4, $\delta_{CA} = .94$.

A complication arises when there are ties in the data such that $\delta_{ij} = \delta_{gh}$ for some pair of data points. If $\delta_{ij} = \delta_{gh}$ and $\hat{d}_{ij}^c = \hat{d}_{gh}^c$, then it does not matter which precedes. If however, $\delta_{ij} = \delta_{gh}$ and $\hat{d}_{ij}^c \neq \hat{d}_{gh}^c$, then the disparity associated with the smaller distance estimate should precede. In Table 5.6, δ_{SI} has been placed ahead of δ_{ER} even though the two data values are identical ($\delta_{SI} = \delta_{ER} = .84$) because the distance estimate (column 4) for the former, $\hat{d}_{SI}^o = .267$, is less than that for the latter, $\hat{d}_{ER}^o = .287$. Similarly δ_{EI} precedes δ_{CI} which precedes δ_{AR} in Table 5.6 even though all three dissimilarities equal .92 because $\hat{d}_{EI}^o < \hat{d}_{CI}^o < \hat{d}_{AR}^o$.

After arranging the dissimilarity data in ascending order, the algorithm begins a series of passes through the data. Once the passes are complete, the nonmetric phase is complete. At the beginning of the first pass in an iteration, the disparities are the current distance estimates from either the starting configuration or the previous iteration. At the beginning of each succeeding pass in that same iteration, the disparities are those obtained in the previous pass. Column 4 of Table 5.6 contains the standardized distance estimates from the starting configuration (Table 5.4) which are the disparities that begin the first pass of the nonmetric phase for the first iteration. The pass begins with the division of disparity estimates into blocks of equal values. For the initial disparity estimates in Table 5.6, there are no tied values, so each disparity constitutes its own block.

The remainder of each pass consists of comparing adjacent blocks. Let m ($m = 1,\ldots, M$) be a subscript designating blocks from lowest ($m = 1$) to highest ($m = M$). The designation of the blocks in Table 5.6 is shown in

Table 5.6. Dissimilarities, Distances, and Disparities from the *Vocational Preference Inventory* Scale Illustration.

Row[a]	Column[a]	Dissimilarity	Before Mergers		After One Merger		After Two Mergers		Distances
			Disparity	Block	Disparity[b]	Block	Disparity[b]	Block	
C	E	.57	.100	1	.100	1	.100	1	.102
E	S	.68	.130	2	.130	2	.130	2	.126
I	R	.73	.158	3	.152	3	.152	3	.155
S	A	.76	.146	4	.152	3	.152	3	.145
C	S	.79	.215	5	.215	4	.215	4	.215
C	R	.80	.246	6	.246	5	.246	5	.246
E	A	.81	.273	7	.273	6	.253	6	.268
A	I	.82	.232	8	.232	7	.253	6	.239
S	I	.84	.267	9	.267	8	.267	7	.270
E	R	.84	.287	10	.287	9	.287	8	.286
S	R	.89	.298	11	.298	10	.298	9	.298
E	I	.92	.324	12	.324	11	.324	10	.324
C	I	.92	.332	13	.332	12	.332	11	.333
A	R	.92	.337	14	.337	13	.337	12	.337
C	A	.94	.347	15	.347	14	.347	13	.346

[a]R = Realistic, I = Investigative, A = Artistic, S = Social, E = Enterprising, and C = Conventional.
[b]Solid lines denote blocks of more than one element.

column 5. Starting with $m = 1$, the elements in the mth block are compared to the elements in the $(m + 1)$st block. If the elements in the mth block are less than those in the $(m + 1)$st block, then one simply moves on to a comparison of the next two blocks. If, however, the elements of the mth block are larger than those of the $(m + 1)$st, then one resets all of the elements in the mth and $(m + 1)$st blocks to be the arithmetic mean of the elements in the two blocks. After resetting the elements in the mth and $(m + 1)$st blocks, all of the elements in both blocks will be equal, and hence one can merge them into a single block which becomes the new mth block. Having merged them, one now proceeds to a comparison of this new mth block with the new $(m + 1)$st block that follows it. The pass ends once all adjacent blocks have been compared. The outcome of the pass is a new set of disparity estimates. If no blocks were merged in the pass, then the nonmetric phase of the iteration ends.

If however, some blocks were merged, then a new pass begins. Each pass begins with a grouping of the current disparity estimates into blocks of equal values. The remainder of the pass consists of comparing pairs of adjacent blocks and merging them as necessary. Passes continue until one is reached in which no merging is required. The disparity estimates derived in this last pass are the disparity estimates for the $(c + 1)$st iteration, $\hat{\delta}_{ij}^{(c+1)}$. The disparity estimates from the last iteration are the final disparity estimates $\hat{\delta}_{ij}$.

In column 4 of Table 5.6, the element in the first block is smaller than the element in the second block, so we can move on to a comparison of the second and third blocks. The element in the second block is smaller than that in the third block, so we move on to blocks 3 and 4. The element in block 3 is larger than that in 4, so these two elements must be replaced by their arithmetic mean, $(.158 + .146)/2.00 = .152$. Column 6 shows the replacement. These two elements become a new block. The pass continues on the elements in column 6.

The elements in the new block 3, column 6, are smaller than that in block 4, block 4 is smaller than block 5, and block 5 is smaller than block 6. Block 6, however, is larger than block 7. The elements in blocks 6 and 7 must be replaced by their arithmetic mean, $(.273 + .232)/2.00 = .253$, and merged into a new block. This new merged block 6 appears in column 8. The pass continues over the elements in column 8.

The elements in the newly created block 6 are smaller than the element in 7, block 7 is smaller than 8, and so forth. Comparison of the remaining adjacent blocks reveals that no more mergers are required. Upon completion of the comparison between the last two adjacent blocks, 12 and 13, pass one would come to an end.

Since the first pass required merging some blocks, a second pass is necessary. In the second pass, made over the elements in column 8, no merging would be necessary. Consequently, the nonmetric phase would end after the second pass. The figures in column 8 would become the final disparity estimates for the $(c + 1) = $ 1st iteration and would be carried into the metric phase of that iteration.

When the passes are complete, the disparities will satisfy the weak monotonicity constraint stated in Expression (5.11). The nonmetric phase is an application of Kruskal's (1964) monotone regression in which the data points are regressed onto the distance estimates. Barlow et al. (1972) contains a general discussion of monotone regression under the heading isotone regression. DeLeeuw (1977) shows that the disparity estimates will minimize the sum of squared discrepancies between the disparities and distance estimates subject to the weak monotonicity constraint in Expression (5.11).

Metric Phase

The metric phase follows the nonmetric phase. It uses the disparities computed in the nonmetric phase $(\hat{\delta}_{ij}^{(c+1)})$, the distance estimates from the previous iteration $(\hat{d}_{ij}^{c})$, and the coordinate estimates from the previous iteration $(\hat{x}_{ik}^{c})$ to obtain new coordinate estimates $[\hat{x}_{ik}^{(c+1)}]$ from which new distance estimates can be computed $[\hat{d}_{ij}^{(c+1)}]$. The disparities remain *unchanged* in this phase. This section begins by describing the function that the metric phase is designed to minimize, and then it proceeds to a description of how one computes the new coordinate estimates.

Having obtained the disparities $\hat{\delta}_{ij}^{(c+1)}$, it is time to enter the metric phase for obtaining new estimates of the coordinates $\hat{x}_{ik}$. If the distances are standardized so that their sum of squares equals 1.00, then STRESS formula one reduces to Eq. (5.28). Minimizing S_1 then is equivalent to minimizing F in Eq. (5.29).

Although the derivation is beyond the scope of this text, nevertheless, Lingoes and Roskam (1973) give the following form for the coordinate estimates $\hat{x}_{ik}^{(c+1)}$:

$$\hat{x}_{ik}^{(c+1)} = \hat{x}_{ik}^{c} - \frac{1}{J}\sum_{j}\left(1 - \frac{\hat{\delta}_{ij}^{(c+1)}}{\hat{d}_{ij}^{c}}\right)\left(\hat{x}_{ik}^{c} - \hat{x}_{jk}^{c}\right). \qquad (5.31)$$

Equation (5.31) gives the equality required to compute the new stimulus coordinate estimates. To avoid division by zero, the ratio $(\hat{\delta}_{ij}^{(c+1)}/\hat{d}_{ij}^{c})$ is arbitrarily set to 1.00 if $\hat{d}_{ij}^{c} = 0.00$.

The right side of Eq. (5.31) utilizes the coordinate estimates from the previous iteration $\hat{x}_{ik}^{c}$, the most recent disparity estimates $\hat{\delta}_{ij}^{(c+1)}$, and the distance estimates from the previous iteration $\hat{d}_{ij}^{c}$. The lower portion of Table 5.5 contains the most recent coordinate estimates in the example, $\hat{x}_{ik}^{0}$.

Column 8 of Table 5.6 contains the disparity estimates, $\hat{\delta}^1_{ij}$, and column 4 contains the distance estimates, $\hat{d}^o_{ij}$. Therefore, the new coordinate estimates $\hat{x}^1_{ik}$ can be calculated using Eq. (5.31) and the information in Tables 5.5 and 5.6.

For instance, the new coordinate estimate along dimension I for the Realistic scale would be

$$\hat{x}^1_{R1} = \hat{x}^o_{R1} - \frac{1}{6} \sum_j \left(1 - \frac{\hat{\delta}^1_{Rj}}{\hat{d}^o_{Rj}}\right)\left(\hat{x}^o_{R1} - \hat{x}^o_{j1}\right)$$

$$= -.088 - 1/6\left\{\left[1 - \frac{0}{0}\right][-.088 - (-.088)]\right.$$

$$+ \left[1 - \frac{.152}{.158}\right][-.088 - (-.179)] \qquad (5.32)$$

$$+ \left[1 - \frac{.337}{.337}\right][-.088 - (-.074)] + \left[1 - \frac{.298}{.298}\right]$$

$$\times (.088 - .052) + \left[1 - \frac{.287}{.287}\right](-.088 - .143)$$

$$+ \left[1 - \frac{.246}{.246}\right](-.088 - .148)\right\}$$

$$= -.089.$$

Or as another example, the second coordinate for the Artistic scale would be

$$\hat{x}^1_{A2} = \hat{x}^o_{A2} - \frac{1}{6} \sum_j \left(1 - \frac{\hat{\delta}^1_{Aj}}{\hat{d}^o_{Aj}}\right)\left(\hat{x}^o_{A2} - \hat{x}^o_{j2}\right)$$

$$= -.173 - \frac{1}{6}\left\{\left[1 - \frac{.337}{.337}\right][-.173 - .163] + \left[1 - \frac{.253}{.232}\right]\right.$$

$$\times [-.173 - .033] + \left[1 - \frac{0}{0}\right][-.173 - (-.173)] + \left[1 - \frac{.152}{.146}\right]$$

$$\qquad (5.33)$$

$$\times [-.173 - (-.100)] + \left[1 - \frac{.253}{.273}\right][-.173 - (-.007)]$$

$$+ \left[1 - \frac{.347}{.347}\right][-.173 - .093]\right\}$$

$$= -.175.$$

Table 5.7. Coordinate Estimates Derived in the First Iteration for the *Vocational Preference Inventory* Scales.

	Dimension	
	I	II
Realistic	$-.089$	.162
Investigative	$-.180$	.037
Artistic	$-.071$	$-.175$
Social	.053	$-.100$
Enterprising	.141	$-.009$
Conventional	.148	.093

Table 5.7 shows the new coordinate estimates $\hat{x}_{ik}^1$ obtained from the metric phase of the first iteration. Column 10 of Table 5.6 shows the new distance estimates $\hat{d}_{ij}^1$ computed from the coordinate estimates in Table 5.7 according to Eq. (5.31). For the first iteration, STRESS formula one would be computed by substituting the disparities in column 8 and the distance estimates in column 10 of Table 5.6 into Eq. (5.30). S_1 equals .023.

After standardization of the new coordinate and distance estimates, the second iteration would begin. Iteration would continue until the improvement in STRESS from one iteration to the next fell below some suitably small amount such as .001.

Alternative Nonmetric Phase

Since Shepard's (1962) original article on nonmetric MDS, authors have proposed various nonmetric algorithms (Guttman, 1968; Johnson, 1973; Kruskal, 1964; Takane et al., 1977). The major algorithms contain the steps in Figure 5.9, but each one executes those steps somewhat differently. Space does not permit a complete description of all the variations on the basic steps. The nonmetric phase proposed by Guttman (1968) and incorporated into the Smallest Space Analysis (Lingoes, 1973) programs is an alternative to Kruskal's (1964) nonmetric phase described above, and it has played such an important role in the MDS literature that it will be outlined here. Like Kruskal's (1964) nonmetric phase, Guttman's (1968) uses the original data and the current distance estimates to calculate new disparities, but it executes those calculations differently.

In Guttman's (1968) nonmetric phase, each disparity is set equal to one of the current distance estimates. Specifically, if the stimulus pair (i, j) corresponds to the rth smallest dissimilarity δ_{ij}, then the corresponding disparity $\hat{\delta}_{ij}^{(c+1)}$ is set equal to the rth smallest distance estimate. That is, if stimulus pair (i, j) corresponds to the smallest dissimilarity δ_{ij}, then $\hat{\delta}_{ij}^{(c+1)}$ is set equal to the smallest distance estimate. If stimulus pair (i, j) corresponds to the second smallest dissimilarity δ_{ij}, then $\hat{\delta}_{ij}^{(c+1)}$ is set equal to the second smallest distance estimate. If stimulus pair (i, j) corresponds to the third smallest dissimilarity, then the corresponding disparity is set equal to the third smallest distance estimate, and so forth until one comes to the stimulus pair (i, j) corresponding to the largest dissimilarity. The corresponding disparity is set equal to the largest distance.

To illustrate Guttman's method, again consider the data in Table 5.6. Column 3 contains the dissimilarity data δ_{ij} and column 4 contains the current distance estimates $\hat{d}_{ij}^o$ from which to calculate the disparities in the first iteration. The smallest data point in column 3 corresponds to stimulus pair (C, E): $\delta_{CE} = .57$. The smallest distance in column 4 is .100, so in the first iteration $\hat{\delta}_{CE}$ would be set equal to .100.

The second smallest dissimilarity in column 3 corresponds to stimulus pair (E, S). The second smallest distance estimate in column 4 is .130, so $\hat{\delta}_{ES}$ would be set equal to .130. The third smallest dissimilarity in column 3 corresponds to stimulus pair (I, R). The third smallest distance estimate in column 4 is .146, so the disparity $\hat{\delta}_{IR}$ would be set equal to .146 in the first iteration, and so forth until one came to the largest dissimilarity in column 3 that corresponded to the stimulus pair (C, A). The largest distance estimate in column 4 is .347, so $\hat{\delta}_{CA}$ would be set equal to .347.

Another way to describe how Guttman's nonmetric phase would work in this example is as follows. Imagine permuting the distance estimates in column 4 of Table 5.6 so that they were in ascending order. After the permutation, column 4 would read as follows: .100, .130, .146, .158, .215, .232, .246, .267, .273, .287, .298, .324, .332, .337, .347. These permuted distance estimates would then constitute the disparities as calculated in the first iteration.

Guttman's (1968) and Kruskal's (1964) nonmetric phases are alike in one respect. Both use the original data δ_{ij} and the current distance estimates $\hat{d}_{ij}^c$ to calculate the new disparities, $\hat{\delta}_{ij}^{(c+1)}$. They differ, however, in the way they use the distance estimates in the calculations. In Kruskal's nonmetric phase, each disparity $\hat{\delta}_{ij}^{(c+1)}$ is set equal to the corresponding distance estimate $\hat{d}_{ij}^c$, or it is set equal to the average of several distance estimates. In Guttman's, the disparity for stimulus pair (i, j), which corresponds to the rth smallest dissimilarity, is set equal to the rth smallest distance estimate. Guttman (1968) and Lingoes and Roskam (1973) describe this alternative nonmetric phase in more detail.

SUMMARY

Shepard (1962) proposed the first major nonmetric, multidimensional scaling algorithm. Any algorithm for estimating stimulus coordinates under the assumption that the data are related to distances in space by an unknown monotone function f is said to be a *nonmetric multidimensional scaling algorithm*. Nonmetric MDS algorithms compute stimulus coordinate estimates $\hat{x}_{ij}$ in a prespecified number of dimensions K so that when distances $\hat{d}_{ij}$ are computed from those coordinate estimates, the rank order of the distance estimates agrees with the rank order of the original data δ_{ij} as closely as possible.

Shortly after Shepard's proposal, Kruskal (1964) followed with another method for estimating stimulus coordinates from data that are monotonically related to distances. Since Kruskal's (1964) seminal work, a series of nonmetric MDS programs have been developed. Each algorithm is designed to provide coordinate estimates and disparities that minimize some measure of fit between the distance estimates and the disparities, subject to the constraint that the disparities and distances be monotonically related. These programs, which are compared by Schiffman et al., (1981), include ALSCAL (Young and Lewyckyj, 1979), SSA (Lingoes, 1973), and TORSCA (Young and Torgerson, 1967). The various fit measures include STRESS formulas one and two, S-STRESS formulas one and two, and the coefficient of alienation.

As in metric MDS, one must decide upon the dimensionality of the solution, the rotation of the configuration, and the interpretation of the solution. The number of dimensions can be decided upon by obtaining solutions in several dimensionalities and choosing among them on the basis of interpretability, reproducibility, and fit. A dimensions-by-fit-measure plot can help in deciding dimensionality. Except in one dimension or if the data contain large amounts of error, one should seldom accept a solution with a STRESS of more than .10, and one seldom needs dimensions beyond the number needed to reduce stress below .05. A C- or U-shaped configuration in two dimensions may, but does not necessarily, indicate an essentially one-dimensional stimulus structure.

Non-Euclidean solutions should not be rotated, because doing so will decrease the fit of the distance estimates to the data. In configural or data reduction applications in one or two dimensions, the important stimulus features should be apparent without rotation. In dimensional applications and in three or more dimensions, rotation may become necessary for interpretation. Either an objective or hand rotation can be used. Interpretation consists of identifying the important stimulus groupings and orderings. Shepard diagrams provide a pictorial representation of the monotone function relating the original data to the disparities and the distance estimates.

Nonmetric MDS algorithms are subject to three problems: local minima, degeneracies, and lack of convergence. To reduce the likelihood of local minima, users can employ a rational starting configuration. In some cases, multiple starting configurations may be required. Fully degenerate solutions can readily be spotted and often have STRESS values very near zero. Faced with a degenerate solution, the user may seek a solution in a higher dimensionality. Lack of convergence can usually be circumvented by increasing the allowable number of iterations.

In one of two examples outlined in this chapter, nonmetric MDS was applied to the intercorrelations of the *Vocational Preference Inventory* scales (Holland, 1965) for a sample of 1234 men. As Holland's (1973) theory of careers might lead one to predict, the stimuli formed a roughly hexagonal shape in two dimensions. For the second example, MDS was applied to confusions between consonant phonemes. In the two-dimensional configuration, phonemes grouped themselves on the basis of several features: whether they were stops or fricatives, whether they were nasal, whether they were voiced, and whether they were pronounced in the front, back, or middle of the mouth.

An illustrative nonmetric algorithm was described. Like all such algorithms, it contained three phases; an initial phase which estimates the starting configuration, a nonmetric phase which estimates the disparities, and a metric phase which estimates the stimulus coordinates. The initial phase is performed only once. After the initial phase, the algorithm proceeds through a series of iterations, each of which contains one nonmetric and one metric phase. Iteration continues until the fit measure fails to improve by some suitably small amount, such as .001, from one iteration to the next.

PROBLEMS

1. Table 5.8. **Letter Confusion Data.**

	b	d	p	q	g	m	n	v	w
b	—								
d	23	—							
p	15	5	—						
q	5	10	16	—					
g	5	10	15	21	—				
m	2	0	1	1	2	—			
n	1	1	0	2	2	21	—		
v	1	0	1	1	2	5	15	—	
w	0	1	0	1	3	15	5	32	—

Imagine that the data in Table 5.8 come from a study in which children are shown a stimulus letter and are asked to name it. Each entry in the table indicates the number of trials in which the row letter was presented and the column letter was named.

Obtain a nonmetric scaling of the above data in one and two dimensions. If possible, use a principal components rotation of the solution, the primary approach to ties, a rational starting configuration, and a Euclidean distance model.

a. What is the one-dimensional stimulus coordinate matrix $\hat{X}$? Describe the curious features of this solution.

b. Plot the two-dimensional solution and indicate the important stimulus groupings as in Figure 5.8.

c. Interpret the important stimulus groupings. What features of the letters appear to account for the more common confusions in children's responses?

2. Assume that in a study of animal behavior, a researcher measured the frequency with which pairs of animals groomed each other, and that the data matrix in Table 5.9 contains a measure of the *relative* frequency for each animal pair. Higher data values indicate more common grooming behavior. The researcher hypothesizes that the animals' social structure is essentially a one-dimensional hierarchical structure, and that the animals are arrayed in alphabetical order along that dimension.

Obtain a nonmetric scaling of the above data in one–two dimensions. If possible, use a principal components rotation of the solution, the primary approach to ties, a rational starting configuration, and a Euclidean distance model.

Table 5.9. Animal Grooming Data.

	A	B	C	D	E	F	G	H	I	J
A										
B	20.25									
C	16.00	20.25								
D	12.25	16.00	20.25							
E	9.00	12.25	16.00	20.25						
F	6.25	9.00	12.25	16.00	20.25					
G	4.00	6.25	9.00	12.25	16.00	20.25				
H	2.25	4.00	6.25	9.00	12.25	16.00	20.25			
I	1.00	2.25	4.00	6.25	9.00	12.25	16.00	20.25		
J	0.25	1.00	2.25	4.00	6.25	9.00	12.25	16.00	20.25	

a. Plot the two-dimensional solution. Describe the significant features of this graph.

b. After inspecting the STRESS values and the two-dimensional solution, how many dimensions do you think should be retained in the final solution? Why?

c. Does the final solution tend to confirm or disconfirm the researchers hypothesis? Why or why not?

Answers

The following results were obtained using KYST (Kruskal et al., 1973). Users who apply other nonmetric scaling algorithms to the data in Problems 1 and 2 should get similar, but not identical, numerical results. Readers who employ a different version of KYST or who employ different options in KYST will get similar, but not identical, results. In other words, readers should not expect the same degree of agreement between their results and answers that they found for Chapters 1–4.

1. a. $\hat{X}' = (-0.90, -0.89, -0.90, -0.90, -0.87, 1.13, 1.12, 1.11, 1.12)$
    The one-dimensional solution is degenerate, and hence should not be used. The first five stimuli, the letters b, d, p, q, and g collapse to one point, and the remaining four stimuli m, n, v, and w collapse to a second point. As often happens with degenerate solutions, STRESS was very low, $S_1 = .005$.

    b.

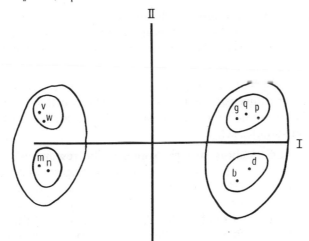

Figure 5.10.   Two-dimensional plot of stimulus coordinates for letter confusion data in Problem 2.

c. There are two major clusters, each of which breaks down into two smaller clusters. The first major cluster contains the five letters composed of a vertical line and a loop {b, d, g, q, p}. This larger cluster breaks down into one set for which the vertical line extends below the loop {g, q, p} and one set for which the vertical line extends above the loop {b, d}. The second major set contains the four letters composed of "arches" or "inverted arches" {m, n, v, w}. The set of four breaks down into the letters composed of arches {m, n} and the letters composed of inverted arches {v, w}.

2. a.

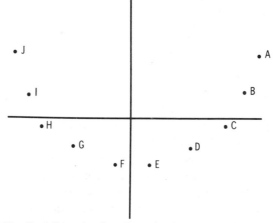

Figure 5.11.   Two-dimensional configuration for the animal grooming data.

The configuration displays the distinctive U-shape characteristic of a one-dimensional set of stimuli. Starting from the upper right and moving clockwise, the stimuli are arrayed in alphabetical order around the U.

b. Everything suggests that only one dimension need be retained. The fit in one dimension is perfect, $S_1 = 0.00$. Further, in two dimensions, the stimuli form the U-shape characteristic of a one-dimensional stimulus set.

c. The MDS analysis strongly supports the researcher's hypothesis. First, as stated in Answer 2b, everything suggests that the structure is one-dimensional. Since the stimuli are arrayed in alphabetical order in the one-dimensional solution and along the U in the two-dimensional solution, the data tend to support the researcher's hypothesized ordering of the animals. The coordinates for the one-dimensional solution are given below.

$$\hat{X}' = \begin{bmatrix} A & B & C & D & E & F & G \\ 1.44 & 1.26 & 0.99 & 0.57 & 0.18 & -0.18 & -0.57 \end{bmatrix}$$

$$\begin{bmatrix} H & I & J \\ -0.99 & -1.26 & -1.44 \end{bmatrix}$$

CHAPTER 6

Individual Differences Models

Torgerson's (1952) original distance model does not allow for any individual differences in the similarity judgment process. Since such individual differences are often of interest, Torgerson's model has been extended by incorporating subject parameters into the basic model. The estimates of these parameters provide a quantitative dimensional description of the subjects analogous to the quantitative dimensional description of stimuli provided by the stimulus coordinate estimates.

The literature contains two commonly cited approaches to individual differences. Bloxom (1968), Carroll and Chang (1970) and Horan (1969) all describe the first model that incorporates subject dimension weights into Torgerson's (1952) original metric distance model. Their model is often called INDSCAL because it is so closely identified with the INDSCAL computer program (Carroll and Chang, 1970) used for estimating the solution parameters. To avoid confusion between the model and the computer program for fitting it, the model will here be called the weighted Euclidean model (WEM).

The second approach is called the three-mode model for MDS (Tucker, 1972). Several psychophysical studies (Krantz and Tversky, 1975; Krumhansl, 1979; Wiener-Ehrlich, 1978) have reported interactions between dimensions not anticipated by the basic Euclidean distance model of Eq. (1.5). Although the dimension interactions in Tucker's model may not be of the form observed in the psychophysical studies, nevertheless, the model can account for some forms of dimension interaction. In the Tucker model, subjects are presumed to differ in their dimension weights and in the degree of interaction between dimensions represented in their judgments.

Individual differences models have been used primarily to characterize variation in judged stimulus structure across individuals—hence the name individual differences models. They can, however, be used to describe variation in the structure across occasions, settings, or treatment conditions. For instance, Hanham (1976) obtained measures of similarity for all possible pairs of elements in an urban environment at several different times during the day. He then used the individual differences parameters—really time parameters in this case—to describe variation in the structure of the city over time. By using an individual differences MDS model, Hanham (1976) developed a more dynamic characterization of the urban environment than he could have done with any of the methods described in Chapters 4 and 5.

This chapter will begin with a discussion of the weighted Euclidean model and finish with a discussion of the three-mode model. Since the weighted Euclidean model has been applied more widely and programs for fitting it are more commonly available, it will receive a more comprehensive treatment.

THE WEIGHTED EUCLIDEAN MODEL

As before, let $\mathbf{X}$ be an $(I \times K)$ matrix of stimulus coordinates. This matrix will be called the group stimulus coordinate matrix. In this model, it is assumed that there exists an idiosyncratic matrix of stimulus coordinates for each subject. Let $\mathbf{X}_s$ with elements x_{iks} be the $(I \times K)$ matrix of stimulus coordinates for subject s. Here x_{iks} is the coordinate of subject s for stimulus i along dimension k. The elements of each subject's coordinate matrix x_{iks} are presumed related to the elements of the group stimulus coordinate matrix by the following equation:

$$x_{iks} = x_{ik}w_{ks}, \tag{6.1}$$

where w_{ks} is an unknown weight for subject s along dimension k. If $\mathbf{W}_s$ is defined as a $(K \times K)$ diagonal matrix with w_{ks} as its kth diagonal element, then Eq. (6.1) can be written in matrix notation as

$$\mathbf{X}_s = \mathbf{X}\mathbf{W}_s. \tag{6.2}$$

According to the model, were it not for measurement and sampling error, subjects' dissimilarity judgments could be expressed as a standard Euclidean distance function of their own stimulus coordinates:

$$\delta_{ijs} = \left[\sum_k (x_{iks} - x_{jks})^2 \right]^{1/2}. \tag{6.3}$$

In Eq. (6.3), δ_{ijs} refers to the dissimilarity judgment of subject s about the stimulus pair (i, j). Substituting the quantity on the right-hand side of Eq. (6.1) for the quantities x_{iks} and x_{jks} in Eq. (6.3) yields

$$\delta_{ijs} = \left[\sum_k w_{ks}^2 (x_{ik} - x_{jk})^2 \right]^{1/2}. \tag{6.4}$$

Equation (6.4) expresses the fundamental assumption of the weighted Euclidean model.

The weights w_{ks} are sometimes called importance weights or salience weights. All other things equal, as w_{ks} increases, differences between stimuli along dimension k have a larger and larger influence on the judged dissimilarity between stimuli i and j. Figure 6.1 shows in graphical form how weighting of dimensions influences the stimulus configuration. The top third

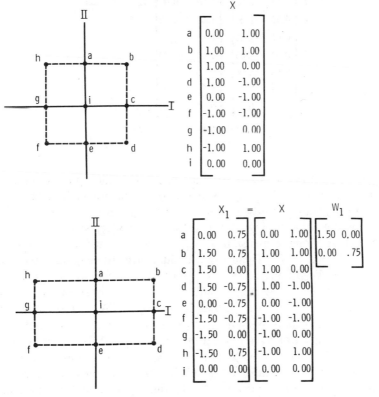

Figure 6.1.   Group stimulus space and two subject spaces for nine hypothetical stimuli.

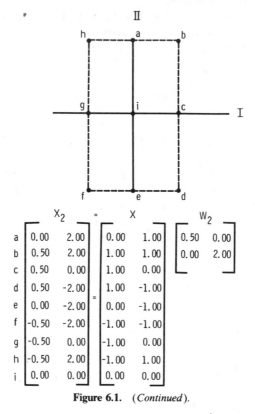

$$
\begin{array}{c}
 \\
a \\
b \\
c \\
d \\
e \\
f \\
g \\
h \\
i
\end{array}
\overset{X_2}{=}
\begin{bmatrix}
0.00 & 2.00 \\
0.50 & 2.00 \\
0.50 & 0.00 \\
0.50 & -2.00 \\
0.00 & -2.00 \\
-0.50 & -2.00 \\
-0.50 & 0.00 \\
-0.50 & 2.00 \\
0.00 & 0.00
\end{bmatrix}
\overset{X}{=}
\begin{bmatrix}
0.00 & 1.00 \\
1.00 & 1.00 \\
1.00 & 0.00 \\
1.00 & -1.00 \\
0.00 & -1.00 \\
-1.00 & -1.00 \\
-1.00 & 0.00 \\
-1.00 & 1.00 \\
0.00 & 0.00
\end{bmatrix}
\overset{W_2}{}
\begin{bmatrix}
0.50 & 0.00 \\
0.00 & 2.00
\end{bmatrix}
$$

Figure 6.1. (*Continued*).

of Figure 6.1 shows a group stimulus space in which nine stimuli array themselves in a square formation centered at the origin. Matrix **X** is the corresponding matrix representation of the group space.

The middle third of Figure 6.1 shows the subject space for a subject whose weight along dimension I, $w_{11} = 1.5$, is twice the weight along dimension II, $w_{21} = .75$. These two weights form the diagonal elements of this subject's weight matrix $\mathbf{W}_1$ in Figure 6.1. This subject's coordinate matrix $\mathbf{X}_1$ was derived by simply multiplying the group stimulus coordinate matrix **X** by the subject's weight matrix $\mathbf{W}_1$: $\mathbf{X}_1 = \mathbf{X}\mathbf{W}_1$. Multiplying **X** by a diagonal matrix such as $\mathbf{W}_1$ simply rescales the columns of **X**. That is, each element in column 1 of $\mathbf{X}_1$ is 1.50 times the corresponding element in **X**; and each element in column 2 of $\mathbf{X}_1$ is 0.75 times the corresponding element in **X**. The effect of this subject's weighting was to transform the square formation at the top of Figure 6.1 into the rectangular formation in the middle of the figure.

The third graph in the lower portion of Figure 6.1 depicts an individual stimulus space in which dimension II, $w_{22} = 2.00$, is four times as salient as dimension I, $w_{12} = .50$. These dimension weights, shown in matrix $\mathbf{W}_2$, were premultiplied by the group stimulus coordinate matrix $\mathbf{X}$ to obtain the individual stimulus coordinate matrix $\mathbf{X}_2$ in Figure 6.1. Multiplying $\mathbf{X}$ by the diagonal matrix $\mathbf{W}_2$ simply rescales the columns of $\mathbf{X}$. That is, each element in column 1 is 0.50 times the corresponding element in $\mathbf{X}$; each element in column 2 of $\mathbf{X}_2$ is 2.00 times the corresponding element in $\mathbf{X}$.

Subjects with different weight matrices would not agree in their judgments about the dissimilarity of stimulus pairs. For instance, hypothetical subject 1 in Figure 6.1 should judge stimulus i to be more similar to a than to g; $d_{gi1} = 1.5$ whereas $d_{ai1} = .75$. Just the opposite should be true for the second hypothetical subject. Stimulus i should be judged less similar to a than to g; $d_{gi2} = .50$, whereas $d_{ai2} = 2.00$.

There are at least three widely distributed computer programs fitting the weighted Euclidean model. The first is INDSCAL (Carroll and Chang, 1970). The second is the closely related, but computationally more efficient, SINDSCAL (Pruzansky, 1975). The ALSCAL program (Young and Lewyckyj, 1979) can also be used to fit the weighted Euclidean model.

Dimensionality, Rotation, and Interpretation

The input into any of the above programs typically includes several similarity or dissimilarity matrices, one for each subject. Table 6.1 shows three dissimilarity matrices, one for each of three subjects. If, however, the user is studying how the stimulus structure varies across occasions, settings, or treatment conditions rather than across individuals, there will be one dissimilarity matrix for each occasion, setting, or treatment condition.

The data in Table 6.1 will be used to illustrate the following discussion of dimensionality, rotation, and interpretation. These data refer to hypothetical dissimilarity data for nine rectangles varying in length and width. Table 6.2 shows the height and width of each stimulus. Three levels of height; 1 in., 2 in., and 3 in.; were crossed with the same three levels of the width variable to create a total of nine stimuli. Imagine that for every pair of the nine stimuli, each of three subjects has indicated the dissimilarity of the rectangle pair and that these dissimilarity data are shown in Table 6.1. The design of this hypothetical study is similar to that reported by Krantz and Tversky (1975) and Wiener-Ehrlich (1978).

The output of an analysis based on the weighted Euclidean model contains the following major elements. The first is the estimate of the $(I \times K)$ group stimulus matrix $\hat{\mathbf{X}}$. The second is an estimate of a $(K \times S)$

Table 6.1. Lower Triangular Portion of Dissimilarity Matrices for Three Subjects and Nine Stimulus Rectangles.

				Subject 1					
Rectangle	a	b	c	d	e	f	g	h	i
a									
b	1.00								
c	1.41	1.00							
d	2.24	2.00	1.00						
e	2.00	2.24	1.41	1.00					
f	2.24	2.83	2.24	2.00	1.00				
g	1.41	2.24	2.00	2.24	1.41	1.00			
h	1.00	2.00	2.24	2.83	2.24	2.00	1.00		
i	1.00	1.41	1.00	1.41	1.00	1.41	1.00	1.41	

				Subject 2					
Rectangle	a	b	c	d	e	f	g	h	i
a									
b	1.50								
c	1.68	0.75							
d	2.12	1.50	0.75						
e	1.50	2.12	1.68	1.50					
f	2.12	3.35	3.09	3.00	1.50				
g	1.68	3.09	3.00	3.09	1.68	0.75			
h	1.50	3.00	3.09	3.35	2.12	1.50	0.75		
i	0.75	1.68	1.50	1.68	0.75	1.68	1.50	1.68	

				Subject 3					
Rectangle	a	b	c	d	e	f	g	h	i
a									
b	0.50								
c	2.06	2.00							
d	4.03	4.00	2.00						
e	4.00	4.03	2.06	0.50					
f	4.03	4.12	2.24	1.00	0.50				
g	2.06	2.24	1.00	2.24	2.06	2.00			
h	0.50	1.00	2.24	4.12	4.03	4.00	2.00		
i	2.00	2.06	0.50	2.06	2.00	2.06	0.50	2.06	

matrix of subject weights $\hat{\mathbf{W}}$ with entries w_{ks}. The entries in column s of $\hat{\mathbf{W}}$ are the diagonal elements in the $(K \times K)$ matrix $\hat{\mathbf{W}}_s$. The matrix $\mathbf{W}$ is said to define the subject space, and each *row* of $\mathbf{W}$ represents one dimension in that subject space. The coordinates along dimension k in the subject space w_{ks} are the salience weights for the various subjects and dimension k.

Note that the output does *not* include a separate stimulus coordinate matrix $\hat{\mathbf{X}}_s$ for each subject. Rather it includes a group stimulus coordinate matrix $\hat{\mathbf{X}}$, with elements $\hat{x}_{ik}$, and a subject coordinate matrix $\hat{\mathbf{W}}$ with elements $\hat{w}_{ks}$. The coordinates in each subject's idiosyncratic stimulus coordinate matrix $\hat{\mathbf{X}}_s$ can be reconstructed from the elements in $\hat{\mathbf{X}}$ and $\hat{\mathbf{W}}$ using Eq. (6.1). Interpreting the solution is a larger task when an individual differences model is employed because one must develop an interpretation of both the group stimulus space, whose matrix representation is $\hat{\mathbf{X}}$, and the subject space, whose matrix representation is $\hat{\mathbf{W}}$.

The third major element of the output is the fit measure, which is used in deciding upon the dimensionality. It is to this issue, deciding dimensionality, to which our attention now turns.

Dimensionality

If the dimensionality is unknown, the user must obtain solutions in several dimensionalities and choose between them on the basis of fit to the data, interpretability, and reproducibility. A reasonable strategy is to develop an *a priori* estimate of the dimensionality K^*, obtain solutions in $(K^* - 3)$ to $(K^* + 3)$ dimensions, and choose from among these seven solutions. If $K^* \leq 3$, then one would obtain solutions in 1 to $(K^* + 3)$ dimensions. A

Table 6.2. Lengths, Widths, and Two-Dimensional Scale Values for Nine Stimulus Rectangles.

Rectangle	Length (inches)	Width (inches)	Dimension I	Dimension II
a	2.00	3.00	.00	.41
b	3.00	3.00	.41	.41
c	3.00	2.00	.41	.00
d	3.00	1.00	.41	−.41
e	2.00	1.00	.00	−.41
f	1.00	1.00	−.41	−.41
g	1.00	2.00	−.41	.00
h	1.00	3.00	−.41	.41
i	2.00	2.00	.00	.00

fit-measure-by-dimensions plot can be useful in deciding among the solutions. Should a clear elbow appear in the plot for the Kth dimension, then K would seem a reasonable number of dimensions to retain.

If the ALSCAL program (Young and Lewyckyj, 1979) is employed, the preferred fit measure is a variation of S-STRESS formula one in Eq. (5.16) adapted for the situation in which there are several data matrices to be analyzed, one for each subject, rather than just one.

$$ SS_1 = \left[\frac{1}{S} \sum_s \frac{\Sigma_{(i,\,j)}\left(\hat{\delta}_{ijs}^2 - \hat{d}_{ijs}^2\right)^2}{\Sigma_{(i,\,j)}\left(\hat{d}_{ijs}^2\right)^2} \right]^{1/2}. \tag{6.5} $$

A corresponding fit statistic can be derived for each subject:

$$ SS_1 = \left[\frac{\Sigma_{(i,\,j)}\left(\hat{\delta}_{ijs}^2 - \hat{d}_{ijs}^2\right)^2}{\Sigma_{(i,\,j)}\left(\hat{d}_{ijs}^2\right)^2} \right]^{1/2}. \tag{6.6} $$

In Eqs. (6.5) and (6.6), $\hat{\delta}_{ijs}$ is a disparity estimate for subject s and stimulus pair (i, j).

If the INDSCAL (Carroll and Chang, 1970) or SINDSCAL (Pruzansky, 1975) program is employed, the fit statistic is the correlation between scalar products and estimated scalar products. Before describing the fit measure, the INDSCAL scalar product matrices must be described. At the beginning of an INDSCAL analysis, an $(I \times I)$ scalar products matrix is computed for each subject by squaring the entries in and double-centering each subject's data matrix. The elements of the scalar products matrix Δ_s^* for subject s are computed as follows.[†]

$$ \delta_{ijs}^* = -\tfrac{1}{2}\left(\delta_{ijs}^2 - \delta_{i.s}^2 - \delta_{.js}^2 + \delta_{..s}^2\right). \tag{6.7} $$

[†]In the literature on the weighted Euclidean distance model, the terms "dissimilarity" and "Euclidean distance" are sometimes given meanings different from those in the present chapter. According to this alternative usage, dissimilarities are data that were it not for error, would take the form $\delta_{ijs} = d_{ijs} + c_s$ where c_s is an additive constant unique to subject s. Euclidean distances are data that, were it not for error, would take the more restrictive form $\delta_{ijs} = d_{ijs}$. It is assumed throughout this discussion that the dissimilarity data are of the latter form. If the data are of the form $\delta_{ijs} = d_{ijs} + c_s$, then most algorithms use some solution to the additive constant problem (see Chapter 4) to estimate c_s for each person and subtract it from each data value to obtain transformed data values of the form $\delta_{ijs} = d_{ijs}$, the form assumed in this chapter.

In Eq. (6.7),

$$\delta_{i.s}^2 = \frac{1}{J} \sum_j \delta_{ijs}^2, \tag{6.8}$$

$$\delta_{.js}^2 = \frac{1}{I} \sum_i \delta_{ijs}^2, \tag{6.9}$$

and

$$\delta_{..s}^2 = \frac{1}{IJ} \sum_{(i,\,j)} \delta_{ijs}^2. \tag{6.10}$$

Equation (6.7) is an application to individual subject dissimilarity matrices of the squaring and double-centering used by Torgerson (1952) and shown in Eq. (4.3). If the dissimilarities data are of the form specified by Eq. (6.4), then the scalar products will be of the form

$$\delta_{ijs}^* = \sum_k x_{ik} x_{jk} w_{ks}^2$$

$$= \sum_k x_{iks} x_{jks}. \tag{6.11}$$

In matrix form, Eq. (6.11) can be written as

$$\Delta_s^* = \mathbf{X} \mathbf{W}_s^2 \mathbf{X}' \tag{6.12}$$

Here $\mathbf{W}_s^2 = \mathbf{W}_s \mathbf{W}_s'$ is the diagonal matrix with w_{ks}^2 as its kth diagonal element.

Once stimulus coordinate estimates $\hat{x}_{ik}$ and subject weight estimates $\hat{w}_{ks}$ have been obtained, estimated scalar products can be calculated by substituting stimulus coordinate and subject weight estimates into the right side of Eq. (6.11) to yield

$$\hat{\delta}_{ijs}^* = \sum_k \hat{x}_{ik} \hat{x}_{jk} \hat{w}_{ks}^2. \tag{6.13}$$

In matrix form, Eq. (6.13) is

$$\hat{\Delta}_s^* = \hat{X} \hat{W}_s^2 \hat{X}'. \tag{6.14}$$

The fit statistic used by the INDSCAL algorithm is simply the correlation between the actual (δ^*_{ijs}) and the estimated ($\hat{\delta}^*_{ijs}$) scalar products:

$$r = \frac{\sum_{(i,j,s)}\left(\delta^*_{ijs} - \delta^*_{...}\right)\left(\hat{\delta}^*_{ijs} - \hat{\delta}^*_{...}\right)}{\left[\sum_{(i,j,s)}\left(\delta^*_{ijs} - \delta^*_{...}\right)^2 \sum_{(i,j,s)}\left(\hat{\delta}^*_{ijs} - \hat{\delta}^*_{...}\right)^2\right]^{1/2}} \qquad (6.15)$$

In Eq. (6.15), $\delta^*_{...}$ is the grand mean of the actual scalar products,

$$\delta^*_{...} = \frac{1}{IJS} \sum_{(i,j,s)} \delta^*_{ijs}, \qquad (6.16)$$

and $\hat{\delta}^*_{...}$ is the grand mean of the estimated scalar products,

$$\hat{\delta}^*_{...} = \frac{1}{IJS} \sum_{(i,j,s)} \hat{\delta}^*_{ijs}. \qquad (6.17)$$

A fit measure is also computed for each subject. It is the correlation between the actual and estimated scalar products for subject s:

$$r_s = \frac{\sum_{(i,j)}\left(\delta^*_{ijs} - \delta^*_{..s}\right)\left(\hat{\delta}^*_{ijs} - \hat{\delta}^*_{..s}\right)}{\left\{\left[\sum_{(i,j)}\left(\delta^*_{ijs} - \delta^*_{..s}\right)^2\right]\left[\sum_{(i,j)}\left(\hat{\delta}^*_{ijs} - \hat{\delta}^*_{..s}\right)^2\right]\right\}^{1/2}}. \qquad (6.18)$$

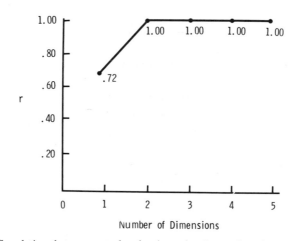

Figure 6.2. Correlations between actual and estimated scalar products in one–five dimensions for the rectangles dissimilarity data.

In Eq. (6.18), $\delta^*_{.s}$ and $\hat{\delta}^*_{.s}$ are, respectively, the mean actual and estimated scalar products for subject s. Unlike the badness-of-fit measures, STRESS and S-STRESS, which decrease as the fit to the data improves, r is a goodness-of-fit measure which increases as the fit to the data improves.

Figure 6.2 shows the fit measures r that were obtained when the dissimilarity data in Table 6.1 were submitted to a SINDSCAL (Pruzansky, 1975) analysis in 1–5 dimensions. There is a sharp elbow in this plot at $K = 2$, suggesting that 2 is a reasonable number of dimensions to retain. In most real data, the elbow is more ambiguous and, consequently, the fit measure alone does not suffice as a basis for deciding dimensionality. For the three subjects in Table 6.1, the two-dimensional fit statistics are all equal and very high, $r_1 = r_2 = r_3 = 1.00$, indicating that all subjects' data were fit equally and well.

Rotation

Except under exceptional circumstances described by MacCallum (1974b; see also Pruzansky, 1975), the weighted Euclidean solution cannot be rotated.[†] In general, if $\hat{X}$ is a solution, then $\hat{X}^* = \hat{X}T$ is not an alternative solution.[‡] Because the unrotated solution in K dimensions should be the interpretable rotation of the coordinates in the vast majority of cases, the rotation problem all but disappears. This near disappearance greatly facilitates interpretation of solutions in more than two dimensions. The popularity of the weighted Euclidean model stems, in part, from the fact that weighted Euclidean solutions are more easily interpreted than are those derived from other methods for which a subsequent rotation may be necessary.

Interpretation

Interpretation of the stimulus coordinate space consists of identifying the important stimulus groupings and orderings. Since the dimensions cannot

---

[†] MacCallum (1974) and Pruzansky (1975) point out, however, that under some exceptional circumstances, a weighted Euclidean solution can be partially rotated. Consider the following normalized sum of products for dimensions k and k':

$$SP_{kk'} = \frac{\Sigma_s \hat{w}_{ks} \hat{w}_{k's}}{\left(\Sigma_s \hat{w}_{ks}^2\right)^{1/2} \left(\Sigma_s \hat{w}_{k's}^2\right)^{1/2}}.$$

If this quantity is near 1.00, then the subject weights along dimension k are, for all practical purposes, proportional to those along dimension k'. In such cases dimensions k and k' can be rotated in the plane that they define without loss of fit.

[‡] In general, $\hat{X}^* = \hat{X}T$ will be a solution only if T is a diagonal matrix, and every diagonal element in T equals either 1.00 or -1.00.

be rotated, in general, the meaningful orderings should correspond to the orderings of the stimuli along the coordinate axes. For the example of Table 6.1, the coordinate estimates from the SINDSCAL analysis are shown in columns 4 and 5 of Table 6.2. The ordering of the variables by length exactly corresponds to their ordering along dimension I. The correlation between the rectangle lengths in column 2 and the dimension I coordinates in column 4 is 1.00. Similarly, the ordering of the variables by width is the same as their ordering along dimension II. The correlation between the widths in column 3 and the dimension II coordinates in column 5 is 1.00. The length and width attributes of the rectangles provide a ready interpretation for the stimulus dimensions.

The subject space also requires interpretation. None of the subject weights should be negative. Negative weights signify violations of the Euclidean distance assumptions. Vectors, such as those drawn in Figure 6.3, running from the origin to the points representing subjects, are useful devices for thinking about the interpretation of the subject weights.

The length of each vector approximately represents the degree of fit to the subject's data, although the subject's fit statistic r_s is a better index of fit than is the vector length. In Figure 6.3, the three vectors are of equal length as one would expect for three subjects whose data were all fit equally well.

The direction of each vector designates the relative weighting of dimensions. Even if two vectors are of unequal length, they represent the same relative weighting of dimensions if they extend in the same direction from the origin. For subject 1 in Figure 6.3, with weights $\hat{w}_{11} = \hat{w}_{21} = .71$, both

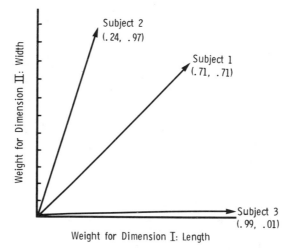

Figure 6.3.   Dimension weights for three subjects judging nine rectangles.

dimensions contribute equally to the judgments. For subject 2, the width dimension, $\hat{w}_{12} = .97$, has more than three times the influence of the length dimension, $\hat{w}_{22} = .24$. The judgments of subject 3 can be accounted for solely in terms of the length dimension; $\hat{w}_{13} = .99$ and $\hat{w}_{23} = .01$.

Young and Lewyckyj (1979) argue that relative dimension weights, defined as follows,

$$w_{ks}^* = \frac{w_{ks}}{\left[\sum_k w_{ks}^2\right]^{1/2}}, \tag{6.19}$$

are more important than the raw weights w_{ks}. The denominator on the right of Eq. (6.19) is the vector length for subject s. Division by that length removes the effect of subject variation in fit to the data and provides a measure of relative dimension weighting unconfounded with effects of fit to the data.

Local Minima and Lack of Convergence

The major algorithms for fitting the weighted Euclidean model are iterative and, therefore, subject to the local minima and convergence problems described in Chapter 5. Although the exact equations differ from one algorithm to the next, nevertheless, for each algorithm there is a set of equations that must be satisfied by the stimulus coordinate estimates and subject weight estimates. These are the solution equations. In general, however, there are several sets of stimulus coordinate estimates and subject weight estimates that satisfy the solution equations. The several sets of estimates will not all fit the data equally well. Of these several sets of parameters, the one that yields the best fit to the data is said to represent a global minimum. All others are local minima. The local minima problem is the problem of ensuring that the parameter estimates represent the global minimum. The best way to avoid a local minimum is to start the iterative process from a rationally derived configuration. The discussion surrounding Eq. (6.23) explains how to derive a rational starting configuration.

The convergence problem arises because the user must often specify the maximum number of iterations allowed. The algorithm may not reach the desired solution in the allowed number of iterations. If the solution does fail to converge, then most programs print a message to that effect, such as "MAXIMUM ITERATIONS REACHED" somewhere near the printing of the fit measure. Users should always examine the messages printed with each solution to ensure that the algorithm did converge in the allowed number of iterations. If not, the user can increase the allowable number of iterations and resolve for the solution.

EXAMPLE

Researchers have commonly employed MDS to study the dimensions underlying subjects' perceptions of other people (Davison and Jones, 1976; Forgas, 1979; Forgas et al., 1977; Isenberg and Ennis, 1980; Jones and Young, 1972; Nygren and Jones, 1977; Rosenberg and Jones, 1972; Rosenberg et al., 1968; Shikiar and Coates, 1978; Wish et al., 1976.) The weighted Euclidean model (WEM) has been used extensively to study how members of small groups perceive each other.

In the first of these studies, Jones and Young (1972, p. 108) used the WEM to "test hypotheses concerning (a) the dimensions of interpersonal perception, (b) changes in perceived social structure, and (c) the relationship of interpersonal perception to interpersonal behavior for members of an intact group."[†] Jones and Young (1972) studied 17 members of an academic unit: seven faculty members, nine graduate students, and one postdoctoral student. These 17 persons were the stimulus persons. The authors report two analyses, one for data collected in 1969 and one for data collected in 1970. Only the 1970 data are discussed here.

In 1970, 31 members of the academic unit rated the similarity of all possible stimulus pairs. The 17 stimulus persons were included among the 31 subjects. The 31 subjects included 14 graduate students, 9 faculty members, 1 postdoctoral fellow, and 7 clerical, technical, and secretarial staff members. The 31 similarity matrices, one for each subject, were analyzed with the INDSCAL program (Carroll and Chang, 1970). Figure 6.4 shows their three-dimensional solution.

The authors had a measure of each subject's academic rank. The correlation between this measure of rank and the coordinates along dimension I was .95. The authors report that the faculty members and the postdoctoral fellow, designated by letters A–I in Figure 6.4, appear at the positive end of dimension I. Full and associate professors appear first followed by assistant professors. Graduate students, letters K–Q, V, and W, appear at the low end of the dimension. Jones and Young (1972) called their dimension I a status dimension.

Their second dimension reflected the political persuasion of the stimulus persons. A measure of each subject's political persuasion, roughly a liberalism–conservatism index, correlated .93 with coordinates along dimension II. A measure of stimulus persons' research area correlated .75 with dimension III. The statisticians appear at the positive end of the dimension. Those who were primarily concerned with substantive problems in psychol-

---

[†]Copyright 1972 by the American Psychological Association. Reprinted by permission of the publisher and author.

EXAMPLE   135

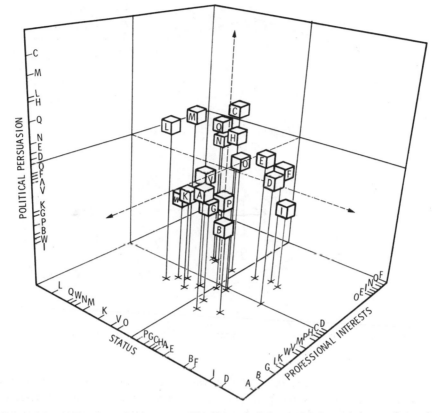

Figure 6.4. 1970 group stimulus space. The letters A–I denote faculty and the postdoctoral fellow. Letters K–Q, V and W denote graduate students. Copyright 1972 by the American Psychological Association. Reprinted by permission of the publisher and author.

ogy appeared at the negative end. Jones and Young (1972) labeled this the professional interest dimension.

Figure 6.5 shows the subject weights from their 31 subjects. An analysis of the subject weights revealed that faculty had generally higher weights on dimension I, the status dimension. Jones and Young (1972) conclude that the faculty were more status conscious. Graduate students, with higher average weights on dimension III, seemed most conscious of professional interests. Clerical staff members and new graduate students had the highest weights along the political persuasion dimension, dimension II.

Jones and Young (1972, p. 119) found that stimulus persons tended to interact most frequently with those who were near them in the stimulus

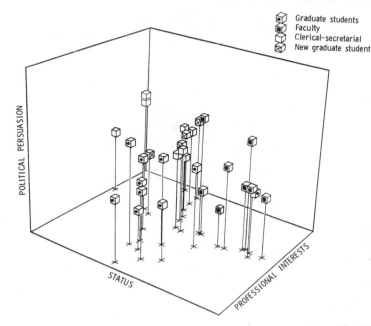

Figure 6.5. Individual differences space based on 31 judges in 1970. Copyright 1972 by the American Psychological Association. Reprinted by permission of the publisher and author.

space. They concluded that "the overall results support the assumed relationship of interpersonal perception to interpersonal behavior."[†] They describe their three-dimensional solution as a representation of perceived group structure because it was derived from subjects' perceptions of the stimulus persons as reflected in similarity judgments. It was not derived from a behavioral measure of stimulus similarity.

THE THREE-MODE MODEL

Carroll and Chang (1972), Harshman (1972a, b), and Tucker (1972) all propose an individual differences MDS model that is more general than the weighted Euclidean model. The distinctions between the Carroll–Chang, Harshman, and Tucker formulations, which need not concern us here, are discussed in Carroll and Wish (1974b). Because the present discussion more

[†]Copyright 1972 by the American Psychological Association. Reprinted by permission of the publisher and author.

closely follows Tucker's formulation, his term, three-mode model, will be used to designate the model.

As in the weighted Euclidean model, there is assumed to exist a group stimulus coordinate matrix $\mathbf{X}$. According to this model, were it not for measurement and sampling error in the data, a subject's dissimilarity judgments could be expressed as a standard Euclidean function of stimulus coordinates idiosyncratic to subject s, Eq. (6.3). Each subject's idiosyncratic coordinate matrix $\mathbf{X}_s$ can be expressed as a function of the group stimulus coordinates, but the function relating $\mathbf{X}$ to $\mathbf{X}_s$ is more complex in the three-mode model. Whereas in the weighted Euclidean model

$$\mathbf{X}_s = \mathbf{XW}_s, \tag{6.20}$$

in the three-mode model,

$$\mathbf{X}_s = \mathbf{XW}_s\mathbf{T}_s. \tag{6.21}$$

Here $\mathbf{W}_s$ is a diagonal weight matrix as before, and $\mathbf{T}_s$ is a transformation matrix. In words, Eq. (6.21) says that each subject's coordinate space can be obtained by combining a weighting and a rotation of the coordinates in the group space. The weighted Euclidean model is a special case of the three-mode model in which $\mathbf{T}_s = \mathbf{I}$ for all subjects.

Figure 6.6 shows in graphical form how a transformation matrix $\mathbf{T}_s$ influences the coordinate estimates. Imagine that these subjects have been asked to judge all possible pairs of the nine rectangles and that the group coordinate space looks like the top graph in Figure 6.1. The top portion of Figure 6.6 shows the stimulus coordinate space for a hypothetical subject with weight matrix $\mathbf{W}_3$ and transformation matrix $\mathbf{T}_3$. This subject's coordinate matrix has been derived by postmultiplying $\mathbf{X}$ by the product $\mathbf{W}_3\mathbf{T}_3$. In this case $\mathbf{W}_3$ has no effect because it is an identity matrix.

The transformation does alter the distances between stimulus points. In the top portion of Figure 6.1, stimulus i is equidistant from stimuli b and h; $d_{bi} = d_{hi} = 1.42$. In the top portion of Figure 6.6, on the other hand, h is closer to i than is b; $d_{bi} = 1.74$ whereas $d_{hi} = 1.00$.

The graph at the bottom of Figure 6.6 shows the combined effect of a weighting and transformation of the group stimulus coordinates. The weighting elongates the configuration, and the transformation converts the square configuration into a parallelogram.

Consider the matrix $\mathbf{R}_s = \mathbf{T}_s\mathbf{T}_s'$ with elements $r_{kk's}$. The three-mode model can be written in terms of the subject parameters w_{ks} and $r_{kk's}$ as follows:

$$\delta_{ijs} = \left[\sum_k w_{ks}^2 (x_{ik} - x_{jk})^2 + \sum_{(k,k')} w_{ks}w_{k's}r_{kk's}(x_{ik} - x_{jk})(x_{ik'} - x_{jk'}) \right]^{1/2}.$$

$$\tag{6.22}$$

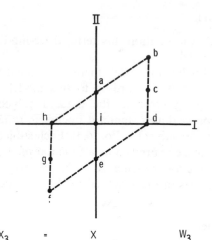

$$X_3 = X \quad W_3 \quad T_3$$

$$
\begin{array}{cc}
\text{I} & \text{II}
\end{array}
$$

$$
\begin{bmatrix}
0.00 & 0.71 \\
1.00 & 1.42 \\
1.00 & 0.71 \\
1.00 & 0.00 \\
0.00 & -0.71 \\
-1.00 & -1.42 \\
-1.00 & -0.71 \\
-1.00 & 0.00 \\
0.00 & 0.00
\end{bmatrix}
=
\begin{bmatrix}
0.00 & 1.00 \\
1.00 & 1.00 \\
1.00 & 0.00 \\
1.00 & -1.00 \\
0.00 & -1.00 \\
-1.00 & -1.00 \\
-1.00 & 0.00 \\
-1.00 & 1.00 \\
0.00 & 0.00
\end{bmatrix}
\begin{bmatrix}
1.00 & 0.00 \\
0.00 & 1.00
\end{bmatrix}
\begin{bmatrix}
1.00 & 0.71 \\
0.00 & 0.71
\end{bmatrix}
$$

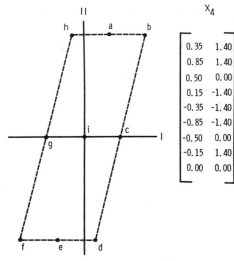

$$X_4 = X \quad W_4 \quad T_4$$

$$
\begin{bmatrix}
0.35 & 1.40 \\
0.85 & 1.40 \\
0.50 & 0.00 \\
0.15 & -1.40 \\
-0.35 & -1.40 \\
-0.85 & -1.40 \\
-0.50 & 0.00 \\
-0.15 & 1.40 \\
0.00 & 0.00
\end{bmatrix}
=
\begin{bmatrix}
0.00 & 1.00 \\
1.00 & 1.00 \\
1.00 & 0.00 \\
1.00 & -1.00 \\
0.00 & -1.00 \\
-1.00 & -1.00 \\
-1.00 & 0.00 \\
-1.00 & 1.00 \\
0.00 & 0.00
\end{bmatrix}
\begin{bmatrix}
.50 & 0.00 \\
0.00 & 2.00
\end{bmatrix}
\begin{bmatrix}
1.00 & .70 \\
0.00 & .70
\end{bmatrix}
$$

Figure 6.6. Stimulus spaces for two hypothetical subjects and nine stimuli.

138

If $r_{kk's}$ equals 0 for all pairs of dimensions (k, k'), then the second sum on the right would disappear and Eq. (6.22) would reduce to the weighted Euclidean model of Eq. (6.4). The summation on the right over dimension pairs (k, k') is a sum of interactions between coordinate differences on all possible pairs of dimensions. The parameter $r_{kk's}$ characterizes the size and direction of the interaction between coordinate differences for dimensions k and k' in the judgments of subject s. The sign of $r_{kk's}$ indicates the direction of the interaction and the absolute value indicates the size of that interaction.

The subject weight matrices $\mathbf{W}_s$ and the subject transformation matrices $\mathbf{T}_s$ do not represent the most concise description of subject characteristics. Such a description would have to contain $2S$ matrices, one weight matrix and one transformation matrix for each of the S subjects. Therefore, Tucker (1972) derives a method of estimating a single set of subject coordinate estimates contained in an $(S \times M)$ matrix $\hat{\mathbf{Z}}$, with elements $\hat{z}_{sm}$. The coordinate estimates in $\hat{\mathbf{Z}}$ provide a quantitative dimensional description of subjects analogous to the description of stimuli provided by matrix $\hat{\mathbf{X}}$. $\hat{\mathbf{Z}}$ has one row for each subject and one column for each dimension in the subject space. M, the number of dimensions in the subject space, need not equal K, the number of dimensions in the stimulus space. This means that there are two dimensionality decisions, one for the subject space and one for the stimulus space.

Dimensionality

As always, dimensionality is decided, in part, by considering the reproducibility and interpretability of several solutions varying in their dimensionalities. As in Torgerson's metric solution, there are eigenvalues that can aid in the dimensionality decision. More precisely, there are two sets of eigenvalues, one for the stimulus space and one for the subject space. Eigenvalues-by-dimensions plots, such as the one in Figure 4.4, can be useful in deciding dimensionality. If an elbow appears over the $(K + 1)$st dimension in the eigenvalues-by-dimensions plot for the stimulus space $\mathbf{X}$, this suggests that K is a reasonable number of dimensions to retain in this space. Similarly, if an elbow appears above the $(M + 1)$st dimension in the eigenvalues-by-dimensions plot for the subject space, then M is a reasonable number of dimensions to retain in the subject space $\mathbf{Z}$.

Rotation

Both the stimulus space and the subject space can be rotated as needed to obtain an interpretable solution. That is, if matrix $\hat{\mathbf{X}}$ represents a solution for the stimulus coordinate estimates, then matrix $\hat{\mathbf{X}}^* = \hat{\mathbf{X}}\mathbf{T}$ is also a solution. Here $\mathbf{T}$ is an orthogonal transformation matrix. Similarly, if matrix $\hat{\mathbf{Z}}$ is a solution for the subject space, then matrix $\hat{\mathbf{Z}}^* = \hat{\mathbf{Z}}\mathbf{T}$ is also a solution. Again, $\mathbf{T}$ is any orthogonal transformation matrix. In general, the transformation matrix that yields the most interpretable rotation of the subject space will not be the same as the rotation yielding the most interpretable rotation of the stimulus space. Both objective and hand rotations can be used to obtain a more interpretable solution if the unrotated solution is difficult to interpret.

One appeal of the weighted Euclidean model is that the rotation of the axes is fixed, in general, which greatly simplifies interpretation of the dimensions. Whereas the rotation problem all but disappears with the weighted Euclidean model, it potentially doubles in the three-mode model: One rotation may be required for the subject space and a second for the stimulus space.

Interpretation

The stimulus coordinate matrix $\hat{\mathbf{X}}$ is interpreted as in all other scaling models. Meaningful stimulus orderings and groupings are identified.

Interpretation of the subject space usually begins with the visual identification of discrete subject clusters in the subject space. Subjects who cluster together in the subject space have approximately the same weight matrices $\mathbf{W}_s$ and transformation matrices $\mathbf{T}_s$. The user must then describe the differences between the stimulus spaces of people in the several clusters. This is often done by identifying real individuals at the center of each cluster. Each real individual serves as a prototype of the individuals in his or her cluster. In Tucker's (1972) work, he describes the several subject clusters by presenting the subject weight matrix and subject transformation matrix for each prototypical subject. If subjects 3 and 4 in Figure 6.6 were individuals at the center of two subject clusters, Figure 6.6 could serve as the description of the transformation $\hat{\mathbf{T}}_s$, weight $\hat{\mathbf{W}}_s$, and stimulus coordinate matrices $\hat{\mathbf{X}}_s$, for the two clusters.

Tucker's three-mode model is the richest of all the multidimensional scaling models, and it includes the weighted Euclidean model as a special case. A three-mode solution provides a description of differences between subjects not only in terms of subject weights, but also in terms of subject transformation matrices. With the increased richness of the three-mode model comes an increased complexity. When the stimulus and subject spaces contain more than a few dimensions, rotation and interpretation of the solution can pose challenging problems for the user. Cooper's (1973) marketing study can provide the reader with an illustration of the complexities involved.

*FITTING THE WEIGHTED EUCLIDEAN MODEL

There are currently several algorithms for fitting the weighted Euclidean model (Bloxom, 1978; Carroll and Chang, 1970; DeLeeuw and Pruzansky, 1978; Lingoes and Borg, 1978). Not all can be described here. The algorithm presented below is a modified version of the one described by Carroll and Chang (1970) and incorporated into the INDSCAL and SINDSCAL (Pruzansky, 1975) algorithms. The rationale behind the algorithm goes well beyond the scope of this book. The purpose of this section is simply to give readers an idea of how such algorithms work. Table 6.3 shows hypothetical dissimilarity matrices for two subjects and three stimuli. These data will be used to illustrate the steps required to obtain a two-dimensional solution.

Table 6.3.   Dissimilarity, Scalar Product, and Starting Configuration Matrices for an Example Involving Three Stimuli and Two Subjects.

Dissimilarity Matrices

Stimulus	A	B	C
A	0.00	1.00	1.00
$\Delta_1 =$ B	1.00	0.00	1.00
C	1.00	1.00	0.00

Stimulus	A	B	C
A	0.00	0.00	1.00
$\Delta_2 =$ B	0.00	0.00	1.00
C	1.00	1.00	0.00

Scalar Product Matrices

Stimulus	A	B	C
A	0.33	-0.17	-0.17
$\Delta_1^* =$ B	-0.17	0.33	-0.17
C	-0.17	-0.17	0.33

Stimulus	A	B	C
A	0.11	0.11	-0.22
$\Delta_2^* =$ B	0.11	0.11	-0.22
C	-0.22	-0.22	0.44

Average Scalar Product Matrix

	Stimulus	A	B	C
	A	0.22	-0.03	-0.20
$\Delta^* = \frac{1}{2}(\Delta_1^* + \Delta_2^*) =$	B	-0.03	0.22	-0.20
	C	-0.20	-0.20	0.34

Starting Configuration

		I	II
	A	-.31	.35
$\hat{X}^o =$	B	-.31	-.35
	C	.63	.00

The first step is to convert each subject's dissimilarity matrix into a scalar product matrix using the transformation in Eq. (6.7). As before, let Δ_s^* be the scalar product matrix for subject s. Matrices Δ_1^* and Δ_2^* in Table 6.3 contain the scalar products for subjects 1 and 2, respectively, in the example.

To prevent any one subject's data from having an undue influence on the final solution, the scalar product matrices may be standardized so that the variance of the elements in each is equal. To streamline the example, however, this step will be skipped.

Before the iterative portion of the algorithm can begin, a starting configuration must be obtained. One way to do so (Schönemann, 1972) requires the computation of an average scalar product matrix Δ^*:

$$\Delta^* = \frac{1}{S} \sum_s \Delta_s^*. \tag{6.23}$$

Using the principal components analysis described in the discussion surrounding Eq. (2.6), a matrix $\tilde{X}$ can be found such that $\tilde{X}\tilde{X}' = \Delta^*$. The first K columns of $\tilde{X}$ make an excellent starting configuration for the K dimensional solution. In Table 6.3, matrix $\Delta^* = \frac{1}{2}(\Delta_1^* + \Delta_2^*)$ contains the average scalar product for the example. $\hat{X}^o$ in Table 6.3 contains the starting configuration for the example, the first two principal components of Δ^*.

The remainder of the algorithm is composed of iterations. Each iteration contains two phases, one to estimate subject weights and one to estimate stimulus coordinates. Figure 6.7 gives a flow chart for such an algorithm.

In the first phase of an iteration, the one in which new weight estimates are obtained, two matrices, A and B, must be constructed. A has S rows, one for each subject, and I^2 columns, one for each stimulus pair. The first I elements in row s are the elements in row 1 of the scalar product matrix for subject s. The second I elements in row s are the elements in row 2 of the

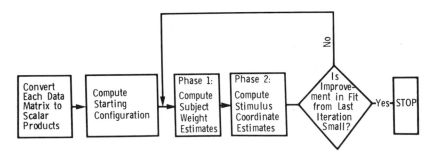

Figure 6.7. Flow chart of an algorithm for fitting the weighted Euclidean model.

scalar product matrix for subject s. The third group of I elements in row s comes from row 3 of the scalar product matrix for subject s, and so forth.

Basically, row s of A is a vector containing all the entries in the scalar product matrix for subject s. Row 1 of matrix A in Table 6.4 contains the nine elements in the scalar product matrix Δ_1^* of Table 6.3. Each group of three elements in row 1 of A in Table 6.4 corresponds to one row of Δ_1^* in Table 6.3. Each group of three elements in row 2 of A corresponds to one row of Δ_2^*.

Matrix B has one column for each stimulus pair and has one row for each dimension k. Thus B is $(K \times I^2)$. The element in the row corresponding to dimension k and the column corresponding to stimulus pair (i, j) is defined as:

$$b_{k(i, j)} = \hat{x}_{ik}\hat{x}_{jk}, \qquad (6.24)$$

where $\hat{x}_{ik}$ and $\hat{x}_{jk}$ are the most recent estimates of the stimulus coordinates. In the first iteration, $\hat{x}_{ik}$ and $\hat{x}_{jk}$ come from the starting configuration. In all subsequent iterations, they are estimates from the previous iteration.

Table 6.4 shows matrix B computed from the starting configuration coordinates $\hat{X}^o$ in Table 6.3. For instance, the element in row 1 column 3 corresponds to dimension I and stimulus pair (A, C). Hence, it was computed from the starting configuration coordinates in Table 6.3 and Eq.

Table 6.4. Matrices Used in Phase 1.

Row Stimulus	A	A	A	B	B	B	C	C	C
Column Stimulus	A	B	C	A	B	C	A	B	C
A = Subject 1	0.33	−0.17	−0.17	−0.17	0.33	−0.17	−0.17	−0.17	0.33
Subject 2	0.11	0.11	−0.22	0.11	0.11	−0.22	−0.22	−0.22	0.44
B = Dimension I	0.10	0.10	−0.20	0.10	0.10	−0.20	−0.20	−0.20	0.40
Dimension II	0.12	−0.12	0.00	−0.12	0.12	0.00	0.00	0.00	0.00

		Subject	
	Dimension	1	2
$\hat{W}^2 = (BB')^{-1}BA' =$	I	0.83	1.11
	II	2.00	0.00

(6.24) as follows:

$$b_{I(A, C)} = \hat{x}^o_{AI}\hat{x}^o_{CI} = (-.31)(.63) = -.20. \qquad (6.25)$$

Once **A** and **B** have been constructed, a $(K \times S)$ matrix $\hat{\mathbf{W}}^2$ with elements $\hat{w}^2_{ks}$ can be estimated as follows:

$$\hat{\mathbf{W}}^2 = (\mathbf{BB'})^{-1}\mathbf{BA'}. \qquad (6.26)$$

The elements of $\hat{\mathbf{W}}^2$, or more precisely, their square roots, become the subject weight estimates for the current iteration.

To start phase 2, matrices **A** and **B** must be reconstructed according to new definitions. **A** again contains scalar products. In this phase, **A** has one row for each stimulus and one column for each possible (subject, stimulus) pair. Thus it has I rows and JS columns. The element in row i and the column corresponding to stimulus j and subject s is δ^*_{ijs}, the scalar product for stimuli i and j in the scalar product matrix of subject s.

Table 6.5 shows matrix **A** as constructed from the scalar product matrices in Table 6.3. The first three elements in row A of **A** come from row A of Δ^*_1 in Table 6.3; the second three elements in row A of **A** come from row A of Δ^*_2 in Table 6.3. The six elements in row B of **A** come from row B in Δ^*_1 and Δ^*_2, and so forth.

B is reconstructed so as to have K rows, one for each dimension, and JS columns, one for each pairing of a stimulus and a subject. The element in

Table 6.5. Matrices Used in Phase 2.

Subject	1	1	1	2	2	2
Stimulus	A	B	C	A	B	C
A A = B C	0.33	−0.17	−0.17	0.11	0.11	−0.22
	−0.17	0.33	−0.17	0.11	0.11	−0.22
	−0.17	−0.17	0.33	−0.22	−0.22	0.44
I B = II	−0.26	−0.26	0.52	−0.34	−0.34	0.70
	0.70	−0.70	0.00	0.00	0.00	0.00

		Dimension	
	Stimulus	I	II
$\hat{\mathbf{X}} = \mathbf{AB'(BB')}^{-1} =$	A	−0.32	0.36
	B	−0.32	−0.36
	C	0.63	0.00

row k corresponding to subject s and stimulus j is defined as follows:

$$b_{k(sj)} = \hat{w}_{ks}^2 \hat{x}_{jk}.$$

(6.27)

Here $\hat{w}_{ks}$ and $\hat{x}_{jk}$ are the most recent estimates of these quantities. Table 6.5 shows matrix **B** constructed from the starting configuration coordinates in Table 6.3 and the weight estimates in Table 6.4. For example, the element in row 1 and column 3 of **B**, which corresponds to dimension I, subject 1, and stimulus C, was computed as follows:

$$b_{I(1C)} = \hat{w}_{I1}^2 \hat{x}_{CI}^o = (.83)(.63) = .52.$$

(6.28)

Once **A** and **B** have been reconstructed, a new matrix of coordinate estimates $\hat{\mathbf{X}}$ can be obtained as follows:

$$\hat{\mathbf{X}} = \mathbf{AB}'(\mathbf{BB}')^{-1}.$$

(6.29)

The elements of $\hat{\mathbf{X}}$ become the current stimulus coordinate estimates. Matrix $\hat{\mathbf{X}}$ at the bottom of Table 6.5 shows the new scale value estimates obtained by substituting matrices **A** and **B** into Eq. (6.29). After computing $\hat{\mathbf{X}}$, the first iteration would be complete.

The algorithm described above is designed to minimize the sum of squared discrepancies between predicted and actual scalar products:

$$F = \sum_{(i,j,s)} \left(\delta_{ijs}^* - \hat{\delta}_{ijs}^* \right)^2,$$

(6.30)

where the predicted scalar product $\hat{\delta}_{ijs}^*$ is defined as

$$\hat{\delta}_{ijs}^* = \sum_k \hat{x}_{ik} \hat{x}_{jk} \hat{w}_{ks}^2.$$

(6.31)

Iteration would continue until the improvement in F from one iteration to the next fell below some suitably small value, say .001.

Table 6.6 shows the predicted scalar products $\hat{\boldsymbol{\Delta}}_s^*$ and the estimated distances $\hat{\mathbf{D}}_s$:

$$\hat{d}_{ijs} = \left[\sum_k \hat{w}_{ks}^2 (\hat{x}_{ik} - \hat{x}_{jk})^2 \right]^{1/2}$$

(6.32)

computed for both subjects from the weight estimates $\hat{\mathbf{W}}^2$ in Table 6.4, and the coordinate estimates $\hat{\mathbf{X}}$ in Table 6.5. Comparison of the predicted scalar products in Table 6.6 and the actual scalar products in Table 6.3 reveals that they are identical except for the first two diagonal elements in the matrices of subject one. The sum of squared discrepancies F equals .0002 after the first iteration. To two decimal places, the correlation between predicted and actual scalar products, the fit measure in Eq. (6.15), equals 1.00. The estimated distances in Table 6.6 agree very closely with the actual dissimilarities shown in Table 6.3.

After completion of the iterations, the scale values in each column of $\hat{\mathbf{X}}$ would be standardized so that the variance of the scale values along every dimension equalled 1.00. Then the weights $\hat{\mathbf{W}}^2$ would be estimated one more time by using Eq. (6.26) in another repetition of phase one.

To summarize, the algorithm begins with the conversion of each subject's dissimilarity matrix to scalar product form. Each subject's scalar product matrix may be standardized, and then a starting configuration would be obtained. A series of iterations form the major portion of the algorithm. Each iteration would contain one phase to estimate subject weights and one phase to estimate stimulus coordinates. Iteration would continue until improvement in fit from one iteration to the next fell below some suitably small amount. After iteration had ceased, the scale value estimates would be standardized so that the variance of the estimates equalled 1.00 along each dimension, and then the weights would be estimated one last time.

SUMMARY

The weighted Euclidean distance model and the three-mode model provide the bases for the major individual differences MDS analyses for dissimilar-

Table 6.6.   Estimated Distances and Scalar Product Matrices for Three Stimuli and Two Subjects.

Stimulus		A	B	C	Stimulus	A	B	C
				Estimated Distance Matrices				
	A	0.00	1.02	1.00	A	0.00	0.00	1.00
$\hat{\Delta}_1 =$	B	1.02	0.00	1.00	$\hat{\Delta}_2 =$ B	0.00	0.00	1.00
	C	1.00	1.00	0.00	C	1.00	1.00	0.00
				Predicted Scalar Product Matrices				
	A	0.34	-0.17	-0.17	A	0.11	0.11	-0.22
$\hat{\Delta}_1^* =$	B	-0.17	0.34	-0.17	$\hat{\Delta}_2^* =$ B	0.11	0.11	-0.22
	C	-0.17	-0.17	0.33	C	-0.22	-0.22	0.44

ity data. Both approaches provide a quantitative dimensional description of subjects and stimuli, thus providing a richer analysis then the approaches of earlier chapters.

In the weighted Euclidean model, subjects are presumed to vary in the weights they assign to dimensions. Several programs for fitting the model have been widely disseminated: INDSCAL (Carroll and Chang, 1970), SINDSCAL (Pruzansky, 1976), and ALSCAL (Young and Lewyckyj, 1979).

The programs for fitting the weighted Euclidean model, which are compared by Schiffman et al. (1981), provide estimates of subject weights and stimulus coordinates. In general, the solution cannot be rotated without loss of fit to the data. The stimulus coordinate matrix is interpreted by identifying substantively meaningful orderings and groupings of the stimuli. The estimates of raw subject weights convey information about the relative salience of dimensions and about the fit of the model to subjects' data. The weighted Euclidean model has proved particularly useful in studying the perceived social structure of small groups.

The three-mode model, programmed by MacCallum (1979), includes the weighted Euclidean model as a special case. In this model, subjects are presumed to vary not only in the weights they assign to dimensions, but also in the degree and direction of the interactions between pairs of dimensions reflected in their judgments. From a three-mode analysis, one can derive estimates of stimulus coordinates, subject weights, and subject transformation matrices. The three-mode solution is the richest of all MDS solutions. That richness brings complexity, however, because both the stimulus space and the subject space may need to be rotated separately to achieve an interpretable solution.

PROBLEMS

Imagine that four people made dissimilarity judgments for all possible pairs of countries used in Problem 1, Chapter 4. Their dissimilarity matrices are given in Table 6.7. Apply a computer program that fits the weighted Euclidean model to these data. Obtain a solution in one–six dimensions. Then answer the following questions.

1. Draw a dimensions-by-fit-measure plot. Then decide how many dimensions should be retained. Defend your answer.

2. In the three-dimensional solution, which subjects' data were fit least well? Which subjects' data were fit best? Defend your answer on the basis of statistics printed by the program.

3. What is the three-dimensional stimulus coordinate matrix $\hat{X}$? What are your interpretations of the dimensions?

4. In the three-dimensional solution, what is the subject weight matrix $\hat{W}$? Describe the differences between subjects as represented in $\hat{W}$.

Table 6.7. Dissimilarity Judgments for Four Subjects and Eight Stimulus Countries.

	An	Ar	Au	Ch	Cu	J	US	Z
				Subject 1				
Angola								
Argentina	1.41							
Australia	1.00	1.00						
China	1.00	1.73	1.41					
Cuba	1.41	1.41	1.73	1.00				
Japan	1.41	1.41	1.00	1.00	1.41			
United States	1.73	1.00	1.41	1.41	1.00	1.00		
Zimbabwe	0.71	1.41	1.00	1.00	1.41	1.41	1.73	

	An	Ar	Au	Ch	Cu	J	US	Z
				Subject 2				
Angola								
Argentina	1.00							
Australia	2.00	2.00						
China	3.00	3.00	2.00					
Cuba	1.00	1.00	3.00	1.00				
Japan	2.00	2.00	1.00	2.00	1.00			
United States	3.00	3.00	2.00	3.00	2.00	2.00		
Zimbabwe	1.00	1.00	3.00	1.00	3.00	3.00	1.00	

	An	Ar	Au	Ch	Cu	J	US	Z
				Subject 3				
Angola								
Argentina	1.41							
Australia	1.41	1.00						
China	1.00	1.41	1.41					
Cuba	1.00	1.41	1.41	1.00				
Japan	1.41	1.00	1.00	1.41	1.41			
United States	1.41	1.00	1.00	1.41	1.41	1.00		
Zimbabwe	1.00	1.41	1.41	1.00	1.00	1.41	1.41	

Table 6.7. (*Continued*).

	An	Ar	Au	Ch	Cu	J	US	Z
				Subject 4				
Angola								
Argentina	1.00							
Australia	0.00	1.00						
China	1.00	0.00	1.00					
Cuba	1.41	1.00	1.41	1.00				
Japan	1.00	1.41	1.00	0.00	1.00			
United States	1.41	1.00	1.41	1.00	0.00	1.00		
Zimbabwe	0.00	1.00	0.00	1.00	1.41	1.00	1.41	

Answers

The following results (Figure 6.8) were obtained using SINDSCAL (Pruzansky, 1975). Other programs should yield similar, but not identical, numerical results. Readers who employ a different version of SINDSCAL or who employ different options in SINDSCAL will also get similar, but not identical, results. In other words, readers should not expect the same degree of agreement between their results and answers that they found for Chapters 1–4.

1.

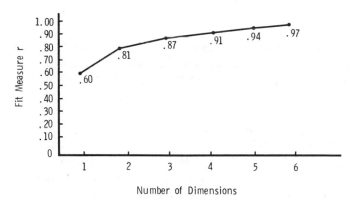

Figure 6.8. Correlations between actual and estimated scalar products in one–six dimensions for the countries dissimilarity data.

There is an elbow at two dimensions and a somewhat smaller one at three dimensions. On the basis of the fit measure, one could justify selecting either the two- or three-dimensional solution.

Applying the criterion of interpretability does not unambiguously settle the issue. In the two-dimensional solution, both dimensions have a clear-cut interpretation. One dimension has the Marxist countries at one end and the capitalist countries at the other. The second dimension has countries in the southern hemisphere at one end and countries in the northern hemisphere at the other.

In the three-dimensional solution, the first two dimensions are easily interpretable, but the interpretation of the third dimension is problematic (see Problem 4 below). On the basis of the interpretability or fit criterion, one could decide to retain either a two- or three-dimensional solution.

2. The data of subject 2 are fit least well: $r_2 = .63$. The data of subject 3 are fit the best: $r_3 = 1.00$. for the remaining two subjects, the fit statistics are $r_1 = .95$ and $r_4 = .87$.

3.

		Dimensions		
$\hat{\mathbf{X}} =$	Stimulus	I	II	III
	Angola	.33	.37	−.32
	Argentina	−.35	−.13	−.56
	Australia	−.38	.43	.03
	China	.40	.00	.45
	Cuba	.34	−.53	.06
	Japan	−.33	.02	.54
	United States	−.36	−.51	.08
	Zimbabwe	.34	.35	−.28

Along dimension I, the Marxist countries of Angola, China, Cuba, and Zimbabwe appear at the positive end. The capitalist countries of Argentina, Australia, Japan, and the United States fall at the negative end. This dimension will be called the Marxist-capitalist dimension.

The countries in the eastern hemisphere, Angola, Australia, China, and Japan, appear at the positive end or in the middle of dimension II. Argentina, Cuba, and the United States, the Western countries, fall at the negative end. This will be called the east–west dimension.

Except for the location of Australia and the United States, dimension III would clearly be a north–south dimension. Three of the nations in the southern hemisphere, Angola, Argentina, and Zimbabwe, have negative coordinates. Japan and China, which have the large positive coordinates, are in the northern hemisphere. Given that Cuba is the closest of all these countries to the Equator, its small positive coordinate along dimension III is consistent with the north–south interpretation of this dimension.

4.

$$
\hat{\mathbf{W}} =
\begin{array}{cccc}
 & & \text{Subject} & \\
1 & 2 & 3 & 4
\end{array}
\quad \text{Dimension}
$$

	1	2	3	4	Dimension
	.57	.34	1.00	.05	Marxist–capitalist
	.66	.24	.00	.78	East–west
	.33	.46	.00	.35	North–south

For the first subject, the Marxist–capitalist and east–west dimensions are the most salient, with a somewhat lesser amount of weight being given to the north–south dimension, dimension III. The second subject weights the dimensions more equally than do any of the others. The judgments of the third subject seem to reflect only the Marxist–capitalist dimension. The east–west dimension is most salient to the fourth subject, although his or her judgments also reflect the north–south dimension.

CHAPTER 7

Preference Models

As explained in Chapter 1, Coombs (1964) proposed a distance model for preference data, often called the unfolding model. Here, however, it will be called the distance model for preferences. According to this model, persons can be characterized by a set of parameters x_{sk} that are their ideal point coordinates. The coordinate x_{sk} designates the level along dimension k that the subject considers ideal. Taken together, the K ideal point coordinates for subject s specify that combination of stimulus characteristics that the subject considers ideal. According to the model, the more closely a stimulus resembles the ideal, the more it will be preferred.

Let δ_{is} represent the strength of person s' preference for stimulus i. It will be assumed that higher values of δ_{is} designate lesser amounts of preference. In other words, δ_{is} is a measure of dislike for stimulus i rather than a measure of like. In the simplest metric version of the model, preferences are assumed to be of the following form:

$$\delta_{is} = d_{is} = \left[\sum_k (x_{ik} - x_{sk})^2 \right]^{1/2}. \qquad (7.1)$$

As always, x_{ik} refers to the location of stimulus i along attribute k. In this model, it is as if the subject arrives at a preference judgment by comparing the stimulus coordinates to his or her ideal point coordinates. Those stimuli whose coordinates place them farthest from the ideal are the least liked.

Carroll (1972) divides MDS analyses of preference into two classes: internal and external. Internal analyses provide estimates of the stimulus coordinates, subject ideal points, and a fit measure. In external analyses, the stimulus coordinates are presumed known, either because they are given by theory or because the stimuli were previously scaled. External analyses provide a measure of fit and estimates of various subject parameters, including the ideal point coordinates. Some external analyses permit formal tests of hypotheses about preference models in ways that internal analyses do not.

This chapter contains two sections. The first describes nonmetric internal analyses of preference data. These analyses closely resemble those encountered in Chapter 5, except that the data matrix is now a matrix of preferences rather than dissimilarities, and ideal point coordinates as well as stimulus coordinates must be estimated. Further, the monotone function relating preferences to distances is defined somewhat differently than the monotone function in Chapter 5.

The second section describes external analyses of preference data and outlines a hierarchy of four preference models for preference data, each of which can be fitted to data with standard multiple regression techniques. The regression techniques provide estimates of the subject parameters in the various models, and they lead to statistical tests for various hypotheses about the fit of the several models to data.

In preference models, the ideal point coordinates x_{sk} are subject parameters, but subject parameters very different from the ones encountered in the last chapter, the weights w_{ks}. Subject weights define their own space, one that is separate from the stimulus space. Ideal point coordinates, on the other hand, are locations in the same space as the one that contains the stimulus points. For the next section of this chapter, the one on internal analyses, the readers should revise their conceptions of the matrix **X**. **X** will contain not only the stimulus coordinates x_{ik}, but also ideal point coordinates x_{sk}. It will contain K columns, as before, and $(I + S)$ rows, one for each stimulus and one for each subject. Correspondingly, a graphical representation of **X** will show points representing stimuli and points representing subjects.

NONMETRIC INTERNAL ANALYSES

This section begins with a discussion of the data used to illustrate a nonmetric internal analysis of preference data. It then proceeds to describe the nonmetric model for preference data with emphasis on the monotone function presumed to relate the observed preferences to theoretical distances in a Euclidean space. The section finishes with discussions of the issues that any user must face in applying an analysis of preference data: issues of dimensionality, rotation, and interpretation.

Table 7.1 shows the data that will be used to illustrate an internal analysis of preference data. In this hypothetical study, married couples ranked nine stimuli according to preference. Rank one represents the most

Table 7.1. Rank Order Preferences of Married Couples for Nine Family Compositions.[a]

Number of Girls	Number of Boys	Couple A	B	C	D	E	F
		Preference Ranking					
0	0	1	9	5	6	6	7
0	1	2	8	3	7	2	3
0	2	5	5	1	9	7	8
1	0	3	7	8	2	3	4
1	1	4	4	4	4	1	1
1	2	8	2	2	8	4	5
2	0	6	6	9	1	8	9
2	1	7	3	7	3	5	2
2	2	9	1	6	5	9	6

[a]Rank 1 is the most preferred composition.

preferred stimulus; rank nine represents the least preferred stimulus. Table 7.1 presumes that the subjects performed a ranking task, but the data for an internal analysis may come from any task that serves to rank order the stimuli from most to least preferred for each subject.

Each stimulus in Table 7.1 describes the composition by sex of children in a family. Column 1 shows that hypothetical couple A most preferred the child-free family, zero girls and zero boys. They least preferred the four-child family, two girls and two boys. For the data in Table 7.1 the stimulus dimensions, number of girls and number of boys, are obvious, but the data will adequately illustrate the technique. These data are hypothetical, but they are based on an actual study of family composition preferences by Coombs, et al. (1973). Throughout this chapter, the data matrix is presumed to be an $I \times S$ matrix with one row for each stimulus and one column for each person.

In its most common nonmetric form, the distance model for preferences assumes that, were it not for error, the observable preferences would be related to distances as follows:

$$\delta_{is} = f_s(d_{is}) = f_s \left[\sum_k (x_{ik} - x_{sk})^2 \right]^{1/2}. \qquad (7.2)$$

In Eq. (7.2), $\dot{f}_s$ designates a monotone function unique to subject s. By allowing a separate monotone function for each subject, one can avoid the assumption that every subject expresses his or her preferences on a common scale. When a separate monotone function is allowed for each column s of the data matrix, the analysis is said to be column conditional.[†]

A column conditional, nonmetric analysis constrains the disparities so as to preserve the ordinal information in every column. It does not, however, constrain them so as to preserve the ordinal information in the rows. Specifically, in a nonmetric, column conditional analysis, the data δ_{is} and disparities $\hat{\delta}_{is}$ must satisfy the following restriction:

$$\delta_{is} < \delta_{js} \Rightarrow \hat{\delta}_{is} \leqslant \hat{\delta}_{js} \qquad \text{for all } (i, j). \tag{7.3}$$

The column conditional restriction in Expression (7.3) is much weaker than the unconditional restriction employed in nonmetric MDS of dissimilarity data, Expression (5.11).

Most of the nonmetric computer programs described in Chapter 5 can perform nonmetric internal analyses of preference data such as that in Table 7.1. Aside from the form of the nonmetric distance model [Compare Eq. (5.1) to Eq. (7.2)], there are some other differences between nonmetric analyses of dissimilarity and preference data. First, whereas a matrix of similarities is usually square and symmetric, a preference matrix is typically an $(I \times S)$ rectangular array with one row for each stimulus and one column for each subject. Second, STRESS formula two is preferred over STRESS formula one and S-STRESS formula two is preferred over S-STRESS formula one, because the former are less prone to certain degeneracies unique to preference analyses (Kruskal and Carroll, 1969; Roskam, 1969; Young, 1972).

The output from a nonmetric analysis of preference rankings is very similar to that from a corresponding analysis of dissimilarity data. The one exception is that the analysis provides estimates of stimulus and subject ideal point coordinates. Decisions about dimensionality, rotation, and interpretation proceed in much the same manner for either an analysis of preference or similarity data.

Dimensionality

If K, the number of dimensions, is unknown, then solutions must be obtained in several dimensionalities. As in the analyses of Chapters 5 and 6, a reasonable approach is to obtain solutions in $K^* - 3$ to $K^* + 3$ dimen-

---

[†] The analysis is said to be row conditional if a separate monotone function is allowed for each row of the data matrix.

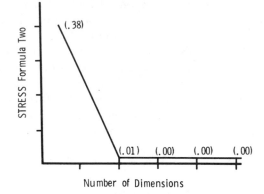

Figure 7.1. Fit-measure-by-dimensions plot for the nonmetric internal analysis of the family composition rankings in Table 7.1

sions (or 1 to K^* + 3 dimensions), where K^* is the best a priori estimate of K. Having obtained the several solutions, a user can choose between them on the basis of fit, interpretability, and reproducibility.

Figure 7.1 shows the fit-measure-by-dimensions plot for the data in Table 7.1. It clearly levels off at $K = 2$. Therefore, the two-dimensional solution, with a STRESS statistic of .01, would be retained. Table 7.2 shows the coordinate matrix for this solution. The first nine rows of this matrix $\hat{\mathbf{X}}$ contain stimulus coordinate estimates. The last six rows contain subject ideal point coordinate estimates.

Rotation

Because Eq. (7.2) is a Euclidean model, an orthogonal rotation can be applied to the coordinate matrix without any loss of fit to the data. That is, if the $(I + S) \times K$ matrix $\hat{\mathbf{X}}$ comprises a solution for the stimulus and ideal point coordinate estimates, then matrix $\hat{\mathbf{X}}^* = \hat{\mathbf{X}}\mathbf{T}$ also comprises a solution. Here $\mathbf{T}$ is an orthogonal transformation matrix. Objective rotations or hand rotations can be used as needed to achieve an interpretable solution.

Interpretation

The interpretation of the output for a nonmetric preference analysis proceeds much like the interpretation of a dissimilarity analysis. One begins by identifying the substantively important stimulus orderings or groupings. Having done so, one attempts to identify interpretable subject orderings and groupings.

Table 7.2.   Two-Dimensional Stimulus and Subject Ideal Point Coordinate Estimates from a Nonmetric Internal Analysis of the Family Composition Rankings in Table 7.1.

Stimuli		Dimension	
Number of			
Girls	Boys	I	II
0	0	−.873	−.716
0	1	−.726	−.028
0	2	−.531	.966
1	0	−.040	−.774
1	1	−.154	.033
1	2	.079	.853
2	0	.647	−.967
2	1	.592	−.165
2	2	1.025	.443
Couple			
A		−.974	−.625
B		1.193	.985
C		−.702	1.141
D		.782	−1.180
E		−.331	.052
F		.011	−.018

Figure 7.2 contains a plot of the coordinates in Table 7.2. Note that the plot contains two kinds of points, stimulus points represented by circles and subject ideal points represented by squares. The locations of the points place the various stimuli and subjects in a space defined by two subjective dimensions. The locations of the points along the two subjective dimensions, however, correspond roughly to their locations on the two objective attributes, number of boys and number of girls. Coordinates along dimension I roughly correspond to the number of girls in each configuration. The three configurations with no girls have scale values ranging from −.90 to −.50 along dimension I. Those with one girl fall in the range −.04 to .08. Those with two girls have scale values of .59 or better.

Dimension II reflects the number of boys in each family composition. Compositions with no boys have scale values below −.70. The range −.20 to .10 contains the three compositions with one boy. All three compositions with two boys fall above .40 along the second dimension.

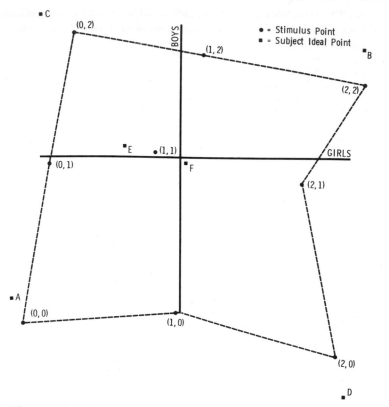

Figure 7.2. Two-dimensional plot of stimulus coordinates and subjects' ideal coordinates in Table 7.2. Numbers in parentheses beside each stimulus point indicate the number of girls and boys, respectively, in the stimulus.

With so little information given about the couples, little interpretation of their ideal point estimates can be made. All ideal points fall nearest the couple's most preferred stimulus.

To estimate the stimulus and subject ideal point coordinates, a column conditional analysis must rely solely on the ordinal information in each column of the data matrix. This means that the analysis has very little information from which to recover the coordinate estimates. As a consequence, the coordinate estimates are not generally estimated with the same precision as in an unconditional analysis of dissimilarity data. Degeneracies and local minima occur much more frequently in a column conditional analysis than in an unconditional one. Partly for these reasons, the literature contains relatively few examples of nonmetric internal preference analyses.

EXTERNAL MODELS

This section describes the four models in Carroll's hierarchy of preference models: the vector model, the simple Euclidean model, the weighted Euclidean model, and the general Euclidean model. It also describes the fit statistics for the various models and the kinds of hypotheses that can be tested in an external analysis. The next section of this chapter will describe the procedures for estimating the subject parameters and for calculating the various statistics used in testing hypotheses.

Although readers will not see how parameters are estimated until the following section, they should keep in mind two things about parameter estimation: Carroll's estimation procedures use standard multiple regression techniques, and the various subject parameter estimates are regression weights or are derived from regression weights. Special computer programs exist for fitting one or more of the four models (Carroll and Chang, 1967; Davison, 1976, 1980; Srinivasan and Shocker, 1973), but multiple regression programs in social science computer packages can be used to fit each model in its metric form. The basic input to such an analysis includes the subject's preference data and the stimulus coordinate estimates. Output contains subject parameter estimates and a measure of fit, one for each subject.

In Carroll's hierarchy, the distinction between the vector model and the three Euclidean models is, in some respects, more fundamental than the distinctions between the three Euclidean models. Before launching into a detailed description of all four models, the distinction between the vector and Euclidean models will be developed further.

Vector Model Versus Distance Models

Carroll's (1972) four models include one linear model, the vector model, and three nonlinear distance models: the simple Euclidean model, the weighted Euclidean model, and the general Euclidean model. Because they are nonlinear, the three distance models are distinctly different from the vector model.

In the vector model, a subject's liking for a stimulus is presumed to increase (or decrease) linearly with stimulus scale values along each dimension. For instance, in our family composition study, if a couple wanted a large number of children so that their liking for family compositions increased linearly as the number of girls increased and it increased linearly as the number of boys increased, then their preferences would satisfy the vector model. If a couple wanted no children, then their preferences would satisfy the vector model as long as their liking for stimuli increased linearly as the number of boys fell to zero and the number of girls fell to zero. A couple who enjoyed girls, but not boys, would satisfy the vector model if their liking for compositions increased linearly as the number of girls increased but decreased linearly as the number of boys increased. In the vector model, a subject's preferences are presumed to be a monotone function of stimulus scale values along each dimension, and the monotone function must have a particular form: linear.

In the Euclidean distance models, the function relating preferences to stimulus scale values need not be linear or even monotone. The distance models permit the preferences and scale values to be related by a curvilinear monotone function or a single-peaked nonmonotone function. To clarify these two kinds of relations—curvilinear monotone and single-peaked non-monotone—let's return to the family composition example.

Imagine a couple who likes a lot of children. Their liking for family compositions might steadily increase as the number of boys increased and as the number of girls increased, but not in a linear fashion. Curve D in Figure 7.3 shows a "liking" function in which liking, plotted along the vertical axis, increases as a function of scale values along the stimulus dimension plotted along the horizontal axis, but in a nonlinear fashion. If a subject's liking for stimuli increases monotonically, but nonlinearly, with scale values along a dimension, the preferences may satisfy one of the distance models, but they cannot satisfy the vector model. Similarly, if liking decreases monotonically, but nonlinearly, as a function of stimulus scale values along a dimension (curve A in Figure 7.3), the subject's

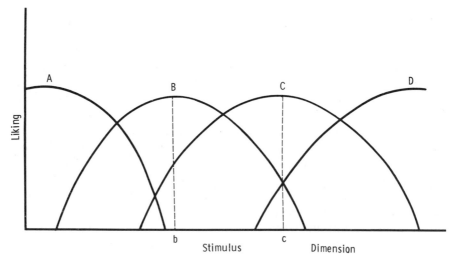

Figure 7.3. Single-peaked and monotone liking functions for four subjects.

preference data may satisfy one of the distance models, but it cannot satisfy the vector model.

The distance models can accommodate curvilinear monotone functions, such as curves A and D in Figure 7.3. They can also accommodate single-peaked nonmonotone liking functions. Imagine a couple who wants two girls—no more, no less. They might prefer a family composition with zero girls over a family with one girl; they would prefer a family with two girls over a family with one girl; they would prefer a family with two girls over a family with three girls; they might prefer a family with three girls over a family with four girls; and so forth. If one were to plot their liking for family compositions as a function of the number of girls in it, that function would increase over the range zero to two girls, reach a peak at the ideal of two girls, and then decline over the range of two girls or more. This couple's liking function would be single-peaked because it has a single maximum at the ideal of two girls. It would also be nonmonotone because it increases over part of the stimulus range (zero to two girls) and decreases over part of the range (two girls and above).

Curves B and C in Figure 7.3 show two single-peaked nonmonotone liking functions. Curve B rises over the initial portion of the stimulus range, reaches a peak at the ideal represented by point b, and then declines over the last portion of the dimension. Curve C follows a similar pattern, rising to a peak at ideal point c and then declining. Taken together, curves A to D in Figure 7.3 illustrate the kinds of liking functions consistent with the distance models, but not the vector model; monotone, but not linearly, increasing (curve A), single-peaked nonmonotone (curves B and C), and monotone, but nonlinearly, decreasing (curve D). The vector model is satisfied only if preferences and stimulus coordinates are linearly related along each dimension.

The Vector Model

Table 7.3 gives the preference data of two couples that will be used to illustrate analyses based on all four preference models in Carroll's hierarchy. In any external analysis, the scale values must be known in advance. For this example, assume that the known scale values along dimensions are the number of girls in each family and the number of boys. That is, assume that the dimension I coordinate (column 3 in Table 7.3) for each stimulus is simply the number of girls in the family composition. The number of boys equals the dimension II coordinate (column 4 in Table 7.3). Columns 5–6 show the hypothetical preference responses of two couples (A and B) whose data will form the basis for the illustration. Again, higher numbers designate greater dislike for the stimulus.

**Table 7.3. Two-Dimensional Stimulus Coordinates and
Preference Ratings for Nine Family Compositions.**

Stimulus		Stimulus Coordinate		Preference Response	
Number of		Dimension		Subject	
Girls	Boys	I	II	A	B
0	0	0.0	0.0	4.1	1.5
0	1	0.0	1.0	2.8	1.0
0	2	0.0	2.0	2.0	0.5
1	0	1.0	0.0	2.8	1.1
1	1	1.0	1.0	2.0	0.0
1	2	1.0	2.0	1.1	1.1
2	0	2.0	0.0	2.0	0.5
2	1	2.0	1.0	0.9	1.0
2	2	2.0	2.0	0.2	1.1

Of the four models outlined by Carroll (1972), the simplest was the *vector model* first proposed by Tucker (1960; Bechtel, 1976; Bechtel et al., 1971). Were it not for error, the model assumes that preferences would have the following form:

$$\delta_{is} = \sum_k b_{ks} x_{ik} + c_s. \qquad (7.4)$$

Here b_{ks} is a linear regression weight and c_s is an additive constant unique to subject s. The unique feature of this model is that preferences (δ_{is}) are assumed linearly related to scale values (x_{ik}) along each dimension.

Fitting the vector model through multiple regression techniques requires one regression for each subject. The analysis yields estimates of the subject parameters $\hat{b}_{ks}$ and $\hat{c}_s$, a multiple correlation coefficient R_V which serves as a measure of fit, and an F-statistic with K and $(I - K - 1)$ degrees of freedom. The F-statistic provides a test of the null hypothesis $R_V^2 = 0$ against the alternative $R_V^2 > 0$. The multiple correlation coefficient R_V carries the subscript V for vector to distinguish it from the fit measures for the remaining three models. R_V^2 equals the proportion of variance in the subject's preference data that can be accounted for by the K stimulus dimensions and the vector model.

If the dimensions are uncorrelated, then the sign of the subject weight indicates whether the preference responses increase ($\hat{b}_{ks} > 0$) or decrease ($\hat{b}_{ks} < 0$) as a function of stimulus dimension k; the absolute value of $\hat{b}_{ks}$ reflects the salience of dimension k to subject s.

Table 7.4 shows the dimension weight estimates, multiple correlation coefficients, and F-statistics derived by fitting the vector model to each

Table 7.4.   The Vector Model Fitted to the Data in Table 7.3.

Couple	Subject Weight Estimates		Squared Multiple Correlation	$F_{(2,6)}$-Statistic for Null Hypothesis
	$\hat{b}_{1s}$	$\hat{b}_{2s}$	R_V^2	$R_V^2 = 0$
A	$-.97$	$-.93$	.99	281.36[a]
B	$-.07$	$-.07$	.03	.10

[a]$p < .01$.

couple's data in Table 7.3. Given the coordinates in Table 7.3, the vector model can account for more than 90% of the variance in couple A's preferences. For couple A the weight estimates were approximately equal along the two dimensions ($\hat{b}_{1A} = -.97$, $\hat{b}_{2A} = -.93$) and suggest that their preferences generally decreased as the number of boys and girls increased. The vector model could account for very little variance in the preferences of couple B ($R_V^2 = .03$, $p > .10$).

The Simple Euclidean Model

According to the *simple Euclidean model*, the more a stimulus resembles a subject's ideal along each dimension, the more the subject will like it. All dimensions are assumed equally salient. It is the first of three models that assumes nonlinear liking functions of the form shown in Figure 7.3. According to this model, preferences have the following form except for error:

$$\delta_{is} = \sum_k w_s^2 (x_{ik} - x_{sk})^2 + c_s^*. \tag{7.5}$$

Fitting the model to a subject's data yields ideal point coordinate estimates $\hat{x}_{sk}$, a subject weight estimate $\hat{w}_s^2$, and a multiple correlation coefficient R_E which serves as a measure of fit. Throughout this chapter, the fit measure for the simple Euclidean model will carry the subscript E to distinguish it from the fit measures for other external analysis models. One can construct an F-statistic with $K + 1$ and $I - K - 2$ degrees of freedom for testing the null hypothesis $R_E^2 = 0$ against the alternative $R_E^2 > 0$. Since the simple Euclidean model includes the vector model as a special case [see the discussion surrounding Eqs. (7.12)–(7.16) below], one can also construct an F-statistic with 1 and $I - K - 2$ degrees of freedom. If the simple Euclidean model fits the data, it can be used to test the null hypothesis $R_E^2 = R_V^2$ against the alternative $R_E^2 > R_V^2$. If the latter F-statistic leads to rejection of the null hypothesis, then one can conclude that the simple

Table 7.5. The Simple Euclidean Model Fitted to the Data in Table 7.3.

Subject	Weight Estimate $\hat{w}_s^2$	Ideal Point Estimates $\hat{x}_{s1}$	$\hat{x}_{s2}$	Squared Multiple Correlation R_E^2	Null Hypothesis $R_E^2 = 0$ F-Statistic $F_{(3,5)}$	$R_E^2 = R_V^2$ $F_{(1,5)}$
A	.08	7.06	6.88	.99	206.15[a]	1.58
B	.25	1.13	1.13	.19	.38	.95

[a] $p < .01$.

Euclidean model accounts for significantly more variance in the preferences of subject s than does the vector model. Further, rejection supports the conclusion that preferences are nonlinearly related to some stimulus dimensions.

Table 7.5 shows the various statistics obtained by fitting the simple Euclidean model to the data in Table 7.3. Columns 5 ($R_E^2 = .99$) and 6 of Table 7.5 show that the simple Euclidean model fit the data of couple A quite well. Using any conventional significance level, however, one would conclude from the statistic in column 7 that it did not account for significantly more variance in their judgments than did the vector model. Little in this analysis suggests nonlinear relationships between the stimulus dimensions and the preferences of couple A.

The simple Euclidean model did not fit the data of couple B well ($R_E^2 = .19$, $F_{(3,5)} = .38$, $p > .10$). This couple's ideal point coordinate estimates ($\hat{x}_{B1} = \hat{x}_{B2} = 1.13$) suggest that ideally, they would choose a family containing one boy and one girl. One does not ordinarily draw conclusions from parameter estimates that did not fit a subject's data, because such parameter estimates can be misleading. Conclusions were drawn about couple B only for purposes of illustration.

The Weighted Euclidean Model

The third model in Carroll's (1972) hierarchy is the *weighted Euclidean model*. The simple Euclidean and weighted Euclidean models differ only in that the former contains a single weight w_s for each dimension, whereas the latter contains a separate weight w_{ks} for each dimension. In other words, the simple Euclidean model assumes an equal weighting for all dimensions. The weighted Euclidean model allows the weighting to differ across dimensions. According to the weighted Euclidean model, preferences have the following form except for error:

$$\delta_{is} = \sum_k w_{ks}^2 (x_{ik} - x_{sk})^2 + c_s^*. \qquad (7.6)$$

Were it not for the exponent $\frac{1}{2}$ on the right side of Eq. (6.4), and the additive constant c_s^* in Eq. (7.6), the weighted Euclidean model for preferences in Eq. (7.6) would closely resemble the weighted Euclidean model for dissimilarity data in Eq. (6.4). The weighted Euclidean model, Eq. (7.6), includes the simple Euclidean model, Eq. (7.5), and the vector model, Eq. (7.4), as special cases.

Fitting the weighted Euclidean model to a subject's data yields ideal point coordinate estimates $\hat{x}_{sk}$, subject weight estimates $\hat{w}_{ks}$, and a multiple correlation coefficient R_W which serves as a measure of fit. The subscript W distinguishes the weighted Euclidean model fit measure R_W from the fit measure for other models.

One can construct an F-statistic with $2K$ and $I - 2K - 1$ degrees of freedom for testing the null hypothesis $R_W^2 = 0$ against the alternative $R_W^2 > 0$. Since the weighted Euclidean model includes the vector and simple Euclidean models as special cases, one can construct two other F-statistics and use those statistics to compare the weighted Euclidean model to the vector and simple Euclidean models.

The first of these two statistics has $K - 1$ and $I - 2K - 1$ degrees of freedom. If the weighted Euclidean model fits the data, it can be used to test the null hypothesis $R_W^2 = R_E^2$, with the alternative being $R_W^2 > R_E^2$. When this statistic leads to rejection of the null hypothesis, one can reasonably conclude that the weighted Euclidean model fits the data better than the simple Euclidean model; further, rejection of the null hypothesis supports the conclusion that the weights for subject s, w_{ks}, are not equal for all K dimensions.

The second of the F-statistics for comparing models has K and $I - 2K - 1$ degrees of freedom. If the weighted Euclidean model fits the data, it can be used to test the null hypothesis $R_W^2 = R_V^2$ against the alternative $R_W^2 > R_V^2$. When this statistic leads to rejection of the null hypothesis, one can conclude that the weighted Euclidean model fits the judgments of subject s better than does the vector model. Further, it supports the conclusion that the preferences are nonlinearly related to the stimulus coordinates along some of the dimensions.

Table 7.6 shows the various statistics obtained by fitting the weighted Euclidean model to the data in Table 7.3. Columns 6 and 7 of Table 7.6 show that the weighted Euclidean model fits the data of couple A quite well. Using any conventional significance level, however, one would conclude from the F-statistics in columns 8 and 9 that it did not account for

Table 7.6. The Weighted Euclidean Model Fitted to the Data in Table 7.3.

	Weight Estimates		Ideal Point Estimates		Squared Multiple Correlation	Null Hypothesis		
						$R_W^2 = 0$	$R_W^2 = R_E^2$	$R_W^2 = R_V^2$
							F-Statistic	
Subject	$\hat{w}_{1s}^2$	$\hat{w}_{2s}^2$	$\hat{x}_{s1}$	$\hat{x}_{s2}$	R_W^2	$F_{(4,4)}$	$F_{(1,4)}$	$F_{(2,4)}$
A	.03	.13	17.17	4.62	.99	139.77[a]	0.00	0.00
B	.20	.30	1.17	1.11	.19	.24	0.00	0.40

[a] $p < .01$.

significantly more variance in their judgments than did the simple Euclidean or vector models. Because the null hypothesis $R_W^2 = R_V^2$ cannot be rejected, there is little reason to suspect serious nonlinearities in the function relating the couples preferences to the stimulus dimensions. The F-statistic in column 7 indicates that the constraint of equal weights in the simple Euclidean model did not seriously decrease the fit of the model to the data for couple A.

The weighted Euclidean model could account for only 19% of the variance in the judgments of couple B. Again, their ideal point estimates suggest that they would choose a family of one boy and one girl.

The General Euclidean Model

The most general distance model in Carroll's (1972) hierarchy is an extension to preference data of Tucker's (1972) three-mode model for dissimilarity data. The model will be presented in a form that is different from Carroll's (1972). This model assumes that there exists a $K \times K$ transformation matrix $\mathbf{T}_s$ and a diagonal weight matrix $\mathbf{W}_s$ for each subject. Applying these matrices to the coordinate matrix $\mathbf{X}$ will yield a new coordinate matrix $\mathbf{X}_s$ idiosyncratic to subject s:

$$\mathbf{X}_s = \mathbf{X}\mathbf{W}_s\mathbf{T}_s. \tag{7.7}$$

According to this model, preferences have the following form except for error:

$$\delta_{is} = \sum_k (x_{iks} - x_{sks})^2 + c_s^*. \tag{7.8}$$

In Eq. (7.8), x_{iks} is the coordinate of stimulus i along the kth dimension in $\mathbf{X}_s$. Similarly, x_{sks} is the ideal point of subject s along this same dimension.

Equation (7.8) expresses the general Euclidean model in terms of stimulus and ideal point coordinate estimates idiosyncratic to subject s. One can show that Eq. (7.8) can be re-expressed in terms of the original stimulus coordinates $\mathbf{X}$ as follows:

$$\delta_{is} = \sum_k w_{ks}^2 (x_{ik} - x_{sk})^2 + \sum_{(k,\,k')} w_{ks} w_{k's} r_{kk's} (x_{ik} - x_{sk})(x_{ik'} - x_{sk'}) + c_s^*.$$

(7.9)

Except for the next to last term on the right in Eq. (7.9), the term that expresses the interaction between dimensions k and k', Eq. (7.9) is the same as the weighted Euclidean model in Eq. (7.6). Were it not for the exponent $\frac{1}{2}$ on the right side of Eq. (6.22), the general Euclidean model for preferences, Eq. (7.9), would exactly parallel the three-mode model for dissimilarity data, Eq. (6.22). The uniqueness of both models stems from the fact that they posit interactions between stimulus dimensions. The sign and absolute value of $r_{kk's}$ in Eq. (7.9) characterizes the direction and magnitude, respectively, of the interaction between dimensions k and k' in the judgments of subject s.

The general Euclidean model includes the prior three models, vector, simple Euclidean, and weighted Euclidean, as special cases. If $r_{kk's} = 0$ for all pairs of dimensions (k, k'), then the next to last term on the right of Eq. (7.9) drops out, and it becomes identical to the expression for the weighted Euclidean model in Eq. (7.6). If, in addition, the subject weights are identical across all K dimensions (i.e., $w_{ks}^2 = w_s^2$ for all dimensions), then the general Euclidean model reduces to the simple Euclidean model in Eq. (7.5). Proof that the general Euclidean model includes the vector model as a special case will have to wait until a later section.

Fitting the general Euclidean model yields subject weight estimates $\hat{w}_{ks}^2$, ideal point coordinate estimates $\hat{x}_{sk}$, subject interaction parameter estimates $\hat{r}_{kk's}$, and a multiple correlation coefficient R_G, which serves as a measure of fit. The fit measure R_G for the general Euclidean model carries the subscript G to distinguish it from the fit measure for other models. One can construct an F-statistic with $\frac{1}{2}K(K + 3)$ and $I - \frac{1}{2}K(K + 3) - 1$ degrees of freedom for testing the null hypothesis $R_G^2 = 0$ against the alternative $R_G^2 > 0$.

One can also construct three other F-statistics that are used to compare the general Euclidean model to the remaining three models. If the general Euclidean model fits the data, there exists an F-statistic with $\frac{1}{2}K(K - 1)$ and $I - \frac{1}{2}K(K + 3) - 1$ degrees of freedom for testing the null hypothesis $R_G^2 = R_W^2$ against the alternative $R_G^2 > R_W^2$. Rejection of the null hypothesis suggests that the interaction term $r_{kk's}$ is not equal to zero for one or more of the dimension pairs.

The second F-statistic, used to test the null hypothesis $R_G^2 = R_E^2$ against the alternative $R_G^2 > R_E^2$, when the general Euclidean model fits the data has $\frac{1}{2}K(K + 1) - 1$ and $I - \frac{1}{2}K(K + 3) - 1$ degrees of freedom. Rejection of the null indicates that the general Euclidean model accounts for significantly more variance in the judgments of subject s than does the simple Euclidean model, either because it contains interaction terms or because it does not presume equal weights for all dimensions.

The third statistic, with $\frac{1}{2}K(K + 1)$ and $I - \frac{1}{2}K(K + 3) - 1$ degrees of freedom, can be used to test the null hypothesis $R^2_G = R^2_V$ against the alternative $R^2_G > R^2_V$ when the general Euclidean model fits the data. Rejection of the null indicates that the general Euclidean model accounts for significantly more variance than the vector model either because of interactions between dimensions or because of nonlinearities in the judgments of subject s.

Table 7.7 shows the various statistics obtained by fitting the general Euclidean model to the data in Table 7.3. The general Euclidean model fit the data of couple A quite well ($R^2_G = .99$, $p < .01$). Columns 9–11, however, show that it did not fit this couple's data significantly better than did the previous three models. Like the other models, the general Euclidean model failed to account for a significant proportion of variance in the judgments of couple B ($R^2_G = .59$, $p > .10$). Again the ideal point estimates for this couple suggest they would most prefer a family containing one boy and one girl.

Table 7.7. The General Euclidean Model Fitted to the Data in Table 7.3.

Subject	Interaction Parameters $\hat{r}_{12s}$	Weight Estimates $\hat{w}^2_{1s}$	$\hat{w}^2_{2s}$	Ideal Point Estimates $\hat{x}_{s1}$	$\hat{x}_{s2}$	Squared Multiple Correlation R^2_G
A	0.60	.03	.13	16.69	0.09	.99
B	0.82	.20	.30	1.17	1.00	.59

	Null Hypothesis			
	$R^2_G = 0$	$R^2_G = R^2_W$	$R^2_G = R^2_E$	$R^2_G = R^2_V$
		F-Statistics		
Subject	$F_{(5,3)}$	$F_{(1,3)}$	$F_{(2,3)}$	$F_{(3,3)}$
A	118.24[a]	1.22	0.88	1.09
B	0.86	2.88	1.46	1.35

[a] $p < .01$.

Interpreting Parameter Estimates

For the parameter estimate $\hat{x}_{sk}$ to be interpreted as an ideal point, the corresponding weight estimate $\hat{w}_{ks}^2$ must be positive. Nothing in Carroll's algorithm constrains the weight estimate to be so, and sometimes it does become negative. When $\hat{w}_{ks}^2 < 0$, Carroll suggests interpreting the subject coordinate estimate $\hat{x}_{sk}$ as an "anti-ideal" point. The less a stimulus resembles the "anti-ideal" the more it is liked. Some authors (Davison, 1976; Srinivasan and Shocker, 1973) have questioned whether the "anti-ideal" model corresponds to a plausible psychological process for making preference judgments about most stimuli. When the "anti-ideal" point interpretation seems implausible, then one should view skeptically the statistics obtained by fitting the Euclidean model that resulted in the negative estimate.

Basing conclusions about a subject on subject parameter estimates from a model that does not fit his or her data seems a highly questionable practice. Since none of the above models capture the judgment strategy of couple B, one may want to avoid drawing conclusions about this couple from the parameter estimates obtained by fitting the models to their data.

As seen in the example above, the number of parameters to be estimated increases with each succeeding model, and the parameter estimates become less and less stable as the number estimated grows. Unless the more general model better fits the subject's data, there seems little reason to draw conclusions about that subject from the less stable parameter estimates of the more general model, rather than on the basis of more stable estimates from a less general model that fits the data about equally well. For instance, no model above the vector model accounted for significantly more variance in the judgments of couple A. Hence, one may wish to use the vector model parameter estimates in drawing conclusions about this couple.

Another point to remember in interpreting distance model parameter estimates is the following. If a subject's ideal point estimate falls outside the range of stimuli along dimension k, then the subject's preferences are a monotone function, rather than a single-peaked nonmonotone function, of stimulus dimension k. Assuming that the weight estimate is positive, $\hat{w}_{ks}^2 > 0$, then a value of $\hat{x}_{sk}$ that falls below the stimulus range suggests a monotone increasing function. On the other hand, a value of $\hat{x}_{sk}$ that falls above the stimulus range suggests a monotone decreasing function. For instance, in Table 7.6, the ideal point coordinate estimates for couple A, $\hat{x}_{A1} = 17.17$ and $\hat{x}_{A2} = 4.62$, both fall well above the stimulus range. Stimulus scale values range from 1.00 to 3.00 along both dimensions. Together with the positive dimension weights, $\hat{w}_{1A}^2 = .03$ and $\hat{w}_{2A}^2 = .13$, these ideal point coordinate estimates above the stimulus range suggest that the couple's preferences monotonically decrease as a function of coordinates along both dimensions, at least within the stimulus range included in this study.

All parameter estimates in an external analysis are regression weights or derivatives of regression weights. Cohen (1968) points out that interpreting regression weights is very tricky when the predictors, in this case the stimulus coordinates, are correlated. His comments apply equally well to the parameter estimates in an external analysis.

Even when one of the above models fits the data quite well, it can never be considered anything more than what Hammond et al. (1964) call a paramorphic model for the preference judgments. A good fit means that the judgments predicted by the model closely approximate the actual preference responses. It does not mean, however, that the cognitive process implied by the model—that is, cognitively comparing perceived stimulus attributes to an ideal—approximates the cognitive process through which subjects reach those judgments. The fit statistic indicates how well the model can approximate the outcomes of the subject's judgment process, but not how well the model approximates the actual judgment process.

FITTING EXTERNAL MODELS

Since the vector model, Eq. (7.4),

$$\delta_{is} = \sum_k b_{ks} x_{ik} + c_s \tag{7.10}$$

is linear in terms of the known stimulus coordinates x_{ik}, standard multiple regression techniques can be used to fit the model. The procedure requires one regression for each subject. The I observations on the criterion (or dependent) variable are the I preference judgments of subject s. The I observations on the K predictor variables are the I stimulus scale values on the K stimulus dimensions.

Column 1 of Table 7.8 shows the preference ratings of couple A from Table 7.3. Columns 2 and 3 contain the stimulus scale values from Table 7.3. Taken together, the data in these three columns provide the basis for fitting the vector model to the preference data of couple A. The row labeled "Vector" at the bottom of Table 7.8 shows the regression weights for the two predictors: $\hat{b}_{1A} = -.97$, $\hat{b}_{2A} = -.93$. These are the same estimates shown in Table 7.4.

The F-statistic with K and $I - K - 1$ degrees of freedom for testing the null hypothesis $R_V^2 = 0$ against the alternative $R_V^2 > 0$ is

$$F = \frac{R_V^2}{1 - R_V^2} \cdot \frac{I - K - 1}{K} \tag{7.11}$$

Table 7.8. The Data Used in and the Regression Weights Obtained From External Analyses of Couple A's Preference Data.

Criterion Variable δ_{is}	Predictor Variables					
	x_{i1}	x_{i2}	$(x_{i1}^2 + x_{i2}^2)$	x_{i1}^2	x_{i2}^2	$x_{i1}x_{i2}$
4.1	0.0	0.0	0.0	0.0	0.0	0.0
2.8	0.0	1.0	1.0	0.0	1.0	0.0
2.0	0.0	2.0	4.0	0.0	4.0	0.0
2.8	1.0	0.0	1.0	1.0	0.0	0.0
2.0	1.0	1.0	2.0	1.0	1.0	1.0
1.1	1.0	2.0	5.0	1.0	4.0	2.0
2.0	2.0	0.0	4.0	4.0	0.0	0.0
0.9	2.0	1.0	5.0	4.0	1.0	2.0
0.2	2.0	2.0	8.0	4.0	4.0	4.0

Model	Regression Weight[a]					
	$\hat{b}_{1A}$	$\hat{b}_{2A}$	$\hat{b}_{3A}$	$\hat{b}_{4A}$	$\hat{b}_{5A}$	$\hat{b}_{6A}$
Vector	$-.97$	$-.93$				
Simple Euclidean	-1.13	-1.10	.08			
Weighted Euclidean	-1.03	-1.20		.03	.13	
General Euclidean	-1.11	-1.28		.03	.13	.075

[a]A blank indicates that the predictor does not enter into the model.

For couple A, $R_V^2 = .98945$, $K = 2$, and $I = 9$. Inserting these figures into Eq. (7.11) will yield $F_{(2, 6)} = 281.36$, which is the figure in Table 7.4.

The Simple Euclidean Model

According to the simple Euclidean model, Eq. (7.5), preferences have the following form except for error:

$$\delta_{is} = \sum_k w_s^2 (x_{ik} - x_{sk})^2 + c_s^*. \tag{7.12}$$

Squaring the expression in parentheses and rearranging terms yields

$$\delta_{is} = w_s^2 \sum_k x_{ik}^2 + \sum_k (-2w_s^2 x_{sk} x_{ik}) + \sum_k w_s^2 x_{sk}^2 + c_s^*. \tag{7.13}$$

Setting

$$c_s = \sum_k w_s^2 x_{sk}^2 + c_s^* \tag{7.14}$$

and

$$b_{ks} = -2w_s^2 x_{sk}, \tag{7.15}$$

and substituting these expressions into Eq. (7.13) gives

$$\delta_{is} = w_s^2 \sum_k x_{ik}^2 + \sum_k b_{ks} x_{ik} + c_s. \tag{7.16}$$

Since the simple Euclidean model as expressed in Eq. (7.16) becomes identical to the vector model, Eq. (7.10), when $w_s = 0$, the simple Euclidean model includes the vector model as a special case. Equation (7.16) is a linear function of $K + 1$ variables: the K stimulus coordinate variables x_{ik} plus the $K + 1$st variable $\sum_k x_{ik}^2$. Thus the simple Euclidean model can be fitted to the preferences of subject s in a multiple regression with $K + 1$ predictors. Again, the I preference judgments δ_{is} serve as the I observations on the criterion or dependent variable. The variable $\sum_k x_{ik}^2$ and the K stimulus coordinate variables x_{ik} serve as the independent or predictor variables.

The least squares estimate of w_s^2 is simply the regression weight on the variable $\sum_k x_{ik}^2$. Solving Eq. (7.15) for the ideal point coordinate x_{sk} leads to the conclusion that a reasonable estimate of x_{sk} is the following:

$$\hat{x}_{sk} = \frac{\hat{b}_{ks}}{-2\hat{w}_s^2}. \tag{7.17}$$

Here $\hat{b}_{ks}$ is the regression weight for the predictor x_{ik}.

Columns 1 through 4 of Table 7.8 show the criterion and predictor variables used in fitting the simple Euclidean model to the data of couple A. The row labeled "Simple Euclidean" gives the three regression weights obtained in this analysis. The weight given in column 4 for the predictor variable $\sum_k x_{ik}^2$ equals the estimate of w_s^2, $\hat{w}_s^2 = .08$, shown for couple A in Table 7.5. The ideal point estimates of couple A in Table 7.5 can be derived from the regression weight estimates in Table 7.8 using Eq. (7.17). For instance, the first ideal point coordinate estimate, $\hat{x}_{A1} = 7.06$, in Table 7.5 is $\hat{b}_{1A}/(-2\hat{w}_A^2) = -1.13/[(-2)(.08)] = 7.06$.

The F-statistic with $K + 1$ and $I - K - 2$ degrees of freedom for testing the null hypothesis $R_E^2 = 0$ against the alternative $R_E^2 > 0$ is

$$F = \frac{R_E^2}{1 - R_E^2} \cdot \frac{I - K - 2}{K + 1}. \tag{7.18}$$

For couple A, substituting the value $R_E^2 = .99198$ into Eq. (7.18) yields $F_{(3,5)} = 206.15$, the figure given in Table 7.5.

When the simple Euclidean model fits the data, there exists an F-statistic with 1 and $I - K - 2$ degrees of freedom for testing the null hypothesis $R_E^2 = R_V^2$ against the alternative $R_E^2 > R_V^2$. That statistic takes the form

$$F = \frac{R_E^2 - R_V^2}{1 - R_E^2} \cdot (I - K - 2). \tag{7.19}$$

For couple A, substituting the values $R_E^2 = .99198$, $R_V^2 = .98945$, $I = 9$, and $K = 2$ into this expression gives $F_{(1,5)} = 1.58$, the figure given in Table 7.5.

The Weighted Euclidean Model

According to the weighted Euclidean model, Eq. (7.6), the preferences have the following form except for error:

$$\delta_{is} = \sum_k w_{ks}^2 (x_{ik} - x_{sk})^2 + c_s^*. \tag{7.20}$$

Squaring the expression in parentheses and rearranging terms yields:

$$\delta_{is} = \sum_k w_{ks}^2 x_{ik}^2 + \sum_k \left(-2w_{ks}^2 x_{sk} x_{ik} \right) + \sum_k w_{ks}^2 x_{sk}^2 + c_s^*. \tag{7.21}$$

Setting

$$c_s = \sum_k w_{ks}^2 x_{sk}^2 + c_s^* \tag{7.22}$$

and

$$b_{ks} = -2w_{ks}^2 x_{sk}, \tag{7.23}$$

and substituting these expressions into Eq. (7.21) gives

$$\delta_{is} = \sum_k w_{ks}^2 x_{ik}^2 + \sum_k b_{ks} x_{ik} + c_s. \tag{7.24}$$

If w_{ks}^2 equals a constant w_s^2 for all k, then the weighted Euclidean model, Eq. (7.24), reduces to the simple Euclidean model in Eq. (7.16). Hence, the weighted Euclidean model includes the simple Euclidean model as a special case. Since the simple Euclidean model includes the vector model as a special case, the weighted Euclidean model also subsumes the vector model.

Equation (7.24) is a linear function of $2K$ predictors, the K variables x_{ik}^2 and the K variables x_{ik}. Thus the weighted Euclidean model can be fitted to the preferences of subject s in a multiple regression with $2K$ predictor variables. The I preference judgments δ_{is} serve as the I observations on the dependent variable. The stimulus coordinates x_{ik} and the squared stimulus coordinates x_{ik}^2 serve as the $2K$ independent variables.

The least squares estimates of w_{ks}^2 are simply the K regression weights on the predictor variables x_{ik}^2. Solving Eq. (7.23) for x_{sk} leads to the conclusion that a reasonable estimate of the ideal point coordinate $\hat{x}_{sk}$ can be derived from $\hat{w}_{ks}^2$ and the regression weight estimates $\hat{b}_{ks}$ for the predictors x_{ik} as follows:

$$\hat{x}_{sk} = \frac{\hat{b}_{ks}}{-2\hat{w}_{ks}^2}. \tag{7.25}$$

Columns 1–3 and 5–6 of Table 7.8 show the criterion and predictor variables used in fitting the weighted Euclidean model to couple A's preferences. The row labeled "Weighted Euclidean" gives the regression weights obtained in this analysis. The regression weight estimates given in columns 5 and 6, $\hat{b}_{4A} = .03$ and $\hat{b}_{5A} = .13$, for the predictor variables x_{i1}^2 and x_{i2}^2 equal the weight estimates, $\hat{w}_{1A}^2 = .03$ and $\hat{w}_{2A}^2 = .13$, shown in Table 7.6. The ideal point estimates in Table 7.6 were derived from the regression weight estimates $\hat{b}_{1A} = -1.03$ and $\hat{b}_{2A} = -1.20$ in Table 7.8 using Eq. (7.25). For instance $\hat{x}_{A1} = 17.17$ in Table 7.6 is simply $\hat{b}_{1A}/(-2\hat{w}_{1A}^2)$ which equals $-1.03/[(-2)(.03)] = 17.17$.

The F-statistic with $2K$ and $I - 2K - 1$ degrees of freedom for the null hypothesis $R_W^2 = 0$ is

$$F = \frac{R_W^2}{1 - R_W^2} \cdot \frac{I - 2K - 1}{2K}. \tag{7.26}$$

The F-statistic with $K - 1$ and $I - 2K - 1$ degrees of freedom for the null hypothesis $R_W^2 = R_E^2$ is

$$F = \frac{R_W^2 - R_E^2}{1 - R_W^2} \cdot \frac{I - 2K - 1}{K - 1}. \tag{7.27}$$

Finally, the F-statistic with K and $I - 2K - 1$ degrees of freedom for the null hypothesis $R_W^2 = R_V^2$ is

$$F = \frac{R_W^2 - R_V^2}{1 - R_W^2} \cdot \frac{I - 2K - 1}{K}. \tag{7.28}$$

*The General Euclidean Model

According to the general Euclidean model, Eq. (7.9), preferences have the following form except for error:

$$\delta_{is} = \sum_k w_{ks}^2 (x_{ik} - x_{sk})^2$$

$$+ \sum_{(k, k' \neq k)} w_{ks} w_{k's} r_{kk's} (x_{ik} - x_{sk})(x_{ik'} - x_{sk'}) + c_s^* \quad (7.29)$$

Multiplying the terms in parentheses and rearranging terms gives:

$$\delta_{is} = \sum_k w_{ks}^2 x_{ik}^2 + \sum_k \left(-2 w_{ks}^2 x_{ik} x_{sk} \right) + \sum_k w_{ks}^2 x_{sk}^2$$

$$+ \sum_{(k, k' \neq k)} w_{ks} w_{k's} r_{kk's} x_{ik} x_{ik'}$$

$$+ \sum_{(k, k' \neq k)} \left(-2 w_{ks} w_{k's} r_{kk's} x_{ik} x_{sk'} \right) \quad (7.30)$$

$$+ \sum_{(k, k' \neq k)} w_{ks} w_{k's} r_{kk's} x_{sk} x_{sk'} + c_s^*.$$

Let

$$c_s = \sum_k w_{ks}^2 x_{sk}^2 + \sum_{(k, k' \neq k)} w_{ks} w_{k's} r_{kk's} x_{sk} x_{sk'} + c_s^*, \quad (7.31)$$

$$b_{ks} = -2 w_{ks}^2 x_{sk} - 2 \sum_{(k' \neq k)} w_{ks} w_{k's} r_{kk's} x_{sk'}, \quad (7.32)$$

and

$$b_{kk's} = 2 w_{ks} w_{k's} r_{kk's}. \quad (7.33)$$

In matrix notation, Eq. (7.32) reads as follows:

$$\mathbf{b}_s = -2 \mathbf{R}_s \mathbf{x}_s, \quad (7.34)$$

where $\mathbf{b}_s$ is a $K \times 1$ column vector containing elements b_{ks}, $\mathbf{x}_s$ is a $K \times 1$ column vector containing elements x_{sk}, and $\mathbf{R}_s$ is a symmetric $K \times K$

matrix with w_{ks}^2 as the kth diagonal element and $w_{ks}w_{k's}r_{kk's}$ in row k, column k'.

Substituting Eqs. (7.31) and (7.33) into Eq. (7.30) yields

$$\delta_{is} = \sum_k w_{ks}^2 x_{ik}^2 + \sum_k b_{ks}x_{ik} + \sum_{(k,\,k'<k)} b_{kk's}x_{ik}x_{ik'} + c_s. \qquad (7.35)$$

If $r_{kk's} = 0$ for all dimension pairs $(k, k' \neq k)$, then $b_{kk's} = 0$ for all dimension pairs $(k, k' \neq k)$, and Eq. (7.35) reduces to the weighted Euclidean model, Eq. (7.24). Thus the general Euclidean model, Eq. (7.35), includes the weighted Euclidean model, Eq. (7.24), as a special case. Since the weighted Euclidean model includes the simple Euclidean and vector models as special cases, the general Euclidean model subsumes them all.

Equation (7.35) is a linear equation in $\frac{1}{2}K(K + 3)$ predictors: the K variables x_{ik}^2, plus the K variables x_{ik}, plus the $\frac{1}{2}K(K - 1)$ variables $x_{ik}x_{ik'}(k, k' < k)$. The general Euclidean model can be fitted to the preferences of subject s in a regression analysis with $\frac{1}{2}K(K + 3)$ predictor variables. The I preference judgments δ_{is} serve as the I observations on the dependent variable. The K stimulus coordinates x_{ik}, the K squared stimulus coordinates, x_{ik}^2, and the $\frac{1}{2}K(K - 1)$ cross-product terms $x_{ik}x_{ik'}(k, k' < k)$ serve as the independent variables.

The least squares estimates of w_{ks}^2 are simply the K regression weights on the predictor variables x_{ik}^2. Solving Eq. (7.33) for $r_{kk's}$ leads to the conclusion that a reasonable estimate for the interaction term is

$$\hat{r}_{kk's} = \frac{\hat{b}_{kk's}}{2\hat{w}_{ks}\hat{w}_{k's}}, \qquad (7.36)$$

where $\hat{b}_{kk's}$ is simply the regression weight on the cross-product variable $x_{ik}x_{ik'}$. Similarly, solving Eq. (7.34) for $\mathbf{x}_s$ leads to the conclusion that

$$\hat{\mathbf{x}}_s = -\tfrac{1}{2}\hat{\mathbf{R}}_s^{-1}\hat{\mathbf{b}}_s \qquad (7.37)$$

provides an estimate of the $K \times 1$ column vector of subject ideal point estimates $\hat{x}_{sk}$. $\hat{\mathbf{R}}_s$ contains the estimate $\hat{w}_{ks}^2$ on its kth diagonal element; the off-diagonal element in row k and column k' equals $\frac{1}{2}\hat{b}_{kk's}$ if $k' < k$ or $\frac{1}{2}\hat{b}_{k'ks}$ if $k' > k$.

Columns 1–3 and 5–7 of Table 7.8 show the criterion and predictor variables used in fitting the general Euclidean model to couple A's preference data. The row labeled "General Euclidean" gives the five regression weights obtained in this analysis. The regression weights given in columns 5 and 6 of Table 7.8, .03 and .13, are the subject weight estimates, $\hat{w}_{1A}^2 = .03$ and $\hat{w}_{2A}^2 = .13$, shown for couple A in Table 7.7. The interaction parameter estimate in Table 7.8, $\hat{r}_{kk'A} = .60$, can be obtained by substituting the regression weight estimates in columns 5–7 of Table 7.8 into Eq. (7.36) to yield

$$\hat{r}_{kk's} = \frac{.075}{2[(.03)(.13)]^{1/2}} = .60.$$

As constructed from the regression weights,

$$\hat{\mathbf{R}}_A = \begin{bmatrix} .03 & .04 \\ .04 & .13 \end{bmatrix} \tag{7.38}$$

and

$$\hat{\mathbf{b}}_s = \begin{bmatrix} -1.11 \\ -1.28 \end{bmatrix}. \tag{7.39}$$

Inverting $\hat{\mathbf{R}}_s$ gives

$$\hat{\mathbf{R}}_s^{-1} = \begin{bmatrix} 44.64 & -12.62 \\ -12.62 & 11.11 \end{bmatrix}. \tag{7.40}$$

Substituting the values in Eqs. (7.39) and (7.40) into Eq. (7.37) yields

$$\hat{\mathbf{x}}_s = \begin{bmatrix} 16.69 \\ .09 \end{bmatrix}, \tag{7.41}$$

the ideal point coordinate estimates in Table 7.7.

The F-statistics for testing null hypotheses $R_G^2 = 0$, $R_G^2 = R_W^2$, $R_G^2 = R_E^2$, and $R_G^2 = R_V^2$ are, respectively,

$$F = \frac{R_G^2}{1 - R_G^2} \cdot \frac{I - \frac{1}{2}K(K+3) - 1}{\frac{1}{2}K(K+3)}, \tag{7.42}$$

$$F = \frac{R_G^2 - R_W^2}{1 - R_G^2} \cdot \frac{I - \frac{1}{2}K(K+3) - 1}{\frac{1}{2}K(K-1)}, \tag{7.43}$$

$$F = \frac{R_G^2 - R_E^2}{1 - R_G^2} \cdot \frac{I - \frac{1}{2}K(K+3) - 1}{\frac{1}{2}K(K+1) - 1}, \tag{7.44}$$

and

$$F = \frac{R_G^2 - R_V^2}{1 - R_V^2} \cdot \frac{I - \frac{1}{2}K(K + 3) - 1}{\frac{1}{2}K(K + 1)}. \tag{7.45}$$

The F-statistics in Eq. (7.42) through (7.45) have $\frac{1}{2}K(K + 3)$ and $I - \frac{1}{2}K(K + 3) - 1$, $\frac{1}{2}K(K - 1)$ and $I - \frac{1}{2}K(K + 3) - 1$, $\frac{1}{2}K(K + 1) - 1$ and $I - \frac{1}{2}K(K + 3) - 1$, and $\frac{1}{2}K(K + 1)$ and $I - \frac{1}{2}K(K + 3) - 1$ degrees of freedom, respectively.

EXAMPLE

Jones and Young (1972), the study summarized in Chapter 6, conclude that people who are near each other in their three-dimensional representation of perceived social group structure are more likely to interact. Their results suggest a Euclidean distance model for sociometric preference data. Davison and Jones (1976) designed a study to investigate this possibility.

Besides the earlier Jones and Young (1972) data, Davison and Jones (1976) had theoretical reasons for investigating a Euclidean model for sociometric preferences. In its simplest form, the similarity-attraction hypothesis (Byrne, 1971) states that people are more strongly attracted to people like themselves along salient interpersonal dimensions. If one thinks of x_{sk} the ideal point coordinate of subject s along dimension k as being the subject's perception of her or himself on dimension k, then the similarity-attraction hypothesis can be interpreted as a distance model in which the ideal point of subject s corresponds to the self-perceived attributes of subject s. The more another individual resembles this ideal, the attributes subject s perceives himself or herself to possess, the more subject s will like the individual. The similarity-attraction hypothesis led Davison and Jones (1976) to predict (1) that a Euclidean distance model would better account for sociometric ratings than would the vector model, and (2) that those people with high self-ratings along a dimension of interpersonal perception would also have high ideal point estimates along that same dimension.

To test their predictions, Davison and Jones (1976) studied an Air Force Reserve Officer Training Corps (ROTC) at a large midwestern university. The unit had two formal characteristics of interest for our purposes: each student cadet was assigned a cadet rank, so a formal hierarchy existed among the group members, and there were two auxiliary units, a paramilitary group and a social fraternity, which members could join on a voluntary basis.

EXAMPLE   **179**

The stimulus persons included 19 members of the unit, 3 regular military officers and 16 student cadets. The judges consisted of 45 group members, including the 19 stimulus persons. The judges first rated the similarity of all possible stimulus pairs. Then they rated each stimulus person on nine unidimensional attributes, including "status" and "enthusiasm for giving orders." Finally, the judges made sociometric ratings for each stimulus person: the judges rated the likelihood that they would choose each stimulus person as (1) a fellow member of an ROTC project team, (2) a summer camp roommate, (3) a beer-drinking companion, (4) a fellow officer, and (5) a party guest.

An INDSCAL (Carroll and Chang, 1970) analysis of the similarity judgments yielded a three-dimensional solution. The correlations between the coordinates along the dimensions were low: $r_{I\ II} = .13$, $r_{I\ III} = -.02$, and $r_{II\ III} = .06$. Davison and Jones (1976) interpreted dimension I as a status dimension. Members of the paramilitary unit and social fraternity appeared at opposite ends of dimension II, a finding that may reflect a competition between these groups for members and for the leadership positions in the corps. Dimension III seemed to reflect each stimulus person's perceived enthusiasm for giving orders.

Fitting Preference Models

The vector, simple Euclidean, and weighted Euclidean models were fitted to the composite sociometric ratings of each subject. Table 7.9 summarizes the statistics used to compare the three preference models. Across the 45 subjects, the multiple correlations assessing the amount of variance in each subject's judgments predictable from the various models ranged from .31 to .92, from .34 to .92, and from .42 to .92 for the linear, simple Euclidean, and weighted Euclidean models, respectively. Across the 45 judges, the root mean square multiple correlations were .68, .70, and .76, indicating that the three models accounted for 47, 49, and 54% of the variance in attraction judgments, on the average.

In testing the null hypothesis $R_V^2 = 0$ for each of the 45 subjects, $29[F_{(3, 15)}]$ of the 45 multiple correlations were significant at the .05 level, and 15 were significant at the .01 level. When the null hypothesis $R_E^2 = 0$ was tested for each subject, the $F_{(4, 14)}$ statistic reached the .05 level of significance for 26 subjects, and it reached the .01 level for 13 of the 45 subjects. Finally, the multiple correlation R_W^2 reached the .05 level of significance for 19 subjects $[F_{(6, 12)}]$, and it reached the .01 level for 12 subjects.

Table 7.9 shows that the weighted Euclidean model accounted for more variance, on the average, but the linear model more frequently attained

Table 7.9. Summary of Statistics Comparing Vector, Simple Euclidean, and Weighted Euclidean Models.

	Type of Model		
Statistic	Vector	Simple Euclidean	Weighted Euclidean
Combined judgments			
Root mean square R	.68	.70	.76
Subjects for whom $p < .05$	29	26	19
Subjects for whom $p < .01$	15	13	12
Predicting judgment set 1 from set 2			
Root mean square R	.65	.67	.71
Subjects for whom model was best	5	5	35
Predicting judgment set 2 from set 1			
Root mean square R	.64	.66	.71
Subjects for whom model was best	5	7	33

Source: Davison and Jones (1976). Copyright 1976 by the American Psychological Association. Reprinted by permission of the publisher and author.

conventional significance levels. Both results can be attributed to the fact that fitting the weighted Euclidean model required estimation of the largest number of parameters; fitting the linear model involved estimating the smallest number.

To provide a test of the models based on cross-validation, the five sociometric scales were divided into sets: the first set included the team member, roommate, and drinking companion scales; the second included the fellow officer and party guest scales. The scales in the first set were averaged together to obtain one measure of attraction, and the scales in the second set were averaged together for another measure. The models were then compared by using parameter estimates derived from the first attraction measure to predict the second and vice versa. The results of this analysis are reported in Table 7.9.

The root mean square cross-validated multiple correlations for the weighted Euclidean models were .71 and .71, for the simple Euclidean models .67 and .66, and for the vector models .65 and .64. On cross-validation, the weighted Euclidean model outperformed both the simple Euclidean and vector models, accounting for 5–10% more variance. For 35 of the 45 subjects, the weighted Euclidean model outpredicted both of the other two

EXAMPLE   181

when parameters estimated from the second measure were used to predict the first. When parameters estimated from the first measure were used to predict the second, the weighted Euclidean model outpredicted the other two for 33 of 45 subjects.

Ideal Point Analysis

Since some persons were estimated to have ideal points along each dimension (their subject weights were positive) and others estimated to have anti-ideals (their subject weights were negative), some basis for comparing ideals and anti-ideals had to be derived. There is a similarity between the attraction judgments of subjects having an ideal point above the mean and those having an anti-ideal point below the mean of the stimulus person distribution; both should consistently prefer friends at the high end of the dimension over those at the low end. Conversely, a person with an ideal below the mean should behave in a manner similar in some respects to that of a person having an anti-ideal above the mean; both should generally be more attracted to stimulus persons below the mean. In other words, an ideal point coordinate reflects the strength and direction of a subject's preferences, and an anti-ideal would do the same if changed in sign. Therefore, a transformed ideal point estimate was constructed for each subject; if their subject weight was positive, the transformed ideal point estimate was set equal to the ideal point coordinate, whereas if their subject weight was negative, this transformed estimate was equal to the anti-ideal multiplied by -1.

Referring back to the ROTC data, all but one of the transformed ideals for dimension I was positive, indicating that regardless of the subject's own status, the vast majority were more attracted to high-status others. (The mean stimulus person scale value along each dimension was 0.00). As might be expected, subjects did not unanimously prefer friends at one or the other pole of the remaining two dimensions. Along dimension II, for instance, the transformed ideal was positive for 28 subjects, indicating a preference for friends in the social fraternity, whereas for the remaining 17 it was negative, indicating a preference for friends in the paramilitary unit. Along dimension III, 32 subjects preferred friends below the midpoint on the enthusiasm for giving orders dimension, whereas 13 preferred friends above the midpoint.

Next, subjects were classified along each dimension as highs or lows on the basis of their transformed ideals. A subject was classified as a high if his transformed ideal coordinate fell above the median transformed ideal along that dimension. Lows were people with transformed ideals below the median. The self-ratings of highs and lows were then compared. Those with high transformed ideal points along dimension I, the status dimension, rated themselves as higher in status than did those with a low transformed ideal point along this dimension ($p < .01$). Along dimension II, those with high and low transformed ideal point estimates differed significantly in their subgroup affiliations ($p < .001$). And along dimension III, highs and lows differed in their enthusiasm for giving orders ($p < .10$). All of these differences were in the direction predicted by a similarity-attraction hypothesis. The authors conclude that their comparison of preference models and their ideal point analysis generally support a similarity-attraction hypothesis.

BEYOND PREFERENCE DATA

The ideal point model is plausible for more than just preference data. Building on an earlier suggestion by Wohlwill (1973), Davison (1977; Davison et al., 1978; Davison et al., 1980) propose a unidimensional distance model for developmental replacement sequences, such as Kohlberg's (1976) or Rest's (1979) moral development sequence and Loevinger's (1966) ego development sequence. Davison et al. (1978, 1980) define a replacement sequence as one in which the responses of higher stages gradually replace those of lower stages as development proceeds. In their model, each person's ideal point corresponds to his or her developmental level x_s. Each stage has a scale value x_i. The more closely the developmental level of subject s corresponds to the location of stage i along the developmental continuum [i.e., the smaller the squared distance $d_{is}^2 = (x_i - x_s)^2$], the greater the likelihood that subject s will choose (prefer) a response associated with stage i.

In effect, this stage sequence model asserts that scores on stage-related variables are related to the subject's developmental level by a single-peaked nonmonotone function of the sort shown in Figure 7.4. Higher stage variables peak at higher points along the continumm. Loevinger (1966) suggests just such a form for the major indicators of ego development, which she calls milestone variables. She describes milestones as:

> observable behaviors that tend to rise and then fall off in prominence as one ascends the scale of ego maturity. For example, conformity to generally accepted social standards becomes increasingly characteristic of behavior up to a point, but beyond that point with increasing maturity becomes progressively less compelling, though not necessarily turning into nonconformity (p. 202).

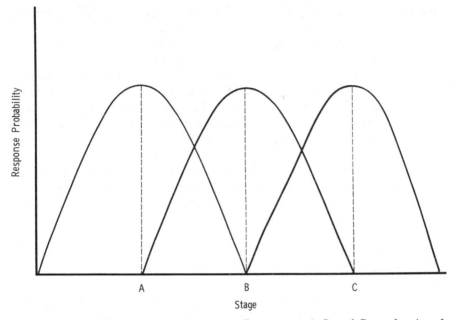

Figure 7.4. Probability of a response corresponding to stages A, B, and C as a function of developmental level.

This passage describes single-peaked nonmonotone response functions like those in Figure 7.4.

The distance model also offers a plausible, if totally untested, model for natural language category behavior (Mervis and Rosch, 1981). In this application, ideal points correspond to categories. The ideal point coordinate x_{sk} designates the level along the kth dimension associated with the prototype for category s. Likewise, each stimulus has a scale value along dimension k. According to a distance model for natural language category behavior, the likelihood that a subject will include stimulus i in category s would be a function of the distance between the stimulus and the prototype for category s in the K-dimensional space. That is, the more stimulus i resembled the prototype for category s, the greater the probability that it would be assigned to that category.

Various theories of vocational counseling (Campbell, 1977; Dawis et al., 1968; Holland, 1973) talk about matching people to careers. Such theories can be interpreted as implying a distance model. In these theories, client s has scores on interest dimensions x_{sk}. One can think of occupations as corresponding to prototypical interest patterns. Let x_{ik} be the interest score along dimension k for the prototypical interest pattern of occupation i. The less the distance between the interest pattern of client s and the prototypical pattern for occupation i, the better the client's interests match those of occupation i. Such theories suggest that people are drawn toward and more satisfied with careers that match their own interests.

Cliff et al. (1973) propose a distance model for self-report personality questionnaire responses. In this model, a subject's ideal point coordinate x_{sk} corresponds to his or her self-perceived location along personality dimension k. Associated with each personality descriptor is a set of coordinates x_{ik} that locate the personality characterization in descriptor i along the K dimensions. The more the subject's self-perception resembles the characterization in the descriptor—that is, the smaller the distance between the person and the descriptor in the K-dimensional space—the more the subject will say the descriptor is true of him or her. Exactly the same model can be proposed for attitude questionnaire responses.

SUMMARY

MDS analyses for preference data include internal analyses and external analyses. The input for a nonmetric internal analysis consists of a stimuli-by-subjects matrix of preferences. Each column contains an ordering of the stimuli by preference for one subject. Preferences are presumed monotonically related to distances between stimulus coordinates and subject ideal points. Analysis of the data proceeds much as in a nonmetric MDS of dissimilarity data except that a column conditional analysis is usually employed. Using STRESS or S-STRESS formula two, instead of formula one, makes the analysis less prone to local minima and degeneracies. Both local minima and degeneracies occur more frequently in an analysis of preference data than in an analysis of dissimilarity data. Further, the coordinates are often estimated with less precision in a preference analysis.

The solution includes estimates of both stimulus coordinates and subject ideal point coordinates along K dimensions. One decides upon the rotation and dimensionality in much the same way whether the data are dissimilarity or preference data. If possible, the researcher may interpret both the stimulus and ideal point coordinates. Substantively important subject groupings and orderings form the basis for interpreting the ideal point coordinates.

In an external analysis, the stimulus coordinates are presumed known. Output includes estimates of the subject parameters in the preference model. Substantively important orderings or groupings of subjects form the basis for interpreting ideal point coordinates, just as in an internal analysis.

Carroll (1972) outlines a hierarchy of four preference models; the vector, simple Euclidean, weighted Euclidean, and general Euclidean models. Each succeeding model includes all prior ones as special cases. If the models are fitted through multiple regression, then the squared multiple correlations equal the proportion of variance in the data of subject s accounted for by the several models and the stimulus coordinates. One can construct F-statistics for testing hypotheses about the fit of each model individually and for comparing the fit of model pairs.

Davison and Jones (1976) use an external analysis to investigate the similarity-attraction hypothesis for sociometric choice behavior. The ideal point concept is one plausible way to model such things as developmental replacement sequences, natural language category behavior, vocational choices, and personality self-descriptions. Readers who desire more on MDS analyses of preference data can consult Bechtel (1976) or Heiser (1981).

PROBLEMS

1. Perform a nonmetric internal analysis in one through five dimensions on the preference data in Table 7.10.
   a. Make a fit-measure-by-dimensions plot. How many dimensions should be retained? Why?
   b. Plot the two-dimensional solution for the stimulus points only. How would you interpret this configuration?
   c. By comparing the stimulus coordinates to the ideal point coordinates for each subject, decide what the favorite color of each subject is.

Table 7.10.   **Rank-Order Color Preferences of Six Subjects.**[a]

	Subject					
	A	B	C	D	E	F
Orange	1	2	3	4	3	2
Red	2	1	2	3	4	3
Violet	3	2	1	2	3	4
Blue	4	3	2	1	2	3
Green	3	4	3	2	1	2
Yellow	2	3	4	3	2	1

[a] 1 = most preferred; 4 = least preferred.

Table 7.11. Family Composition Preference Ratings of a Couple.

	Family Composition								
Number of									
Girls	0	0	0	1	1	1	2	2	2
Boys	0	1	2	0	1	2	0	1	2
Preference	1.2	1.0	1.2	0.5	0.00	0.5	1.2	1.0	1.2

2. Fit the vector, simple unfolding, and weighted unfolding models of Eqs. (7.4)–(7.6) to the following couple's family composition preference ratings. Use the stimulus coordinates in Table 7.11. Assume that higher numbers indicate a greater dislike for the family composition.

   a. What proportion of variance do the models account for?

   b. Using a .05 level of significance, would one reject the null hypothesis $R_V^2 = 0$? $R_E^2 = 0$? $R_W^2 = 0$?

   c. Using a .05 level of significance, would one reject the null hypothesis $R_E^2 = R_V^2$? $R_W^2 = R_E^2$? $R_W^2 = R_V^2$?

   d. Based on the ideal point estimates in the weighted unfolding model, what family composition do you think the couple would ideally choose?

   e. Describe the relative weighting of dimensions in the weighted Euclidean model.

   f. After examining the ideal point coordinate estimates in the weighted unfolding model and the various fit statistics, would it be reasonable to conclude that the couple's preferences are linearly related to the stimulus dimensions? Monotonically related within the range of stimuli included in this study?

Answers

1. a. There is a clear elbow in the plot (Figure 7.5) at $K = 2$ and the two-dimensional solution fits perfectly. Hence, one would retain the two-dimensional solution.

   b. In the two-dimensional plot of Figure 7.6, the colors are arrayed as on the standard color wheel. Complementary colors red and green, violet and yellow, and blue and orange appear opposite each other.

   c. The stimulus coordinates for orange, red, violet, blue, green, and yellow, respectively, are identical to the ideal point coordinates for subjects A–F. Hence, the ideal point coordinates suggest that the

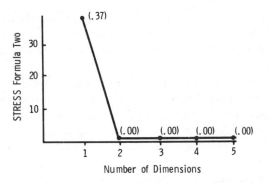

Figure 7.5. Fit-measure-by-dimensions plot for the color preference data in Problem 1.

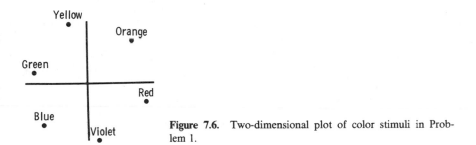

Figure 7.6. Two-dimensional plot of color stimuli in Problem 1.

favorite colors for subjects A–F are orange, red, violet, blue, green, and yellow, respectively.

2. a. The vector, simple Euclidean, and weighted Euclidean models accounted for 0, 81, and 97% of the variance, respectively, in this couple's preference ratings.

   b. One would not reject the null hypothesis $R_V^2 = 0$ [$F_{(2,6)} = 0.00$] at the .05 level, but one would reject the null hypothesis $R_E^2 = 0$ [$F_{(3,5)} = 6.95$], and the null hypothesis $R_W^2 = 0$ [$F_{(4,4)} = 36.50$].

   c. At the .05 level, one would reject the null hypothesis $R_E^2 = R_V^2$ [$F_{(1,5)} = 20.86$], $R_W^2 = R_E^2$ [$F_{(1,4)} = 25.00$], and $R_W^2 = R_V^2$ [$F_{(2,4)} = 72.99$]. The weighted Euclidean model fits significantly better than either of its two special cases, and the simple Euclidean model significantly improves the fit over the vector model.

   d. The ideal point estimates are $\hat{x}_{s1} = \hat{x}_{s2} = 1.00$, suggesting they would choose a family composed of one boy and one girl.

   e. The finding that one would reject the null hypothesis $R_W^2 = R_E^2$ at the .05 or .01 levels of significance leads one to conclude that the weights for the two dimensions are significantly different. Dimension I, the number of girls, received more than twice the weight of dimension II in this couple's weighted Euclidean model; $\hat{w}_{1s} = .80$ and $\hat{w}_{2s} = .30$.

f. At the .05 level, one would reject the null hypothesis $R_E^2 = R_V^2$ and $R_W^2 = R_V^2$. Both findings support the conclusion that the couple's preferences are nonlinearly related to preferences along at least one dimension. Because both ideal points fall in the middle of the stimulus ranges along dimensions I and II, the ideal point estimates suggest that the couple's preferences are nonmonotonically related to both dimensions within the range included in this study.

CHAPTER 8

Examining Prior Hypotheses with Multidimensional Scaling

Very rarely will a researcher conduct a MDS study without some prior hypotheses about the nature of the stimulus configuration. In some cases, the researcher will have a prior hypothesis about the configuration as a whole. That hypothesis may come from a theory or from a previous scaling of the stimuli. For instance, Holland's (1973) theory of careers led Rounds et al. (1979) to postulate the hexagonal configuration in Figure 5.2. If, on the other hand, the hypothesized configuration comes from a prior study, the researcher wishes to see if new data will replicate the earlier findings.

Sometimes, however, the researcher's hypothesis does not constitute a configuration as such. Rather the researcher has some stimulus attributes in mind which he or she suspects will emerge in the stimulus configuration. Again, the hypothesized dimensions may arise from theory or some prior empirical work. The object in this case is to evaluate the hypothesized dimensions individually to assess which, if any, of the hypothesized attributes appear in the MDS solution.

This chapter is divided into two parts: a discussion of the most common methods used to examine hypotheses about separate attributes in the MDS solution, and a discussion of methods for examining hypotheses about the stimulus configuration as a whole.

ATTRIBUTE HYPOTHESES

In the most common method for examining attribute hypotheses, one must have measures of the stimuli on each hypothesized attribute. These measures

189

must be obtained by procedures separate from those used to obtain the proximity data on which the MDS is based. Jones and Young (1972), for example, obtained 10 measures on the stimulus persons in their longitudinal study of perceived group structure described in Chapter 6. Table 8.1 gives the 10 measures they obtained, most of which were subjective ratings. For instance, to get a measure of each stimulus person's political persuasion, they asked subjects to make a 9-point rating of each stimulus person on a "left–right" spectrum. The average rating of a stimulus person on this attribute constituted the measure of their political persuasion. Another of their attributes was academic rank, which was measured objectively. In most MDS studies, the attribute measures contain a mix of both objective and subjective indices.

How one uses the attribute measures to evaluate the hypotheses depends, in part, on whether the solution can be rotated without loss of fit to the data. Since the process is simpler when the solution cannot be rotated, let's begin with that case using the Jones and Young (1972) study as an illustration.

Fixed Rotation

Jones and Young (1972) obtained an INDSCAL solution (Carroll and Chang, 1970). Except in unusual circumstances (see Footnote †, p.131), an

Table 8.1. Correlations of Attribute Measures With INDSCAL Dimensions: 1970 Sample.

		Dimension	
	I	II	III
			Professional
Attribute	Status	Political Persuasion	Interest
Interest in			
Content areas	.50	.05	−.75
Statistical problems	.14	−.25	.78
Computers	.13	−.01	.29
Teaching	.59	.35	−.14
Experimentation	.35	.35	−.83
Perceived status	.96	−.17	−.15
Academic Rank	.95	−.15	−.10
Social–political concern	.14	.83	−.11
Lifestyle	−.10	.86	−.21
Political persuasion	.15	−.93	.23

Source: Jones and Young (1972). Copyright 1972 by the American Psychological Association. Reprinted by permission of the publisher and author.

INDSCAL solution cannot be rotated without loss of fit to the data. If one of the hypothesized attributes corresponds to a dimension, then the measures of that attribute should correlate significantly and highly—generally above .70 in absolute value—with the stimulus coordinates along one of the stimulus dimensions. Ideally, it should be uncorrelated with all but the one dimension.

All but two of Jones and Young's (1972) attribute measures in Table 8.1 (interest in teaching and interest in computers) have correlations above .70 with one dimension. The perceived status and academic rank variables have correlations of .96 and .95 with the stimulus coordinates along dimension I, which the authors interpret as a status dimension. Their interpretation is well supported by the correlations of the stimulus coordinates with the perceived status and academic rank variables.

Dimension II, which they label a political persuasion dimension, has correlations of .83, .86, and −.93 with the subjective ratings of social–political concerns, lifestyle, and political persuasion. The interest in content areas, statistical problems, and experimentation scales all have correlations of .75 or above in absolute value with dimension III. These correlations tend to support their interpretation of this dimension as a professional interest dimension.

The correlations between stimulus attributes and coordinates serve two purposes. They provide a quantitative basis for evaluating the authors' prior hypotheses about the attributes emerging in the solution. All but two of their hypothesized attributes received some support. Furthermore, the correlations aid the interpretation of dimensions. The interpretation of MDS dimensions need not rely solely on the researchers' subjective impression of the configuration.

Indeterminate Rotation

In Torgerson's metric solution, in a nonmetric Euclidean solution, or in a three-mode solution, the configuration can be rotated without loss of fit to the data. To assess an attribute hypothesis in this case, one must determine whether it is possible to rotate the dimensions so that one of the reoriented dimensions corresponds to the hypothesized attribute. It can be shown, although the proof will not be offered here, that the coordinate estimates $\hat{x}_{ik'}$, on a reoriented dimension k' will have the following form:

$$\hat{x}_{ik'} = \sum_k b_{kk'}\hat{x}_{ik} + c_{k'}. \tag{8.1}$$

Here $\hat{x}_{ik}$ refers to the estimated coordinate of stimulus i on unrotated dimension k, $b_{kk'}$ is an unknown multiplicative weight (or multiple regression weight), and $c_{k'}$ is an additive constant.

Using standard multiple regression techniques, one can find the weights $\hat{b}_{kk'}$ and an additive constant $\hat{c}_{k'}$ such that the resulting rotated coordinate estimates $\hat{x}_{ik'}$ are maximally correlated with a given attribute measure. From here on, let $\hat{b}_{kk'}$ refer to a multiplicative constant associated with the unrotated dimension k and the rotated dimension k' that is maximally correlated with attribute measure k'. In the regression analysis, the I observations on attribute measure k', one observation per stimulus, constitute the criterion values. The K predictors are the K unrotated stimulus coordinate dimensions. The resulting regression weights are the empirical estimates of $b_{kk'}$ and $c_{k'}$ in Eq. (8.1). The resulting squared multiple correlation $R_{k'}^2$ gives the proportion of variance in the attribute measure that can be accounted for by the optimally rotated stimulus dimension. A statistically significant and large—generally .75 or above—multiple correlation tends to support the attribute hypothesis.

To illustrate the use of multiple regression in examining attribute hypotheses, consider the data in Table 8.2. Columns 2–4 of Table 8.2 are the unrotated stimulus coordinate dimensions for the countries data in Problem 2 of Chapter 4. The data in that problem are purely hypothetical, but they are based on an actual study of nations by Wish et al. (1970). Columns 5–7 of Table 8.2 give hypothesized attributes. The first attribute is a south–north variable on which countries in the southern hemisphere have a score of .500 and those in the northern hemisphere have a score of $-.500$. The variable in Column 6 is an east–west attribute. Countries in the eastern hemisphere have a score of .375, and those in the western hemisphere have a score of $-.625$. The last column, column 7, contains a Marxist–nonMarxist variable on which Marxist countries have a score of .500 and nonMarxist countries have a score of $-.500$.

Table 8.2. Stimulus Coordinate Dimensions and Attribute Variables for Countries Data.

Country	Coordinates for Dimension			Hypothesized Attributes		
	I	II	III	South–North	East–West	Marxist–nonMarxist
Angola	−.73	.00	−.21	.500	.375	.500
Argentina	.42	.71	−.45	.500	−.625	−.500
Australia	−.28	.71	.26	.500	.375	.500
China	−.28	−.71	.26	−.500	.375	.500
Cuba	.42	−.71	−.45	−.500	−.625	.500
Japan	.24	.00	.77	−.500	.375	.500
United States	.95	.00	.04	−.500	−.625	−.500
Zimbabwe	−.73	.00	−.21	.500	.375	−.500

Table 8.3. Regression of the Attribute Variables onto the Stimulus Dimensions in Table 8.2.

Attribute	Multiple Correlation[a]	Standardized Regression Weights for Dimension			Cosine for Dimension		
		I	II	III	I	II	II
South–north	1.00	−.587	.707	−.391	−.587	.707	−.391
East–west	1.00	−.821	.000	.573	−.821	.000	.573
Marxist–nonMarxist	1.00	−.587	−.707	−.391	−.587	−.707	−.391

[a]$p < .01$

To examine the attribute hypotheses, three multiple regressions were performed, one for each attribute. The three MDS stimulus dimensions, shown in columns 2–4 of Table 8.2, were the predictor variables in all three analyses. Table 8.3 shows the multiple correlations and regression weights obtained in these analyses.

To two decimal places, all three multiple correlations equal 1.00, indicating that the three hypothesized attributes are well represented in the three-dimensional scaling solution. The standardized regression weights in columns 3–5 of Table 8.3 are the empirical estimates of the weights $b_{kk'}$ in Eq. (8.1).

Rotating the Solution

If the unrotated stimulus coordinates are difficult to interpret, then one may use the multiple regression results to obtain a more interpretable rotation if two conditions are met. First, the K hypothesized attributes must have low correlations with each other and second, they must have large multiple correlations with the unrotated stimulus dimensions. To see how the multiple regression results can be used to obtain a more interpretable rotation, let $\hat{b}_{kk'}$ be the standardized regression weight estimate for unrotated dimension k and the hypothesized attribute k'. The following quantity,

$$\hat{t}_{kk'} = \frac{\hat{b}_{kk'}}{R_{k'}}, \tag{8.2}$$

is an estimate of the cosine between unrotated dimension k and the rotated dimension k' that is maximally correlated with attribute measure k'. Let $\hat{T}$ be a $K \times K$ transformation matrix with elements $\hat{t}_{kk'}$ defined as in Eq. (8.2). Let

$$\hat{X}^* = \hat{X}T, \tag{8.3}$$

where $\hat{\mathbf{X}}$ is the unrotated stimulus coordinate matrix. Dimension k' in the rotated stimulus coordinate matrix $\hat{\mathbf{X}}^*$ will correspond to hypothesized attribute k'. The correlation between dimension k' in $\hat{\mathbf{X}}^*$ and hypothesized attribute measure k' will equal $R_{k'}$. Because of their correspondence to and high correlations with the hypothesized attributes, the new dimensions in the rotated stimulus coordinate matrix $\hat{\mathbf{X}}^*$ all have ready interpretations.

One word of caution is in order, however. If the determinant $\hat{\mathbf{T}}'\hat{\mathbf{T}}$, det $\mathbf{T}'\mathbf{T}$, equals zero, then the new matrix $\hat{\mathbf{X}}^*$ does not faithfully reproduce all of the information in $\hat{\mathbf{X}}$. Most textbooks on matrix algebra (Green, 1978; Hohn, 1973) show how to compute the determinant of a matrix. Some (Nie et al., 1975) factor analysis programs contain an option that will print det $\hat{\mathbf{T}}'\hat{\mathbf{T}}$ if $\hat{\mathbf{T}}'\hat{\mathbf{T}}$ is input as if it were a correlation matrix. In any case, before reporting a solution $\hat{\mathbf{X}}^*$, one should always check det $\hat{\mathbf{T}}'\hat{\mathbf{T}}$ to see if it is near zero. If so, the K hypothesized attributes are too highly correlated to serve as a basis for finding a more interpretable rotation.

Table 8.3 shows the quantities $\hat{t}_{kk'}$ computed from the regression weights in that table using Eq. (8.2). Since $R_{k'} = 1.00$ for all k' in this example, $\hat{t}_{kk'} = \hat{b}_{kk'}$ in every instance. When assembled, these cosine estimates form the following matrix $\hat{\mathbf{T}}$:

$$\hat{\mathbf{T}} = \begin{bmatrix} -.587 & -.821 & -.587 \\ .707 & .000 & -.707 \\ -.391 & .573 & -.391 \end{bmatrix} \tag{8.4}$$

Premultiplying $\hat{\mathbf{T}}$ in Eq. (8.4) by the matrix of unrotated stimulus coordinates in Table 8.3 gives:

$$\hat{\mathbf{X}}^* = \hat{\mathbf{X}}\hat{\mathbf{T}} = \begin{bmatrix} -.73 & .00 & -.21 \\ .42 & .71 & -.45 \\ -.28 & .71 & .26 \\ -.28 & -.71 & .26 \\ .42 & -.71 & -.45 \\ .24 & .00 & .77 \\ .95 & .00 & .04 \\ -.73 & .00 & -.21 \end{bmatrix} \begin{bmatrix} -.587 & -.821 & -.587 \\ .707 & .000 & -.707 \\ -.391 & .573 & -.391 \end{bmatrix}$$

$$= \begin{bmatrix} .51 & .48 & .51 \\ .43 & -.60 & -.57 \\ .56 & .38 & -.44 \\ -.44 & .38 & .56 \\ -.57 & -.60 & .43 \\ -.44 & .24 & -.44 \\ -.57 & -.76 & -.57 \\ .51 & .48 & .51 \end{bmatrix} \begin{matrix} \text{Angola} \\ \text{Argentina} \\ \text{Australia} \\ \text{China} \\ \text{Cuba} \\ \text{Japan} \\ \text{United States} \\ \text{Zimbabwe} \end{matrix} \tag{8.5}$$

Along dimension I in rotated stimulus coordinate matrix $\hat{\mathbf{X}}^*$, countries in the southern hemisphere appear at the positive end and countries in the northern hemisphere appear at the negative end. Similarly, countries in the eastern and western hemispheres appear at opposite ends of dimension II. Marxist and nonMarxist countries lie at the positive and negative ends of dimension III. After the rotation, one can readily interpret these as south–north, east–west, and Marxist–nonMarxist dimensions. The determinant of the matrix $\hat{\mathbf{T}}'\hat{\mathbf{T}}$ equals .86 and assures us that the rotated matrix $\hat{\mathbf{X}}^*$ reproduces all of the information in matrix $\hat{\mathbf{X}}$.

CONFIGURATION HYPOTHESES

Schönemann and Carroll (1970) and Gower (1971, 1975) discuss rotations that can serve as the basis for comparing a stimulus configuration to an hypothesized target configuration. Let the $I \times k$ matrix $\hat{\mathbf{X}}$ be the stimulus coordinate matrix, and let the $I \times K$ matrix $\mathbf{Y}$ be the hypothesized configuration. As illustrated in the next section of this chapter, the target matrix may be derived from a theory. Alternatively, it may be a stimulus coordinate matrix obtained in a prior MDS of the stimuli. In comparing the stimulus coordinate matrix $\hat{\mathbf{X}}$ to the target $\mathbf{Y}$, the first step is to standardize the coordinates in $\hat{\mathbf{X}}$ and $\mathbf{Y}$ so that the mean stimulus coordinate along each dimension equals 0; that is, $(1/I)\Sigma_i \hat{x}_{ik} = (1/I)\Sigma_i y_{ik} = 0$ for all k. The discussion that follows presumes that both matrices have been so standardized.

The target matrix $\mathbf{Y}$ and the stimulus coordinate matrix $\hat{\mathbf{X}}$ are presumed to be related by a function of the following form:

$$\mathbf{Y} = c\hat{\mathbf{X}}\mathbf{T}. \tag{8.6}$$

Here c is a multiplicative constant and $\mathbf{T}$ is an orthogonal transformation matrix. The constant c in Eq. (8.6) represents a change of scale or a change in the unit of measurement, such as a shift from feet to inches or a shift from liters to milliliters. In words, Eq. (8.6) states that the stimulus coordinates in $\hat{\mathbf{X}}$ are the same as those in $\mathbf{Y}$ except for a change in the unit of measurement, represented by the multiplicative constant c, and a change of rotation, represented by the transformation matrix $\mathbf{T}$. Schönemann and Carroll (1970) and Gower (1971, 1975) show how to find an estimate of the multiplicative constant $\hat{c}$ and the transformation matrix $\hat{\mathbf{T}}$ which minimizes the following sum of squared errors:

$$\text{SSE} = \sum_{(i,\,k)} (y_{ik} - \hat{y}_{ik})^2. \tag{8.7}$$

In Eq. (8.7), the symbol $\hat{y}_{ik}$ refers to an element of the matrix $\hat{\mathbf{Y}} = \hat{c}\hat{\mathbf{X}}\hat{\mathbf{T}}$. Equations (8.8)–(8.10) and (8.17) below show how to estimate the transformation matrix $\mathbf{T}$ and the multiplicative constant c. For an explanation of the rationale behind these estimates, the interested reader should consult Schönemann and Carroll (1970) or Gower (1971, 1975).

One can estimate c and $\mathbf{T}$ by first forming the following $K \times K$ matrix product:

$$\mathbf{A} = \mathbf{Y}'\hat{\mathbf{X}}\hat{\mathbf{X}}'\mathbf{Y}. \tag{8.8}$$

Using any principal components program (see Chapter 2), one can find a $K \times K$ matrix $\mathbf{B}$ such that

$$\mathbf{A} = \mathbf{B}\mathbf{B}'. \tag{8.9}$$

From the output of such an analysis, one can form a $K \times K$ diagonal matrix $\mathbf{D}$. The kth diagonal element of $\mathbf{D}$, d_{kk}, will equal the kth eigenvalue in the principal components analysis. Using $\mathbf{B}$ and $\mathbf{D}$, one can estimate $\mathbf{T}$ as follows:

$$\hat{\mathbf{T}} = \hat{\mathbf{X}}'\mathbf{Y}\mathbf{B}\mathbf{D}^{(-3/2)}\mathbf{B}'. \tag{8.10}$$

Here $\mathbf{D}^{(-3/2)}$ refers to a diagonal matrix with $1/(d_{kk}^3)^{1/2}$ as the kth diagonal element.

To illustrate this approach, consider the data in Table 8.2. Columns 2–4 are the unrotated stimulus coordinate dimensions $\hat{\mathbf{X}}$ for the countries data in Problem 2 of Chapter 4. The next three columns, 5–7, give an hypothesized configuration, $\mathbf{Y}$. The coordinates along each dimension in $\mathbf{Y}$ have already been standardized so their means equal 0.0. Consequently, the first step can be skipped.

$$\mathbf{A} = \mathbf{Y}'\hat{\mathbf{X}}\hat{\mathbf{X}}'\mathbf{Y} = \begin{bmatrix} 4.150 & 1.835 & .117 \\ 1.835 & 3.936 & 1.835 \\ .117 & 1.835 & 4.150 \end{bmatrix}. \tag{8.11}$$

Factoring $\mathbf{A}$ yields the following matrix $\mathbf{B}$:

$$\mathbf{B} = \begin{bmatrix} 1.335 & 1.420 & .593 \\ 1.771 & .000 & -.894 \\ 1.335 & -1.420 & .593 \end{bmatrix} \tag{8.12}$$

and matrix $\mathbf{D}$:

$$\mathbf{D} = \begin{bmatrix} 6.702 & 0.000 & 0.000 \\ 0.000 & 4.033 & 0.000 \\ 0.000 & 0.000 & 1.501 \end{bmatrix}. \tag{8.13}$$

Computing the matrix product in Eq. (8.10) gives the following estimate of the transformation matrix:

$$\hat{T} = \hat{X}'YBD^{(-3/2)}B' = \begin{bmatrix} -.510 & -.699 & -.510 \\ .706 & .000 & -.706 \\ -.493 & .720 & -.493 \end{bmatrix}. \qquad (8.14)$$

After obtaining the transformation matrix $\hat{T}$, one can then estimate the rotated stimulus coordinate matrix $\hat{X}^*$ with elements $\hat{x}_{ik}^*$:

$$\hat{X}^* = \hat{X}\hat{T}. \qquad (8.15)$$

For the example in Table 8.2,

$$\hat{X}^* = \hat{X}\hat{T} = \begin{bmatrix} .48 & .36 & .48 \\ .51 & -.62 & -.49 \\ .52 & .38 & -.49 \\ -.49 & .38 & .52 \\ -.49 & -.62 & .51 \\ -.50 & .39 & -.50 \\ -.50 & -.64 & -.50 \\ .48 & .36 & .48 \end{bmatrix} \begin{matrix} \text{Angola} \\ \text{Argentina} \\ \text{Australia} \\ \text{China} \\ \text{Cuba} \\ \text{Japan} \\ \text{United States} \\ \text{Zimbabwe} \end{matrix} \qquad (8.16)$$

The multiplicative constant can be estimated according to Eq. (8.17):

$$\hat{c} = \frac{\sum\limits_{(i,k)} \hat{x}_{ik}^* y_{ik}}{\sum\limits_{(i,k)} \hat{x}_{ik}^2}. \qquad (8.17)$$

For the example of Table 8.2, $\hat{c} = 1.00$. Hence $\hat{Y} = \hat{X}^*$ in Eq. (8.17).

The transformation matrix $\hat{T}$ and the multiplicative constant $\hat{c}$ minimize the sum of squared errors shown in Eq. (8.7). They also maximize the following congruence coefficient:

$$r(Y,\hat{X}) = \frac{\sum\limits_{(i,k)} \hat{x}_{ik}^* y_{ik}}{\left[\sum\limits_{(i,k)} \hat{x}_{ik}^{*2}\right]^{1/2}\left[\sum\limits_{(i,k)} y_{ik}^2\right]^{1/2}}. \qquad (8.18)$$

If the mean stimulus coordinate equals 0 for each dimension in $\hat{X}$ and each dimension in Y, then the congruence coefficient is simply the correlation between the elements in the hypothesis matrix y_{ik} and those in the rotated stimulus matrix $\hat{x}_{ik}^*$. It will always range between 0 and 1. The coefficient proposed by Lingoes and Schönemann (1974) in their Eq. 19 equals $1 - r(\mathbf{Y}, \hat{\mathbf{X}})^2$. Inserting the $\hat{x}_{ik}^*$ from Eq. (8.17) and the y_{ik} from Table 8.2 into Eq. (8.19) gives $r(\mathbf{Y}, \hat{\mathbf{X}}) = 1.00$ to two decimal places.

How high should $r(\mathbf{Y}, \hat{\mathbf{X}})$ be before one declares that there is a good correspondence between the hypothesized matrix $\mathbf{Y}$ and the obtained matrix $\hat{\mathbf{X}}$? At the time of this writing, there is no definitive answer to this question. As a rough (very rough) rule of thumb, however, congruence coefficients equal to or greater than .90 generally represent an excellent match between the target matrix $\mathbf{Y}$ and the obtained stimulus configuration $\hat{\mathbf{X}}$. Coefficients of .70 to .90 represent a good to fair match.

If one has two (or more) hypothesis matrices, one can compare the hypothesis matrices on the basis of their congruence statistics $r(\mathbf{Y}, \hat{\mathbf{X}})$ to determine which hypothesis matrix more closely approximates the obtained configuration. Or if one has a single hypothesis matrix $\mathbf{Y}$, but estimates of $\hat{\mathbf{X}}$ for two (or more) subpopulations, one can compare the subpopulations on the basis of their congruence statistics $r(\mathbf{Y}, \hat{\mathbf{X}})$ to determine in which subpopulation the hypothesis better matches the obtained configuration.

If the dimensions in the target matrix $\mathbf{Y}$ have ready interpretations and if the congruence statistic $r(\mathbf{Y}, \hat{\mathbf{X}})$ is high, then the dimensions in the rotated matrix $\hat{\mathbf{X}}^*$ should also be readily interpretable. For instance, in the example of Table 8.2, the unrotated configuration makes very little sense. Each dimension in the rotated configuration $\hat{\mathbf{X}}^*$ can be interpreted in the same fashion as the corresponding dimension in the hypothesis matrix $\mathbf{Y}$. When the rotated matrix $\hat{\mathbf{X}}^*$ is more interpretable than the unrotated matrix, the fitting process outlined in Eqs. (8.6) to (8.17) does more than provide a basis for comparing the hypothesized and obtained configurations. It also aids in locating a meaningful orientation of the stimulus dimensions.

CONFIRMATORY MDS

The preceding section described a method of evaluating an hypothesis about a configuration $\mathbf{Y}$ by assessing its congruence to the obtained configuration $\hat{\mathbf{X}}$. Confirmatory MDS offers a second method of evaluating an hypothesis about the configuration. In confirmatory MDS, the evaluation is based on the degree to which the data can be reproduced by a configuration that conforms to the hypothesis. Hence, the evaluation is based, not on a congruence coefficient, but on some badness-of-fit measure, such as STRESS, or some goodness-of-fit measure, such as the one used by INDSCAL in Eq. (6.15). In short, one method uses a congruence coefficient to assess the match between an obtained and an hypothesized configuration. The other, confirmatory MDS, uses some fit statistic to assess the degree to which the hypothesis matrix reproduces the original data.

Confirmatory MDS has one advantage over the congruence methods described in the previous section of this chapter. Congruence methods require specification of every coordinate in the hypothesis matrix. Confirmatory techniques require that some, but not all, of the coordinates be specified. Hence, if the user's hypothesis specified only a portion of the stimulus coordinates, the confirmatory approach can be employed; the congruence approach cannot.

There are now a number of confirmatory approaches (Bentler and Weeks, 1978; Bloxom, 1978; Borg and Lingoes, 1980; Carroll et al., 1980; Lee and Bentler, 1980; Noma and Johnson, 1979; Ramsey, 1980; Takane, 1981; Zinnes and Griggs, 1974). Most are based on either the nonmetric models described in Chapter 5 or the individual differences models described in Chapter 6. The fit measures described in those earlier chapters are often employed in the confirmatory analyses. In a confirmatory analysis, however, not all stimulus coordinates are estimated by the algorithm. Only those coordinates not specified by the hypothesis must be computed.

To illustrate the general confirmatory approach, again consider the hexagonal hypothesis of Rounds et al. (1979) for the intercorrelations of the six *Vocational Preference Inventory* scales. The intercorrelations are shown in Table 5.1, and the hypothesis itself is graphically depicted in Figure 5.2. Matrix Y of Table 8.4 shows a set of coordinates that, if plotted in two dimensions, would form a hexagon exactly like the one in Figure 5.2, and hence it would represent a suitable hypothesis for use in any confirmatory analysis. The hexagonal configuration formed by the coordinates in Table 8.4 was suggested by Holland's (1973) hexagonal model of career types, and

Table 8.4. Stimulus Coordinate Hypothesis Matrix Y for the Vocational Preference Inventory Data of Table 5.5.

		Dimension	
		I	II
	Realistic	0.00	1.00
	Investigative	0.87	0.50
Y =	Artistic	0.87	−0.50
	Social	0.00	−1.00
	Enterprising	−0.87	−0.50
	Conventional	−0.87	0.50

this hypothesis is an example of one drawn directly from a theory. The coordinates in Table 8.4 were specified in a confirmatory MDS based on a nonmetric Euclidean model (Chapter 5). The STRESS statistic resulting from that analysis was $S_1 = .17$. How is the value of this statistic assessed? In other words, is this a good or a bad fit?

There is no agreed upon way to evaluate a confirmatory fit statistic in the absolute, but one can make relative interpretations about such statistics. For instance, if one has two or more hypotheses that are equally well specified, one can compare the hypotheses on the basis of their respective fit statistics. Here the phrase "equally well specified" means that the number of coordinates that must be estimated is the same for both hypotheses. Or if one has two populations and a sample of similarity data from each, one can compare the fit of a given hypothesis in the two populations.

Ramsey (1978, 1980) has been experimenting with chi square tests of fit that can be used in confirmatory MDS. Ultimately, his significance tests may provide the most useful way to evaluate hypotheses in a confirmatory approach. At present, however, their practical utility in actual applications of MDS remains largely untested. Until the development of some improved method for interpreting such statistics, confirmatory fit statistics are best interpreted in a relative, rather than in an absolute, way.

SUMMARY

Very rarely will a researcher conduct a MDS study without some hypotheses about the configuration or the dimensions that will emerge in the configuration. If one starts with hypotheses about the stimulus attributes, then measures of those attributes can be used to examine the hypotheses. The correlations of the attributes with the dimensions will suffice when the solution cannot be rotated without loss of fit to the data. For an attribute hypothesis to be supported, the corresponding measure should correlate highly—generally above .70—and significantly with one of the dimensions. Ideally, it should be uncorrelated with all but one of the dimensions. A dimension that correlates highly with an hypothesized attribute measure has a ready interpretation corresponding to that attribute.

One can use a multiple regression analysis to examine attribute hypotheses when the solution can be rotated. The attribute measure serves as the criterion variable, and the stimulus dimensions serve as predictors. The squared multiple correlation coefficient equals the proportion of variance in the attribute that can be accounted for by the optimally rotated stimulus dimension. For an attribute hypothesis to be supported, the multiple correlation should be high—generally above .75—and statistically significant. If K attributes can be found that have low correlations with each other and high multiple correlations with the dimensions, the standardized regression weights for the K attribute measures can be used to rotate the dimensions so that each dimension corresponds to one of the attributes.

Schönemann and Carroll (1970) and Gower (1971, 1975) discuss a rotation scheme that can serve as the basis for comparing an obtained stimulus configuration to an hypothesized configuration. It can also serve as a basis for comparing two obtained configurations. The scheme first involves standardizing the dimensions in both the target configuration and the obtained configuration so that the mean stimulus coordinate along each dimension equals zero. Then one must estimate a multiplicative constant and a transformation matrix that minimize the sum of squared discrepancies between corresponding coordinates in the target configuration and the rotated obtained stimulus configuration.

One can assess the congruence between the hypothesized and obtained configurations by computing the correlation between corresponding coordinates in the hypothesized configuration and the rotated obtained configuration. The congruence statistic facilitates comparisons between populations to determine in which of several populations an hypothesized configuration best matches the obtained. It also facilitates comparisons between hypothesized configurations designed to assess which of the hypothesized configurations best matches the obtained one. If the dimensions in the hypothesized target matrix are readily interpretable and if the congruence statistic is high, then the Schönemann–Carroll (1970) transformation matrix can be used to acquire a rotation of the obtained configuration in which each dimension has the same interpretation as a corresponding dimension in the hypothesized configuration.

Congruence coefficients provide one means of examining an hypothesis about a configuration. Confirmatory scaling methods represent another means. In one form of a confirmatory MDS, some or all of the coordinates are specified and the remaining coordinates are estimated. The resulting fit measure indicates the degree to which the data can be reproduced within the limits of the coordinates set by the hypothesis. Although there is no agreed upon method of evaluating confirmatory fit statistics in the absolute, one can use such methods to compare two equally well specified hypotheses or to compare the fit of an hypothesis in two different populations.

PROBLEMS

1. Columns 3 and 4 of Table 8.5 show the stimulus coordinates of the nine family compositions taken from Table 7.2. Column 5 shows the number of children in each composition. Column 6 shows the proportion of

girls. (For the first composition, the proportion of girls has been set to .5.) Use a multiple regression analysis and the data in Table 8.5 to examine the hypothesis that the number of children and the proportion of girls appear as dimensions in the obtained configuration.

a. What are the two multiple correlations? Are they significant at the .01 level?

b. Do the multiple correlations support the number-of-children and proportion-of-girls hypotheses? Why or why not?

c. What are the standardized regression weights obtained in the two analyses?

d. Use the standardized regression weights from Problem 1c and the multiple correlation coefficients from Problem 1a to construct a transformation matrix $\hat{T}$ that will rotate the coordinate matrix so that dimension I is a number-of-children dimension and dimension II is a proportion-of-girls dimension.

e. Apply the tranformation computed in Problem 1d to obtain a rotated coordinate matrix, $\hat{X}^*$.

2. Let columns 3 and 4 of Table 8.5 be the obtained stimulus coordinate matrix $\hat{X}$. Standardize columns 5 and 6 of Table 8.5 so that both columns have a mean of zero, and let the standardized variables serve as the hypothesized configuration Y. Then answer the following questions.

a. Compute $\hat{X}'Y$.

b. Take the result in Problem 2a, $\hat{X}'Y$, and premultiply it by its transpose $Y'\hat{X}$, to obtain $A = Y'\hat{X}\hat{X}'Y$.

Table 8.5. Stimulus Coordinate Dimensions and Attribute Variables for Family Compositions.

Family Composition Number of		Coordinates for Dimension		Number of Children	Proportion of Girls
Girls	Boys	I	II		
0	0	−.873	−.716	0	0.500
0	1	−.726	−.028	1	0.000
0	2	−.531	.966	2	0.000
1	0	−.040	−.774	1	1.000
1	1	−.154	.033	2	0.500
1	2	.079	.853	3	0.333
2	0	.647	−.967	2	1.000
2	1	.592	−.165	3	0.667
2	2	1.025	.443	4	0.500

c. Use a factor analysis program to find a 2×2 matrix $\mathbf{B}$ of unrotated principal components such that $\mathbf{A} \doteq \mathbf{BB}'$. What is $\mathbf{B}$? What is $\mathbf{D}$, the diagonal matrix formed from the eigenvalues?

d. Compute $\mathbf{D}^{(-3/2)}$.

e. Compute $\mathbf{BD}^{(-3/2)}\mathbf{B}'$.

f. Premultiply the result in Problem 2e, $\mathbf{BD}^{(-3/2)}\mathbf{B}'$, by the result in Problem 2a, $\hat{\mathbf{X}}'\mathbf{Y}$, to yield $\hat{\mathbf{T}} = (\hat{\mathbf{X}}'\mathbf{Y})(\mathbf{BD}^{(-3/2)}\mathbf{B}')$.

g. Postmultiply $\hat{\mathbf{X}}$ by $\hat{\mathbf{T}}$ to obtain $\hat{\mathbf{X}}^*$.

h. Compute $r(\mathbf{Y}, \hat{\mathbf{X}})$.

Answers

1. a. For the number-of-children hypothesis, $R = .99$. The corresponding F-statistic for testing the null hypothesis $R = 0$ is $F_{(2,6)} = 209.30$, $p < .01$. For the proportion-of-girls hypothesis, $R = .91$, $F_{(2,6)} = 14.46$, $p < .01$.

b. The multiple correlations tend to support the number-of-children and proportion-of-girls hypotheses. Both multiple correlations are well above .75 and significant at the .01 level.

c. For the number-of-children hypothesis, $b_\mathrm{I} = .82$ and $b_\mathrm{II} = .56$. The corresponding figures for the proportion-of-girls hypothesis are $b_\mathrm{I} = .53$ and $b_\mathrm{II} = -.74$.

d.

		Number of Children	Proportion of Girls
$\hat{\mathbf{T}} =$	I	.83	.57
	II	.58	$-.81$

e.

$$\hat{\mathbf{X}} = $$

	Number of Children	Proportion of Girls
	-1.14	0.08
	-0.62	-0.39
	0.12	-1.09
	-0.48	0.60
	-0.11	-0.11
	0.56	-0.65
	-0.02	1.15
	0.40	0.47
	1.11	0.23

2. a. $\hat{\mathbf{X}}'\mathbf{Y} = \begin{bmatrix} 5.233 & 1.018 \\ 3.808 & -1.510 \end{bmatrix}$

   b. $\mathbf{A} = (\mathbf{Y}'\hat{\mathbf{X}})(\hat{\mathbf{X}}'\mathbf{Y}) = \begin{bmatrix} 41.885 & -.423 \\ -.423 & 3.316 \end{bmatrix}$

   c. $\mathbf{B} = \begin{bmatrix} 6.472 & .020 \\ -.071 & 1.820 \end{bmatrix}$

   $\mathbf{D} = \begin{bmatrix} 41.890 & 0.000 \\ 0.000 & 3.311 \end{bmatrix}$

   d. $\mathbf{D}^{(-3/2)} = \begin{bmatrix} .004 & .000 \\ .000 & .166 \end{bmatrix}$

   e. $\mathbf{B}\mathbf{D}^{(-3/2)}\mathbf{B}' = \begin{bmatrix} .168 & .004 \\ .006 & .550 \end{bmatrix}$

   f. $\hat{\mathbf{T}} = \begin{bmatrix} .885 & .580 \\ .631 & -.815 \end{bmatrix}$

   g. $\hat{\mathbf{X}}^* = \begin{bmatrix} -1.22 & .08 \\ -.66 & -.40 \\ .14 & -1.10 \\ -.52 & .61 \\ -.12 & -.12 \\ .61 & -.65 \\ -.04 & 1.16 \\ .42 & .48 \\ 1.19 & .23 \end{bmatrix}$

   h. $r(\mathbf{Y}, \hat{\mathbf{X}}) = .87$

CHAPTER 9

Multidimensional Scaling and its Alternatives

This chapter discusses the relationship between MDS and other methods employed in the social and behavioral sciences. The first section discusses the use of nonmetric MDS algorithms to estimate scale values in Thurstone's (1927) unidimensional scaling technique, the method of paired comparisons. The second section compares MDS and hierarchical cluster analysis. In the last section, MDS and factor analysis are contrasted.

MDS AND THURSTONE SCALING

Thurstone (1927; Torgerson, 1958) proposes a method of scaling stimuli along a unidimensional continuum. The judgment task employed by his method has become known as the paired comparisons method. Subjects are presented all possible stimulus pairs and they are asked to choose that member of the pair that in their judgment possesses more of the attribute being scaled. Subjects' responses permit derivation of a data matrix such as **P** in Table 9.1. These data come from a study in which subjects were presented pairs of vegetables. For each pair, they chose their preferred vegetable. The element p_{ij} in row i column j gives the proportion of subjects who preferred stimulus j over stimulus i. The unidimensional continuum being scaled in this case is a preference dimension.

Thurstone (1927) assumes that there is a scale value x_i for each stimulus along the dimension being scaled. In the most commonly applied form of his model, Thurstone's case five, he assumes the probability that stimulus j

Matrix P

Vegetable	T	Cab	B	A	Car	Sp	Sb	P	Co
Turnips	—	.818	.770	.811	.878	.892	.899	.892	.926
Cabbage	.182	—	.601	.723	.743	.736	.811	.845	.858
Beets	.230	.399	—	.561	.736	.676	.845	.797	.818
Asparagus	.189	.277	.439	—	.561	.588	.676	.601	.730
Carrots	.122	.257	.264	.439	—	.493	.574	.709	.764
Spinach	.108	.264	.324	.412	.507	—	.628	.682	.628
String Beans	.101	.189	.155	.324	.426	.372	—	.527	.642
Peas	.108	.155	.203	.399	.291	.318	.473	—	.628
Corn	.074	.142	.182	.270	.236	.372	.358	.372	—

Matrix Δ of Dissimilarities

Vegetables	T	Cab	B	A	Car	Sp	Sb	P	Co
Turnips	—								
Cabbage	.318	—							
Beets	.270	.101	—						
Asparagus	.311	.223	.061	—					
Carrots	.378	.243	.236	.061	—				
Spinach	.392	.236	.176	.088	.007	—			
String Beans	.399	.311	.345	.176	.074	.128	—		
Peas	.392	.345	.297	.101	.209	.182	.027	—	
Corn	.426	.358	.318	.230	.264	.128	.142	.128	—

Thurstone Scale Values

−2.029	−.955	−.684	−.016	.265	.320	.846	.936	1.318

Nonmetric MDS Scale Values

−2.210	−.661	−.671	−.028	.320	.288	.814	.881	1.267

would be chosen over stimulus i on a given trial p_{ij}, would be of the form

$$p_{ij} = \frac{1}{(2\pi)^{1/2}} \int_{-\infty}^{(x_j - x_i)} e^{-t^2} dt. \tag{9.1}$$

Equation (9.1) is a cumulative, standard normal density function. It states that p_{ij} equals that proportion of the area under a normal curve that falls below the standard normal deviate $z = (x_j - x_i)$. Thurstone and others (Torgerson, 1958) have proposed various methods for estimating the scale values x_i, x_j from the probability estimates obtained in the paired comparisons task.

MDS provides one way of estimating those scale values. Davison and Wood (1981) show that if the probabilities satisfy Eq. (9.1), then the quantity δ_{ij}

$$\delta_{ij} = |p_{ij} - .50| \tag{9.2}$$

is a monotonically increasing function of the distances between stimuli along the continuum being scaled. That is,

$$\delta_{ij} = f(d_{ij}) = f(|x_i - x_j|) \tag{9.3}$$

where f is a monotonically increasing function. Therefore, one can use empirical estimates of δ_{ij} as a measure of dissimilarity for input into a nonmetric algorithm.

Matrix Δ in Table 9.1 is the dissimilarity matrix derived from the probabilities in **P**. As an example, the element in row 2 column 1 of Δ was computed from the corresponding elements in **P** as follows:

$$\delta_{21} = |p_{21} - .50|$$

$$= |.182 - .500| \tag{9.4}$$

$$= .318.$$

The bottom of Table 9.1 shows the scale values derived from matrix **P** using Thurstone's (1927) estimation scheme. Below the Thurstone scale values, Table 9.1 shows the scale values from a one-dimensional nonmetric MDS analysis based on the dissimilarity matrix. The correlation between these two sets of scale values is .99. If the empirical estimates of the quantities in Eq. (9.2) are used as dissimilarity data, and if the choice probabilities satisfy Eq. (9.1), then nonmetric MDS should provide scale value estimates from paired comparisons data that closely approximate Thurstone's (1927) estimates.

MDS AND HIERARCHICAL CLUSTER ANALYSIS

Hierarchical cluster analysis and MDS are two methods often used to investigate the structure of stimuli. There are at least three parallels between the methods: one can analyze proximity data using either hierarchical cluster analysis or MDS, both methods are built on distance models, and one can represent either a hierarchical cluster or MDS solution in terms of dimension coordinates, although cluster solutions are seldom represented in such terms.

Despite these three parallels, cluster analysis and MDS fundamentally differ. First, the relationship between the proximity data δ_{ij} and the distances d_{ij} in the cluster analysis often cannot be expressed by a linear or even a monotone function as in MDS. Second, cluster distances are not spatial distances as in MDS. The distinction between the tree distances or ultrametric distances of hierarchical cluster analysis and the spatial distances of MDS will be described below. Third, the coordinate dimensions in MDS are continuous variables whereas those in cluster analysis are discrete.

Since hierarchical cluster solutions are not usually represented in terms of stimulus coordinates, the present discussion will begin by describing the more typical representation of cluster solutions in terms of stimulus groupings and tree diagrams. Then the tree diagrams will be related to distances and the stimulus groupings will be related to a stimulus coordinate system. Finally, the distances and stimulus coordinates in hierarchical cluster analysis will be related to the corresponding concepts in MDS. Various authors have described nonhierarchical cluster methods (Sarle, 1981; Sattath and Tversky, 1976; Shepard and Arabie, 1979). Only hierarchical methods will be discussed below, however, because most applications of clustering involve hierarchical rather than nonhierarchical techniques.

A stimulus cluster is any subset of stimuli. The object of hierarchical cluster analysis is to divide the stimuli into subsets, each of which corresponds to a meaningful feature of the stimuli. If the solution is a hierarchical cluster solution, then any two distinct subsets A and B must be related in one of three ways: $A \cap B = A$, $A \cap B = B$, $A \cap B = \varnothing$ ($\varnothing$ refers to the empty set). In other words, the elements in B must include all the elements in A, the elements in A must include all the elements in B, or A and B must share no common elements. The two sets *cannot* be partially overlapping.

Figure 9.1 shows a tree diagram representing the cluster structure of the 16 consonant phonemes in Figure 5.8. The diagram consists of nodes (the circles) and edges (the lines) connecting the nodes. Nodes 1–16, called the terminal nodes, represent trivial clusters containing only one stimulus. Nodes 17–29 represent the nontrivial clusters. The cluster corresponding to any node includes all of the stimuli connected to that node either directly or

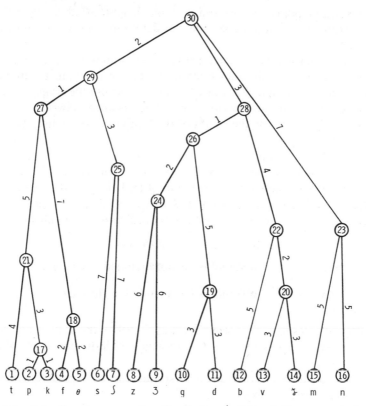

Figure 9.1. Tree diagram representing the cluster structure of 16 consonant phonemes. Adapted from "Psychological Representation of Speech Sounds" by R. N. Shepard. Copyright 1972 by McGraw-Hill. Used with permission of the McGraw-Hill Book Company.

through other nodes. For instance, the cluster corresponding to node 17 includes stimuli /p/ and /k/ because node 17 is connected to the terminal nodes for these two stimuli. Node 29 corresponds to the cluster containing /t/, /p/, /k/, /f/, /θ/, /s/, and /ʃ/ because node 29 is connected through other nodes to the terminal nodes for these seven stimuli.

On each edge, there appears a number stating the vertical height of that edge. The height of any node (other than a terminal node whose height is 0) is the sum of the heights of edges connecting that node to a terminal node. For instance, if one follows the edges leading from terminal node 11 (stimulus /d/) to node 26, the combined heights of these edges is eight, leading to the conclusion that the height of node 26 is eight. One will reach the same conclusion no matter which terminal node (nodes 8–11) is chosen as the starting point for determining the height of node 26. Likewise, starting from any of nodes 1–5, one can determine that the height of node 27 is nine.

In a tree diagram, the distance between two stimuli is represented by the height of the lowest node connecting them. For instance, in Figure 9.1, the distance between stimuli /f/ and /θ/ is two, because the height of the first node connecting them (node 18) is two. The distance between stimuli /z/ and /d/ is eight, because the height of the first node connecting them (node 26) is eight.

There exists a coordinate representation for any structure such as that in Figure 9.1. The coordinate set will contain one dimension for each node except the highest one (node 30 in Figure 9.1). Let x_k be the vertical height of the edge leading upward from node k in the tree diagram representing the cluster structure. Along dimension k, the coordinate for stimulus i is defined as

$$x_{ik} = 0 \qquad \text{if stimulus } i \text{ is not included in cluster } k,$$
$$x_{ik} = \tfrac{1}{2}x_k \quad \text{if stimulus } i \text{ is included in cluster } k. \tag{9.5}$$

When coordinates have the form shown in Eq. (9.5), the scale values for any dimension take on only two values, and hence each dimension is a dichotomous variable.

The tree distance between any two stimuli can be expressed in terms of coordinates defined as in Eq. (9.5):

$$d_{ij} = \sum_k |x_{ik} - x_{jk}|. \tag{9.6}$$

The tree distances in Eq. (9.6) are city-block distances defined over dichotomous coordinate dimensions.

The above example illustrates certain contrasts between MDS and hierarchical cluster conceptions of stimulus structure. First, the coordinates in a cluster representation are coordinates along dichotomous dimensions, whereas MDS yields continuous dimensions. Second, in practice, the number of dichotomous dimensions needed to reproduce a set of data is often quite large. In other words, whereas hierarchical cluster analysis often uses many simple two-valued dimensions to reproduce the structure, MDS uses a few complex multivalued dimensions to accomplish the same goal.

There exists a third difference between MDS and hierarchical cluster distances. In addition to the triangular inequality, hierarchical cluster distances must satisfy the much stronger ultrametric inequality (Hartigan,

1967; Holman, 1972; Jardine et al., 1967; Johnson, 1967):

$$d(a, c) \leqslant \max[d(a, b), d(b, c)]. \tag{9.7}$$

Since hierarchical cluster analysis and MDS employ such different representations of structure, they are often viewed as complementary methods for highlighting different features of the stimuli. Most complex stimuli vary in terms of continuous and dichotomous attributes. People, for instance, vary in terms of continuous attributes such as age and intelligence. They also differ in terms of discrete features such as sex and eye color. When the important stimulus features are all dichotomous or all continuous, then one of the two methods may be clearly superior to the other. Even when the stimulus attributes are all discrete, however, MDS often provides a convenient method for reducing the data to a form in which the cluster structure can be represented pictorially as in Figure 5.8. In most instances, however, the stimulus features are neither all continuous nor all discrete, and hence neither method will be clearly superior. Cluster analysis and MDS then represent alternative methods for representing complementary stimulus features.

Since many complex stimuli vary along discrete and continuous attributes, it seems quite natural to posit hybrid models that assume a combination of discrete and continuous dimensions. Both Degerman (1970) and Carroll (1976) discuss such models, but as yet hybrid models have received little application. One would hope that the future will bring continued experimentation with techniques that combine continuous and discrete dimensions. Readers interested in more information about cluster analysis can consult Anderberg (1973), Hartigan (1975), or Sneath and Sokal (1973). Kruskal (1977) contains a more extensive comparison between MDS and cluster analysis.

MDS AND FACTOR ANALYSIS

MDS is more closely related to factor analysis than to cluster analysis. The basic data in most factor analyses are measures of proximity for object pairs. In practice, the objects are often psychological tests or test items, and the proximity measure is frequently the correlation coefficient. Like MDS, factor analysis yields a quantitative dimensional representation of the structure among the objects.

With these parallels between factor analysis and MDS, it should come as no surprise that MDS and factor analysis are sometimes used to study the same research issues. Both have been used to study the dimensions of

interpersonal perception, the structure of human abilities, and the organization of urban environments. One could cite many more examples.

In his comparison of the two techniques, Shepard (1972a) emphasizes that in nonmetric MDS, a small number of dimensions often suffices to represent the structure. Ten or more factors are extracted in some factor analytic studies. "Such results cannot, of course, be cast into a readily visualizable picture" (Shepard, 1972a, p. 3). At another point, Shepard says that

This matter of dimensionality and hence visualizability tends, in practice, to distinguish these relatively new methods of multidimensional scaling proper from the related methods that have long been used in the social sciences under such names as "factor analysis" and "principal components analysis." (Shepard, 1972a, p. 2)

Schlessinger and Guttman (1969) draw much the same conclusion.

MacCallum (1974a) largely restricted his comparison to MDS group solutions of the type described in Chapters 4 and 5: Torgerson's metric model and the nonmetric models. He emphasized the fact that group MDS solutions yield only a quantitative dimensional description of objects. In addition, factor analysis provides a quantitative dimensional description of people in the form of factor scores. "In general, the model underlying factor analysis is much richer than that underlying multidimensional scaling in that the former is capable of describing individual differences and the latter is not" (MacCallum, 1974a, p. 512). A comparison of factor analysis and individual differences MDS would not have led to the same conclusion.

When factor analysis and MDS are used to study the same issue, there are three reasons why the conclusions may differ, two of which have nothing to do with the method of data analysis. First, the studies may employ different measures of object similarity. Factor analysts have favored the correlation coefficient. In addition to the correlation coefficient, MDS studies have employed profile dissimilarity measures, direct similarity judgments, and joint or conditional probabilities.

Second, factor analytic and MDS studies of the same issue often employ very different experimental procedures. This may be the biggest single source of variation between MDS and factor analytic studies. In the Smith and Siegel (1967) study of job dimensions, for instance, the investigators asked job incumbents to rate the similarity of job task pairs. Most factor analytic studies of job dimensions have employed a very different experimental procedure. Supervisors have rated job incumbents on various job performance scales. The factors needed to reproduce the intercorrelations of the performance scales have served as the representation of job dimensions.

The data analytic methods themselves represent the third source of differences. Both factor analysis and MDS yield a representation of the stimulus structure in terms of spatial coordinates. Those coordinates are called factor loadings in factor analysis, and they are called scale values in MDS. The factor model and the MDS model, however, contain very different assumptions about the relationship between the coordinates and the observed proximity data. In principal components analysis, for instance, the correlations r_{ij} (or some other proximity measures) are presumed related to the coordinates x_{ik} and x_{jk} by a function of the following form:

$$r_{ij} = \sum_k x_{ik} x_{jk}.$$ (9.8)

In metric MDS, on the other hand, the dissimilarities are presumed related to the coordinates by a function of the form shown in Eq. (4.1).

Such differences in assumptions about the data should lead to different results. But what kinds of differences? To this author's knowledge, there exists no analytical study to suggest what kinds of differences one might generally expect to find between a MDS and a factor analysis of the same data. A comparison of two studies into the structure of vocational interests (Hanson et al., 1977; Rounds et al., 1979), one of which employed MDS and one of which employed factor analysis, shows how the two solutions compared in one instance. These studies are the subject of the next section.

MDS and Factor Analytic Studies of Vocational Interest Scales

As discussed in Chapter 5, Holland's (1973) theory of career choice includes six occupational types and six corresponding interest types. Several vocational interest inventories now include separate scales for each type. Prediger (Hanson et al., 1977; Prediger, 1980) factor analyzed the intercorrelations of the six Holland scales from several vocational interest inventories and several samples. Results vary from sample to sample and inventory to inventory, but three factors emerge fairly consistently. Prediger calls the second and third factors theory-based dimensions. In the plane defined by these two factors, the six scales form a roughly hexagonal configuration as predicted by Holland's theory. Hanson et al. (1977) call the first factor a response level factor:

Not shown... is a general factor common to interest inventories using response categories such as "like," "indifferent," and "dislike." When such categories are used, the frequency with which a particular response is chosen tends to vary from person to person, regardless of

Table 9.2. Factor Loadings and Nonmetric Scale Values for the Six Vocational Preference Inventory Scales.

Scale	Factor I	Dimension I	Factor II	Dimension II	Factor III
Realistic	.595	.369	.324	.491	.598
Investigative	.555	.683	.685	.061	.158
Artistic	.568	.133	.335	−.696	−.607
Social	.736	−.236	−.080	−.294	−.371
Enterprising	.803	−.492	−.437	.020	−.055
Conventional	.711	−.456	−.496	.418	.307

item content. That is, some persons tend to choose "indifferent" more often, etc. Hence, there is a general response-related factor affecting the scores on each scale. The chief identifying feature of this factor, to be called the "response level factor," is that all *interest scales have relatively high loadings on it.* (Hanson et al., 1977, p. 20, italics added.)[†]

In the Rounds et al. (1979) study cited earlier, five sets of correlations between Holland scales from different inventories were analyzed. In only one of the five analyses were more than two dimensions needed to reduce STRESS below .05. Even in the one exception, the STRESS for the two-dimensional solution was a relatively low .06. In two dimensions, the scales consistently formed a roughly hexagonal configuration, although the configuration deviated further from a hexagonal shape in the female samples than in the male samples. In other words, the MDS configuration found by Rounds et al. (1979) resembled that found by Hanson et al. (1977) in the plane defined by their two theoretical factors. The MDS analyses of Rounds et al. (1979) turned up nothing resembling the response level factor of Hanson et al. (1977).

To contrast the results of these two studies, consider the data in Table 9.2. To obtain the factor loadings in this table (columns 2, 4, and 6), the intercorrelations of the six *Vocational Preference Inventory* scales (Table 5.1) were submitted to a principal components analysis without rotation.

The scale values in columns 3 and 5 of Table 9.2 were obtained from a two-dimensional nonmetric scaling of these same data. The scale values were rotated to a principal components orientation. Then each scale value was multiplied by −.59. The original solution before multiplication by −.59 is shown in Table 5.2.

[†]Copyright 1969 by the American College Testing Program. Reprinted with permission.

The column labeled "Factor I" in Table 9.2 contains the general factor. This factor displays the distinctive characteristic described in the italicized phrase of the Hanson et al. (1977) quotation above: "All interest scales have relatively high loadings on it" (Hanson et al., 1977, p. 20). This factor has no counterpart in the two scaling dimensions.[‡]

The remaining two factors, however, do have counterparts in the scaling dimensions. Compare the scale values along dimension I to the factor loadings along factor II. For each *Vocational Preference Inventory* scale, the scale value along dimension I is of the same sign and approximately the same magnitude as the loading along factor II. Similarly, the scale values along dimension II closely match the loadings along factor III.

The loadings along factors II and III were assembled into an hypothesis matrix Y. Then the congruence coefficient in Eq. (8.18) was used to assess the congruence between the two-dimensional scaling solution and the hypothesis matrix. The computed coefficient, $r(Y, \hat{X})$ was very high, .97.

Davison (1981) reports a comparison between a three-dimensional principal components solution and a two-dimensional scaling solution. He analyzes the intercorrelations of ability tests, rather than vocational interest scales, but his results are very similar to those in Table 9.2. The principal components solution for his ability data contain a general factor on which all tests had high positive loadings. The general factor has no counterpart in the scaling solution. After multiplying the scale values in his MDS solution by a constant of proportionality, however, it becomes apparent that the second and third principal components each have a counterpart among the scaling dimensions. For each ability test, its scale value along dimension I is of the same sign and approximately the same magnitude as the loading along factor II. Similarly, the scale values along dimension II closely match the loadings along factor III.

Results such as those in Table 9.2 and those of Davison (1981) suggest the following two relationships between a $(K + 1)$-factor principal components analysis and a K-dimensional MDS of the same test intercorrelations. First, the principal components analysis will often contain a general factor on which all tests load highly, and that general factor will have no counterpart in the scaling solution. Second, once the MDS scale values have been multiplied by an appropriate transformation matrix and constant of proportionality, the scale values on one or more of the dimensions will closely resemble the factor loadings on corresponding factors. Results such as those in Table 9.2 are only suggestive. As this book is being written, it is not clear how often the above two relationships hold.

[‡]Copyright 1969 by the American College Testing Program. Reprinted with permission.

MDS and Factor Analysis of Simplex Correlation Matrices

Guttman (1954) describes a distinctive pattern for the intercorrelations between psychological measures. If a correlation matrix fits the pattern, then there exists a unidimensional ordering of the variables. Let h, i, and j refer to three variables that fall in that order ($h < i < j$) in the unidimensional ordering of variables. For the correlation matrix to fit the pattern, called the simplex pattern, the following equality must hold:

$$r_{hj} = r_{hi}r_{ij} \qquad (9.9)$$

for all (h, i, j) such that $h < i < j$ in the ordering. If the rows and columns of the correlation matrix are rearranged so their ordering corresponds to the unidimensional ordering of the variables, then the correlation matrix will look very distinctive; in any row (column) of the matrix, the correlations will consistently descend as one moves to the left or right (up or down) away from the diagonal element. Table 9.3 shows a correlation matrix that closely approximates the simplex pattern. Note, for instance, the elements in row 4, which descend from .37 to .18 as one moves away from the main diagonal to the left and which descend from .69 to .47 as one moves away from the main diagonal to the right. Several different process models have been proposed to account for the simplex pattern (Davison, 1977; Humphreys, 1960; Humphreys and Parsons, 1979; Jöreskog, 1970). Visually, the correlational patterns predicted by these several process models are indistinguishable, but there are subtle differences between them.

Nonmetric MDS provides the most convenient way to determine whether a one-dimensional ordering can account for the correlations, and if so, what that ordering is. No matter which process model best accounts for the correlations, a unidimensional MDS configuration should fit the correlation matrix well. Indeed, if the correlations perfectly satisfy Eq. (9.9), then the correlations can be fitted perfectly by a nonmetric one-dimensional distance

Table 9.3. "Intercorrelations of the Six Subscales for the Defining Issues Test, a Measure of Moral Reasoning Development.

1.00	.59	.59	.18	.15	−.05
.59	1.00	.59	.33	.29	.19
.59	.59	1.00	.37	.36	.32
.18	.33	.37	1.00	.69	.47
.15	.29	.36	.69	1.00	.54
−.05	.19	.32	.47	.54	1.00

model. The underlying unidimensional ordering of the variables should correspond to their ordering along the one dimension.

Factor analysis does not provide a convenient method for recovering the unidimensional ordering, but it can provide a method for distinguishing between the several process models. Each model leads to the prediction of a different factor structure (Davison, 1977; Jöreskog, 1970). Whereas only one MDS dimension is ever needed to account for the data arising from any one of the several process models, anywhere from 2 to $I - 1$ factors will be needed to account for the intercorrelations of I variables. Unlike nonmetric MDS, factor analytic methods are sensitive to the subtle differences between the process models. This sensitivity is an advantage if one is trying to distinguish between process models, but not if one is trying to recover the ordering of variables.

SUMMARY

Researchers can use MDS to estimate unidimensional scale values from paired comparisons data. If p_{ij} is the proportion of trials in which stimulus j is chosen over stimulus i, then the empirical dissimilarity estimate for stimuli i and j is $|p_{ij} - .50|$. For data that satisfy Thurstone's (1927) case five assumptions reasonably well, applying a nonmetric MDS to these dissimilarity estimates should yield scale values that closely approximate Thurstone's estimates.

Both MDS and hierarchical cluster analysis provide representations of stimulus structure based on proximity data. Cluster solutions represent stimulus structure in terms of qualitative stimulus groupings. MDS uses a quantitative dimensional representation.

Of the various techniques for representing stimulus structure, factor analysis more closely resembles MDS than does any other technique. Both provide quantitative dimensional representations of stimuli. Shepard (1972a) emphasizes that nonmetric MDS often provides a simpler and therefore more easily interpreted solution. MacCallum (1974a) concludes that the factor scores and loadings of factor analysis provide a richer solution than do the stimulus coordinates of MDS. Individual differences MDS models are no less rich than the factor models.

MDS and factor analytic studies often vary in their experimental procedures and their similarity measures. When MDS and factor analytic studies lead to different conclusions about the same issue, some or all of the conflict may be attributable to variation in experimental procedures rather than to variation in data analytic methods.

A comparison between the principal components analysis of Hanson et al. (1977) and the MDS study of Rounds et al. (1979) reveals that the factor solutions were more complex. A general factor consistently emerged in the principal components analysis, and that general factor had no counterpart among the scaling dimensions. The second and third principal components closely resembled the two dimensions in the MDS analysis. That is, the interest scales formed much the same configuration in the plane defined by the second and third principal components and in the plane defined by the two scaling dimensions.

MDS and factor analysis have both been used to study simplex correlation matrices. Several different process models have been posited to account for such matrices. Anywhere from 2 to $I - 1$ factors may be required to account for such a matrix, depending on which process gives rise to the structure. In nonmetric MDS, one dimension can always account for the correlations. Factor analysis is sensitive to differences between the process models, but nonmetric MDS is not.

References

Adkins, D. C. (1973). A simpler structure of the American Psychological Association. *American Psychologist* **28**, 47–54.

Anderberg, M. R. (1973). *Cluster analysis for applications.* New York: Academic.

Arabie, P. (1973). Concerning Monte Carlo evaluations of nonmetric multidimensional scaling algorithms. *Psychometrika* **38**, 607–608.

Arabie, P. (1978). Random versus rational strategies for initial configurations in nonmetric multidimensional scaling. *Psychometrika* **43**, 111–113, 119.

Arabie, P. and Boorman, S. A. (1973). Multidimensional scaling of measures of distance between partitions. *Journal of Mathematical Psychology* **10**, 148–203.

Arnold, J. B. (1971). A multidimensional scaling study of semantic distance. *Journal of Experimental Psychology Monograph* **90**, 349–372.

Attneave, F. (1950). Dimensions of similarity. *American Journal of Psychology* **63**, 516–556.

Barlow, R. E., Bartholomew, D. J., Bremner, J. M. and Brunk, H. D. (1972). *Statistical inference under order restrictions.* New York: Wiley.

Bass, B. M., Cascio, W. F., and O'Connor, E. J. (1974). Magnitude estimation of frequency and amount. *Journal of Applied Psychology* **59**, 313–320.

Beals, R., Krantz, D. H., and Tversky, A. (1968). Foundations of multidimensional scaling. *Psychological Review* **75**, 127–142.

Bechtel, G. G. (1976). *Multidimensional preference scaling.* The Hague, Netherlands: Mouton.

Bechtel, G. G., Tucker, L. R., and Chang, W. A. (1971). A scalar product model for multidimensional scaling of choice. *Psychometrika* **36**, 369–388.

Bentler, P. M. and Weeks, D. G. (1978). Restricted multidimensional scaling models. *Journal of Mathematical Psychology* **17**, 138–151.

Bloxom, B. (1968). *Individual differences in multidimensional scaling.* Research Bulletin 68-45. Princeton, NJ: Educational Testing Service.

Bloxom, B. (1978). Constrained multidimensional scaling in *N* spaces. *Psychometrika* **43**, 397–408.

Borg, I. and Lingoes, J. C. (1980). A model and algorithm for multidimensional scaling with external constraints on the distances. *Psychometrika* **45**, 25–38.

Borman, W. C., Hough, L. M., and Dunnette, M. D. (1976). *Development of behaviorally-based rating scales for evaluating the performance of U. S. Navy recruiters*. (Technical Report NPRDC TR 76-31). San Diego, CA: Navy Personnel Research and Development Center.

Byrne, D. (1971). *The attraction paradigm*. New York: Academic.

Campbell, D. P. (1977). *Manual for the Strong–Campbell Interest Inventory* (2nd ed.). Stanford, CA: Stanford.

Carroll, J. D. (1972). Individual differences and multidimensional scaling. In R. N. Shepard, A. K. Romney, and S. B. Nerlove (Eds.), *Multidimensional scaling: Theory and applications in the behavioral sciences* (Vol. I). New York: Seminar Press.

Carroll, J. D. (1976). Spatial, non-spatial and hybrid models for scaling. *Psychometrika* **41**, 439–470.

Carroll, J. D. and Arabie, P. (1980). Multidimensional scaling. In M. R. Rosenzweig and L. W. Porter (Eds.), *Annual Review of Psychology* **31**, 607–649.

Carroll, J. D. and Chang, J. J. (1967). *Relating preference data to multidimensional scaling via a generalization of Coombs' unfolding model*. Paper presented at the meeting of the Psychometric Society, Madison, WI, April.

Carroll, J. D. and Chang, J. (1970). Analysis of individual differences in multidimensional scaling via an *N*-way generalization of "Eckart–Young" decomposition. *Psychometrika* **35**, 283–319.

Carroll, J. D. and Chang, J. J. (1972). *IDIOSCAL (Individual Differences In Orientation Scaling): A generalization of INDSCAL allowing idiosyncratic reference systems as well as an analytic approximation to INDSCAL*. Paper presented to the Psychometric Society, Princeton, NJ, March.

Carroll, J. D., Pruzansky, S., and Kruskal, J. B. (1980). CANDELINC: A general approach to multidimensional analysis of many-way arrays with linear constraints on parameters. *Psychometrika* **45**, 3–24.

Carroll, J. D. and Wish, M. (1974a). Multidimensional perceptual models and measurement methods. In E. C. Carterette and M. P. Friedman (Eds.), *Handbook of perception* (Vol. 2). New York: Academic.

Carroll, J. D. and Wish, M. (1974b). Models and methods for three-way multidimensional scaling. In D. H. Krantz, R. C. Atkinson, R. D. Luce, and P. Suppes (Eds.), *Contemporary developments in mathematical psychology* (Vol. 2). San Francisco: W. H. Freeman.

Clark, A. K. (1976). Re-evaluation of Monte Carlo studies in nonmetric multidimensional scaling. *Psychometrika* **41**, 401–403.

Cliff, N., Bradley, P., and Girard, R. (1973). The investigation of cognitive models for inventory responses. *Multivariate Behavioral Research* **8**, 407–425.

Cohen, H. S. and Davison, M. L. (1973). Jiffy-scale: A FORTRAN IV program for generating Ross-ordered pair comparisons. *Behavioral Science* **18**, 76.

Cohen, J. (1968). Multiple regression as a general data-analytic system. *Psychological Bulletin* **70**, 426–443.

Coombs, C. H. (1964). *A theory of data*. New York: Wiley.

Coombs, C. H., McClelland, G. H., and Coombs, L. C. (1973). *The measurement and analysis of family composition preferences*. Michigan Mathematical Psychology Program, MMPP 73-5.

Cooper, L. G. (1972). A new solution to the additive constant problem in metric multidimensional scaling. *Psychometrika* **37**, 311–322.

Cooper, L. G. (1973). A multivariate investigation of preferences. *Multivariate Behavioral Research* **8**, 253–272.

Coxon, A. P. M. and Jones, C. L. (1974a). Occupational similarities: Subjective aspects of social stratification. *Quality and Quantity* **22**, 369–384.

Coxon, A. P. M. and Jones, C. L. (1974b). Problems in selection of occupational titles. *The Sociological Review* **22**, 369–384.

Cronbach, L. J. (1955). Processes affecting scores on "understanding of others" and "assumed similarity." *Psychological Bulletin* **52**, 177–193.

Davison, M. L. (1972). *An empirical comparison of card sorting and paired comparisons judgments as methods for gathering data in a multidimensional scaling study: An exploratory study.* Unpublished masters thesis, University of Illinois at Urbana–Champaign.

Davison, M. L. (1976). Fitting and testing Carroll's weighted unfolding model for preferences. *Psychometrika* **41**, 233–248.

Davison, M. L. (1977). On a unidimensional, metric unfolding model for attitudinal and developmental data. *Psychometrika* **42**, 523–548.

Davison, M. L. (1980). DACAR: A FORTRAN program for fitting linear and distance models of preference. *Applied Psychological Measurement* **4**, 419.

Davison, M. L. (1981). *Multidimensional scaling versus factor analysis of tests and items.* Address to the American Psychological Association, Los Angeles, August 26.

Davison, M. L. and Jones, L. E. (1976). A similarity-attraction model for predicting sociometric choice from perceived group structure. *Journal of Personality and Social Psychology* **33**, 601–612.

Davison, M. L., King, P. M., Kitchener, K. S., and Parker, C. A. (1980). The stage sequence concept in cognitive and social development. *Developmental Psychology* **16**, 121–131.

Davison, M. L., Robbins, S., and Swanson, D. (1978). Stage structure in objective moral judgments. *Developmental Psychology* **14**, 137–146.

Davison, M. L. and Wood, P. K. (1981). *Fitting unidimensional choice models with nonmetric multidimensional scaling.* Unpublished manuscript, University of Minnesota.

Dawis, R. V, Lofquist, L. H., and Weiss, D. J. (1968). A theory of work adjustment: A revision. *Minnesota Studies in Vocational Rehabilitation* **23**.

De Leeuw, J. (1977). Correctness of Kruskal's algorithms for monotone regression with ties. *Psychometrika* **42**, 141–144.

De Leeuw, J. and Pruzansky, S. (1978). A new computational method to fit the weighted Euclidean distance model. *Psychometrika* **43**, 479–490.

Degerman, R. (1970). Multidimensional analysis of complex structure: Mixtures of class and quantitative variation. *Psychometrika* **35**, 475–491.

Dixon, W. J. and Brown, M. D. (Eds.) (1979). *Biomedical computer programs, P-series.* Los Angeles: University of California.

Forgas, J. P. (1979). Multidimensional scaling: A discovery method in social psychology. In G. P. Ginsburg (Ed.), *Emerging strategies in social psychological research.* New York: Wiley-Interscience.

Forgas, J. P., Kagen, C., and Frey, D. (1977). The cognitive representation of political personalities: A cross-cultural comparison. *International Journal of Psychology* **12**, 19–30.

Gower, J. C. (1966). Some distance properties of latent root and vector methods used in multivariate analysis. *Biometrika* **53**, 325–388.

Gower, J. C. (1971). Statistical methods of comparing different multivariate analyses of the same data. In F. R. Hodson, D. G. Kendall, and P. Tatu (Eds.), *Mathematics in the archaeological and historical sciences*. Edinburgh: Edinburgh University.

Gower, J. C. (1975). Generalized Procrustes analysis. *Psychometrika* **40**, 33–51.

Gower, J. C. (1982). Euclidean distance geometry. *Mathematical Scientist* **7**, 1–14.

Green, P. E. (1978). *Mathematical tools for applied multivariate analysis*. New York: Academic.

Green, P. F. and Carmone, F. J. (1972). Marketing research applications of nonmetric scaling methods. In A. K. Romney, R. N. Shepard, and S. B. Nerlove (Eds.), *Multidimensional scaling: Theory and application in the behavioral sciences* (Vol. 2). New York: Seminar Press.

Guilford, J. P. (1954). *Psychometric methods*. New York: McGraw-Hill.

Guttman, L. (1954). A new approach to factor analysis: The radex. In P. F. Lazarsfeld (Ed.), *Mathematical thinking in the social sciences*. Glencoe, IL:. Free Press.

Guttman, L. (1968). A general nonmetric technique for finding the smallest coordinate space for a configuration of points. *Psychometrika* **33**, 469–504.

Hammond, K. R., Hursch, C. J., and Todd, F. J. (1964). Analyzing the components of clinical inference. *Psychological Review* **71**, 438–456.

Hanham, R. Q. (1976). Factorial ecology in space and time. *Environment and Planning* **8**, 823–828.

Hanson, G. R., Prediger, D. J., and Schussel, R. H. (1977). *Development and validation of sex-balanced interest inventory scales*. Iowa City, IA: The American College Testing Program (ACT Research Report 78).

Harman, H. H. (1976). *Modern factor analysis* (3rd ed.). Chicago: University of Chicago.

Harshman, R. A. (1972a). *Determination and proof of minimum uniqueness conditions for PARAFAC 1*. U.C.L.A., Working Papers in Phonetics 22, March.

Harshman, R. A. (1972b). *PARAFAC 2: Mathematical and technical notes*. U.C.L.A., Working Papers in Phonetics 22, March.

Hartigan, J. A. (1967). Representation of similarity matrices by trees. *Journal of the American Statistical Association* **62**, 1140–1158.

Hartigan, J. A. (1975). *Clustering algorithms*. New York: Wiley.

Heiser, W. J. (1981). *Unfolding analysis of proximity data*. Leiden, The Netherlands: Reprodienst Psychologie.

Hohn, F. E. (1973). *Elementary matrix algebra* (3rd ed.). New York: MacMillan.

Holland, J. L. (1965). *Manual for the Vocational Preference Inventory* (6th ed.). Palo Alto, CA: Consulting Psychologists Press.

Holland, J. L. (1973). *Making vocational choices: A theory of careers*. Englewood Cliffs, NJ: Prentice-Hall.

Holland, J. L., Whitney, D. R., Cole, N. S., and Richards, J. M., Jr. (1969). *An empirical occupational classification derived from a theory of personality and intended for practice and research* (ACT Research Report No. 29). Iowa City, IA: The American College Testing Program.

Holman, E. W. (1972). The relation between hierarchical and Euclidean models for psychological distances. *Psychometrika* **37**, 417–423.

Horan, C. B. (1969). Multidimensional scaling: Combining observations when individuals have different perceptual structures. *Psychometrika* **34**, 139–165.

Hubert, L. (1974). Problems in seriation using a subject-by-item response matrix. *Psychological Bulletin* **81**, 976–983.

Humphreys, L. G. (1960). Investigations of the simplex. *Psychometrika* **25**, 313–323.

Humphreys, L. G. and Parsons, C. K. (1979). A simplex process model for describing differences between cross-lagged correlations. *Psychological Bulletin* **86**, 325–334.

Isenberg, D. J. and Ennis, J. G. (1980). *A comparison of derived and imposed dimensions of group structure.* Unpublished manuscript, Harvard University.

Jardine, C. J., Jardine, N., and Sibson, R. (1967). The structure and construction of taxonomic hierarchies. *Mathematical Biosciences* **1**, 173–179.

Johnson, P. E., Cox, D. L., and Curran, T. E. (1970). Psychological reality of physical concepts. *Psychonomic Science* **19**, 245–247.

Johnson, R. M. (1973). Pairwise nonmetric multidimensional scaling. *Psychometrika* **38**, 11–18.

Johnson, S. C. (1967). Hierarchical clustering schemes. *Psychometrika* **32**, 241–254.

Jones, L. E. and Young, F. W. (1972). Structure of a social environment: Longitudinal individual differences scaling of an intact group. *Journal of Personality and Social Psychology* **24**, 108–121.

Jöreskog, K. G. (1970). Estimation and testing of simplex models. *The British Journal of Mathematical and Statistical Psychology* **23**, 121–145.

Kaiser, H. F. (1958). The varimax criterion for analytic rotation in factor analysis. *Psychometrika* **23**, 187–200.

Kendall, D. G. (1971). Maps from marriages: An application of nonmetric multidimensional scaling to parish register data. In F. R. Hodson, D. G. Kendall, and P. Tatu (Eds.), *Mathematics in the archeological and historical sciences.* Edinburgh: Edinburgh University.

Kohlberg, L. (1976). Moral stages and moralization: The cognitive-developmental approach. In T. Lickona (Ed.), *Moral development and behavior.* New York: Holt, Rinehart & Winston.

Krantz, D. H. and Tversky, A. (1975). Similarity of rectangles: An analysis of subjective similarity. *Journal of Mathematical Psychology* **12**, 4–34.

Krumhansl, C. L. (1979). The psychological representation of musical pitch in a tonal context. *Cognitive Psychology* **11**, 346–374.

Kruskal, J. B. (1964). Multidimensional scaling by optimizing goodness-of-fit to a nonmetric hypothesis. *Psychometrika* **29**, 1–28, 115–129.

Kruskal, J. B. (1977). The relationship between multidimensional scaling and clustering. In J. Van Ryzin (Ed.), *Classification and clustering.* New York: Academic.

Kruskal, J. B. and Carmone, F. (undated). *How to use M-D-SCAL (Version 5M) and other useful information.* Murray Hill, NJ: Unpublished manuscript, Bell Laboratories.

Kruskal, J. B. and Carroll, J. D. (1969). Geometric models and badness-of-fit functions. In P. R. Krishnaiah (Ed.), *Multivariate analysis* (Vol. 2), New York: Academic.

Kruskal, J. B. and Wish, M. (1978). *Multidimensional scaling.* Beverly Hills, CA: Sage.

Kruskal, J. B., Young, F. W., and Seery, J. B. (1973). *How to use KYST, a very flexible program to do multidimensional scaling and unfolding.* Murray Hill, NJ: Unpublished manuscript, Bell Laboratories.

Lee, S. and Bentler, P. M. (1980). Functional relations in multidimensional scaling. *British Journal of Mathematical and Statistical Psychology* **33**, 142–150.

Lingoes, J. C. (1973). *The Guttman-Lingoes nonmetric program series.* Ann Arbor, MI: Mathesis Press.

Lingoes, J. C. and Borg, I. (1978). A direct approach to individual differences scaling using increasingly complex transformations. *Psychometrika* **43**, 491–519.

Lingoes, J. C. and Roskam, E. E. (1973). A mathematical and empirical analysis of two multidimensional scaling algorithms. *Psychometrika Monograph Supplement* **38**, 1–93.

Lingoes, J. C. and Schönemann, P. H. (1974). Alternative measures of fit for the Schönemann–Carroll matrix fitting algorithm. *Psychometrika* **39**, 423–427.

Loevinger, J. (1966). The meaning and measurement of ego development. *American Psychologist* **21**, 195–206.

MacCallum, R. C. (1974a). Relations between factor analysis and multidimensional scaling. *Psychological Bulletin* **81**, 505–516.

MacCallum, R. C. (1974b). *A comparison of two individual differences models for multidimensional scaling: Carroll and Chang's INDSCAL and Tucker's three-mode factor analysis.* Unpublished doctoral dissertation, University of Illinois.

MacCallum, R. C. (1978). Recovery of structure in incomplete data by ALSCAL. *Psychometrika* **44**, 69–74.

MacCallum, R. C. (1979). 3-MODE-MDS: A computer program to execute Tucker's three-mode multidimensional scaling. *Applied Psychological Measurement* **3**, 24.

Mauser, G. A. (1972). A structural approach to predicting patterns of electoral substitution. In A. K. Romney, R. N. Shepard, and S. B. Nerlove (Eds.), *Multidimensional scaling: Theory and applications in the behavioral sciences* (Vol. 2). New York: Seminar Press.

Mervis, C. B. and Rosch, E. (1981). Categorization of natural objects. In M. R. Rosenzweig and L. W. Porter (Eds.), *Annual review of psychology* (Vol. 32). Palo Alto: Annual Reviews Inc.

Miller, G. and Nicely, P. E. (1955). An analysis of perceptual confusions among some English consonants. *Journal of the Acoustical Society of America* **27**, 338–352.

Monahan, J. S., and Lockhead, G. R. (1977). Identification of integral stimuli. *Journal of Experimental Psychology: General* **106**, 94–110.

Nie, N. H., Hull, C. H., Jenkins, J. G., Steinbrenner, K., and Bent, D. H. (1975). *Statistical package for the social sciences* (2nd ed.). New York: McGraw-Hill.

Noma, E. and Johnson, J. (1979). *Constrained nonmetric multidimensional scaling* (Tech. Rep. MMPP 1979-4). Ann Arbor, MI: University of Michigan, Michigan Mathematical Psychology Program.

Nygren, T. E. (1978). ADDIMOD: A program to test the axioms of the additive difference model for multidimensional scaling. *Applied Psychological Measurement* **2**, 338, 360.

Nygren, T. E. (1979). A theoretical framework for testing the additive difference model for dissimilarities data: Representing gambles as multidimensional stimuli. *Journal of Mathematical Psychology* **20**, 53–77.

Nygren, T. E. and Jones, L. E. (1977). Individual differences in perceptions and preferences for political candidates. *Journal of Experimental Social Psychology* **13**, 182–197.

Prediger, D. J. (1980). *Mapping occupations and interests: A graphic aid for vocational guidance and research.* Unpublished manuscript, American College Testing Service, Iowa City, IA.

Pruzansky, S. (1975). *How to use SINDSCAL: A computer program for individual differences in multidimensional scaling.* Unpublished manuscript, Bell Laboratories, Murray Hill, NJ.

Ramsey, J. O. (1978). *MULTISCALE: Four programs for multidimensional scaling by the method of maximum likelihood.* Chicago: International Education Services.

Ramsey, J. O. (1980). Some small sample results for maximum likelihood estimation in multidimensional scaling. *Psychometrika* **45**, 139–144.

Rest, J. R. (1979). *Development in judging moral issues*. Minneapolis, MN: University of Minnesota.

Richardson, M. W. (1938). Multidimensional psychophysics. *Psychological Bulletin* 35, 659–660.

Rosenberg, S. and Jones, R. (1972). A method of investigating and representing a person's implicit theory of personality: Theodore Dreiser's view of people. *Journal of Personality and Social Psychology* 22, 372–386.

Rosenberg, S. and Kim, M. P. (1975). The method of sorting as a data-gathering procedure in multivariate research. *Multivariate Behavioral Research* 10, 489–502.

Rosenberg, S., Nelson, C., and Vivekananthan, P. S. (1968). A multidimensional approach to the structure of personality impressions. *Journal of Personality and Social Psychology* 9, 283–294.

Roskam, E. E. (1969). *Data theory and algorithms for nonmetric scaling* (Parts 1 and 2). Unpublished manuscript, Catholic University, Nijmegan, The Netherlands.

Ross, R. T. (1934). Optimum orders for presentation of pairs in paired comparisons. *Journal of Educational Psychology* 25, 375–382.

Rothkopf, E. Z. (1957). A measure of stimulus similarity and errors in some paired-associate learning tasks. *Journal of Experimental Psychology* 53, 94–104.

Rounds, J. B., Jr., Davison, M. L., and Dawis, R. V. (1979). The fit between Strong–Campbell Interest Inventory general occupational themes and Holland's hexagonal model. *Journal of Vocational Behavior* 15, 303–315.

Rummelhart, D. E. and Abrahamson, A. A. (1973). A model for analogical reasoning. *Cognitive Psychology* 5, 1–28.

Sarle, W. S. (1981). The ADCLUS procedure (Technical Report S-124). Cary, NC: SAS Institute.

Sattath, S. and Tversky, A. (1976). *Additive similarity trees*. Unpublished manuscript, Hebrew University.

Saunders, D. R. (1960). A computer program to find the best-fitting orthogonal factors for a given hypothesis. *Psychometrika* 25, 207–210.

Schiffman, S. S., Reynolds, M. L., and Young, F. W. (1981). *Introduction to multidimensional scaling*. New York: Academic.

Schlessinger, I. M. and Guttman, L. (1969). Smallest space analysis of intelligence and achievement tests. *Psychological Bulletin* 71, 95–100.

Schönemann, P. H. (1972). An algebraic solution for a class of subjective metrics models. *Psychometrika* 37, 441–451.

Schönemann, P. H. and Carroll, R. M. (1970). Fitting one matrix to another under choice of a central dilation and a rigid motion. *Psychometrika* 35, 245–255.

Shepard, R. N. (1962). The analysis of proximities: Multidimensional scaling with an unknown distance function. *Psychometrika* 27, 125–140, 219–246.

Shepard, R. N. (1972a). Introduction to volume I. In R. N. Shepard, A. K. Romney, and S. B. Nerlove (Eds.) *Multidimensional scaling: Theory and applications in the behavioral sciences* (Vol. 1). New York: Seminar Press.

Shepard, R. N. (1972b). Psychological representation of speech sounds. In E. E. David and P. B. Denes (Eds.), *Human communication: A unified view*. New York: McGraw-Hill.

Shepard, R. N. (1974). Representation of structure in similarity data: Problems and prospects. *Psychometrika* 39, 373–422.

Shepard, R. N. (1980). Multidimensional scaling, tree-fitting, and clustering. *Science* **210**, 390–398.

Shepard, R. N. and Arabie, P. (1979). Additive clustering: Representation of similarities as combinations of discrete overlapping properties. *Psychological Review* **86**, 87–123.

Shepard, R. N., Kilpatrick, D. W., and Cunningham, J. P. (1975). The internal representation of numbers. *Cognitive Psychology* **7**, 82–138.

Sherman, C. R. (1972). Nonmetric multidimensional scaling: A Monte Carlo study of the basic parameters. *Psychometrika* **37**, 323–355.

Shikiar, R. and Coates, C. (1978). A multidimensional scaling study of person perception in children. *Multivariate Behavioral Research* **13**, 363–370.

Smith, R. J. and Siegel, A. I. (1967). A multidimensional scaling analysis of the job of civil defense director. *Journal of Applied Psychology* **51**, 476–480.

Sneath, P. H. and Sokal, R. R. (1973). *Numerical taxonomy*. San Francisco: W. H. Freeman.

Soli, S. D. and Arabie, P. (1979). Auditory versus phonetic accounts of observed confusions between consonant phonemes. *Journal of the Acoustical Society of America* **66**, 46–52.

Spence, I. (1972). A Monte Carlo evaluation of three nonmetric multidimensional scaling algorithms. *Psychometrika* **37**, 461–486.

Spence, I. (1974). On random ranking studies in nonmetric scaling. *Psychometrika* **39**, 267–268.

Spence, I. and Domoney, D. W. (1974). Single subject incomplete designs for nonmetric multidimensional scaling. *Psychometrika* **39**, 469–490.

Spence, I. and Young, F. W. (1978). Monte Carlo studies in nonmetric scaling. *Psychometrika* **43**, 115–117.

Srinivasan, V. and Shocker, A. D. (1973). Linear programming techniques for multidimensional analysis of preferences. *Psychometrika* **38**, 337–369.

Stevens, S. S. (1971). Issues in psychophysical measurement. *Psychological Review* **78**, 426–450.

Subkoviak, M. J. (1975). The use of multidimensional scaling in educational research. *Review of Educational Research* **45**, 387–423.

Swann, B. B. (1978). *Affines, office, and factionalism in three rural Japanese settlements*. Unpublished doctoral dissertation, Brandeis University.

Takane, Y. (1981). Multidimensional successive-categories scaling: A maximum likelihood method. *Psychometrika* **46**, 9–28.

Takane, Y., Young, F. W., and De Leeuw, J. (1977). Nonmetric individual differences multidimensional scaling: An alternating least squares method with optimal scaling features. *Psychometrika* **42**, 7–67.

Thurstone, L. L. (1927). A law of comparative judgment. *Psychological Review* **34**, 273–286.

Thurstone, L. L. (1947). *Multiple-factor analysis*. Chicago: University of Chicago.

Torgerson, W. S. (1952). Multidimensional scaling: I. Theory and method. *Psychometrika* **17**, 401–419.

Torgerson, W. S. (1958). *Theory and methods of scaling*. New York: Wiley.

Tucker, L. R. (1960). Intra-individual and inter-individual multidimensionality. In H. Gulliksen and S. Messick (Eds.), *Psychological scaling: Theory and applications*. New York: Wiley.

Tucker, L. R. (1967). The objective definition of simple structure in linear factor analysis. In D. N. Jackson and S. Messick (Eds.), *Problems in human assessment*. New York: McGraw-Hill.

Tucker, L. R. (1972). Relations between multidimensional scaling and three-mode factor analysis. *Psychometrika* **37**, 3–28.

Tversky, A. (1977). Features of similarity. *Psychological Review* **84**, 327–352.

United States Employment Service Dictionary of Occupational Titles (4th ed.) (1977). Washington, DC: United States Department of Labor.

Wainer, H. and Berg, W. (1972). The dimensions of De Maupassant: A multidimensional analysis of students' perception of literature. *American Educational Research Journal* **9**, 485–491.

Wiener-Ehrlich, W. K. (1978). Dimensional and metric structures in multidimensional stimuli. *Perception and Psychophysics* **24**, 399–414.

Wish, M., Deutsch, M., and Biener, L. (1970). Differences in conceptual structures of nations: An exploratory study. *Journal of Personality and Social Psychology* **16**, 361–373.

Wish, M., Deutsch, M., and Kaplan, S. J. (1976). Perceived dimensions of interpersonal relations. *Journal of Personality and Social Psychology* **33**, 409–420.

Wohlwill, J. (1973). *The study of behavioral development*. New York: Academic.

Young, F. W. (1972). A model for polynomial conjoint analysis algorithms. In R. N. Shepard, A. K. Romney, and S. B. Nerlove (Eds.), *Multidimensional scaling: Theory and applications in the behavioral sciences* (Vol. 1). New York: Seminar Press.

Young, F. W., Hamer, R. M., and Lewyckyj, R. (1980). Nonmetric multidimensional scaling under SAS. In *Proceedings of the fifth annual SAS users group international conference*. Cary, NC: SAS Institute Inc.

Young, F. W. and Lewyckyj, R. (1979). *ALSCAL 4 User's Guide*. (2nd ed.). Chapel Hill, NC: Data Analysis and Theory Associates.

Young, F. W. and Torgerson, W. S. (1967). TORSCA: A FORTRAN IV program for Shepard–Kruskal multidimensional scaling analysis. *Behavioral Science* **12**, 498.

Young, G. and Householder, A. S. (1938). Discussion of a set of points in terms of their mutual distances. *Psychometrika* **3**, 19–22.

Young, G. and Householder, A. S. (1941). A note on multidimensional psychophysics. *Psychometrika* **6**, 331–333.

Zinnes, J. L. and Griggs, R. A. (1974). Probabilistic, multidimensional unfolding analysis. *Psychometrika* **39**, 327–350.

Zinnes, J. L. and Wolff, R. P. (1977). Single- and multi-dimensional same–different judgments. *Journal of Mathematical Psychology* **16**, 30–50.

List of Symbols

$\hat{\mathbf{b}}_s$ = vector of k regression weight estimates $\hat{b}_{ks}$.

$b_{kk'}$ = multiple regression weight for predictor variable k and criterion variable k'.

$b_{kk's}$ = regression weight attached to criterion variable s and a predictor variable representing the interaction between variables k and k'.

$\hat{b}_{kk'}$ = multiple regression weight estimate for predictor variable k and criterion variable k'.

$\hat{b}_{kk's}$ = estimate of a regression weight attached to criterion variable s and a predictor variable representing the interaction between variables k and k'.

b_{ks} = regression weight for predictor variable k and criterion variable s.

$\hat{b}_{ks}$ = estimated regression weight for predictor variable k and criterion variable s.

c = subscript used to designate an iteration; an additive or multiplicative constant.

c_s = additive or intercept constant unique to subject s.

c_s^* = additive constant unique to subject s.

$\hat{\mathbf{D}}_s$ = matrix of estimated distances $\hat{d}_{ijs}$ in the stimulus space of subject s.

$\mathbf{\Delta}$ = matrix of proximity data with elements δ_{ij}.

$\mathbf{\Delta}_s$ = matrix of proximity data for subject s.

$\mathbf{\Delta}^*$ = matrix of scalar products with elements δ_{ij}^*.

$\mathbf{\Delta}_s^*$ = matrix of scalar products for subject s with elements δ_{ijs}^*.

228

$\hat{\boldsymbol{\Delta}}_s^*$ = matrix of estimated scalar products for subject s with elements $\hat{\delta}_{ijs}^*$.

$d(\mathrm{a,b})$ = distance between points a and b.

$d(\mathrm{a,c})$ = distance between points a and c.

$d(\mathrm{b,c})$ = distance between points b and c.

d_{ij} = distance between points i and j.

d_{ijs} = distance between points i and j in the stimulus space of subject s.

d_{is} = distance between points i and s.

$\hat{d}_{ij}$ = estimate of the distance between points i and j.

$\hat{d}_{ijs}$ = estimate of the distance between points i and j in the stimulus space of subject s.

$\hat{d}_{ij}^o$ = estimate of the distance between points i and j computed from the coordinates in the starting configuration.

$\hat{d}_{ij}^c$ = estimate of the distance between points i and j computed in the cth iteration.

$\hat{d}_{ij}^{c+1}$ = estimate of the distance between points i and j computed in iteration $(c + 1)$.

δ_{ij} = measure of the proximity between stimuli i and j.

δ_{ijs} = proximity measure about stimulus pair (i, j) for subject s.

δ_{is} = preference of subject s for stimulus i.

δ_{js} = preference of subject s for stimulus j.

δ_{ij}^* = scalar product for stimulus pair (i, j). See Eq. (4.3).

δ_{ijs}^* = scalar product for subject s and stimulus pair (i, j). See Eq. (6.7).

$\hat{\delta}_{ij}$ = disparity or rank image for stimulus pair (i, j). See Eq. (5.11).

$\hat{\delta}_{ijs}$ = disparity or rank image for stimulus pair (i, j) and subject s.

$\hat{\delta}_{is}$ = disparity or rank image corresponding to δ_{is}, the preference of subject s for stimulus i. See Eq. (7.3).

$\hat{\delta}_{js}$ = disparity or rank image corresponding to δ_{js}, the preference of subject s for stimulus j. See Eq. (7.3).

$\hat{\delta}_{ijs}^*$ = estimate of the scalar product δ_{ijs}^*. See Eq. (6.13).

$\hat{\delta}_{ij}^{c+1}$ = disparity for stimuli i and j computed in the $(c + 1)$st iteration.

F = statistic conforming to the F-distribution; least squares loss function.

f = monotone function.

f_s = monotone function unique to subject s.

$\mathbf{I}$	=	identity matrix.
I	=	number of stimuli.
i	=	subscript designating a stimulus.
i'	=	subscript designating a stimulus.
J	=	number of stimuli.
j	=	subscript designating a stimulus.
j'	=	subscript designating a stimulus.
K	=	number of dimensions in a space; number of measures in a profile of measures.
K^*	=	*a priori* estimate of the number of dimensions in the stimulus space.
κ	=	coefficient of alienation defined in Eq. (5.20).
k	=	subscript designating a dimension or a measure in a profile of measures.
k'	=	subscript designating a dimension.
λ_k	=	eigenvalue for dimension k: $\lambda_k = \sum_i x_{ik}^2$.
M	=	number of judgments for each pair of stimuli; number of dimensions in the subject space of a three-mode solution.
m	=	subscript designating a dimension in the subject space of a three-mode MDS; subscript designating a block of disparities in Kruskal's monotone regression.
$\mathbf{P}$	=	matrix of probabilities with elements p_{ij}.
p	=	superscript designating the Minkowski metric in a Minkowski distance function.
p_{ij}	=	probability defined for stimulus pair (i, j).
$\mathbf{R}_s$	=	matrix of interaction parameters $r_{kk's}$ unique to subject s: $\mathbf{R}_s = \mathbf{T}_s\mathbf{T}_s'$.
$\hat{\mathbf{R}}_s$	=	matrix of interaction parameter estimates $\hat{r}_{kk's}$ unique to subject s.
R_{E}	=	multiple correlation obtained by fitting the simple Euclidean model for preferences.
R_{G}	=	multiple correlation obtained by fitting the general Euclidean model for preferences.
$R_{k'}$	=	multiple correlation obtained by regressing predictors onto criterion variable k'.
R_{W}	=	multiple correlation obtained by fitting the weighted Euclidean model for preferences.

R_V	=	multiple correlation obtained by fitting the vector model for preferences.
r	=	correlation between estimated and actual scalar products used as a fit measure by some MDS algorithms. See Eq. (6.15).
r_{ij}	=	correlation between scores on measures i and j.
$r_{kk's}$	=	parameter characterizing the size and direction of the interaction between dimensions k and k' in the judgments of subject s.
r_s	=	correlation between estimated and actual scalar products of subject s. See Eq. (6.18).
$r(\mathbf{Y}, \hat{\mathbf{X}}) =$		congruence coefficient for target matrix $\mathbf{Y}$ and stimulus coordinate matrix $\hat{\mathbf{X}}$.
$\hat{r}_{kk's}$	=	estimate of a parameter characterizing the size and direction of the interaction between dimensions k and k' in the judgments of subject s.
S_1	=	STRESS formula one, which indexes the degree to which the model fits the data. See Eq. (5.13).
S_2	=	STRESS formula two, which indexes the degree to which the model fits the data. See Eq. (5.14).
SS_1	=	S-STRESS formula one, which indexes the degree to which the data fit the model. See Eqs. (5.16), (6.5), and (6.6).
SS_2	=	S-STRESS formula two, which indexes the degree to which the data fit the model. See Eq. (5.17).
s	=	subscript designating a subject.
$\mathbf{T}$	=	transformation matrix with elements $t_{kk'}$.
$\mathbf{T}_s$	=	transformation matrix unique to subject s with elements $t_{kk's}$.
$\hat{\mathbf{T}}$	=	estimated transformation matrix with elements $\hat{t}_{kk'}$.
$\hat{\mathbf{T}}_s$	=	estimate of the transformation matrix for subject s with elements $\hat{t}_{kk's}$.
$t_{kk'}$	=	cosine of the angle between dimension k and rotated dimension k'.
$t_{kk's}$	=	cosine of the angle between dimension k and dimension k' in the stimulus space of subject s.
$\hat{t}_{kk'}$	=	estimate of the cosine of the angle between dimension k and rotated dimension k'.
$\hat{t}_{kk's}$	=	estimate of the angle between dimension k and dimension k' in the stimulus space of subject s.
μ	=	coefficient of monotonicity defined in Eq. (5.19).
$\mathbf{W}$	=	matrix of subject weights with elements w_{ks}.

$\mathbf{W}_s$ = diagonal matrix of weights for subject s in which the kth diagonal element is w_{ks}.

$\mathbf{W}_s^2$ = diagonal matrix of weights for subject s with w_{ks}^2 as its kth diagonal element.

$\hat{\mathbf{W}}$ = matrix of subject weight estimates with elements $\hat{w}_{ks}$.

$\hat{\mathbf{W}}_s$ = diagonal matrix of weight estimates for subject s in which the kth diagonal element is $\hat{w}_{ks}$.

$\hat{\mathbf{W}}^2$ = matrix of squared subject weight estimates with elements $\hat{w}_{ks}^2$.

w_{ks} = weight for subject s along dimension k; coordinate of subject s along dimension k in the subject weight space.

w_s = dimension weight for subject s common to all K dimensions.

w_{ks}^* = relative weight for subject s along dimension k. See Eq. (6.19).

$\hat{w}_{ks}$ = estimate of the subject weight w_{ks}.

$\hat{w}_s$ = estimate of the dimension weight w_s common to all k dimensions.

$\mathbf{X}$ = matrix of stimulus coordinates with elements x_{ik}, x_{jk}; matrix of stimulus and ideal point coordinates with elements x_{ik}, x_{jk}, and x_{sk}.

$\mathbf{X}_s$ = matrix of stimulus coordinates for subject s with elements x_{iks}, x_{jks}.

$\mathbf{X}^*$ = rotation of the coordinate matrix $\mathbf{X}$: $\mathbf{X}^* = \mathbf{XT}$.

$\hat{\mathbf{X}}$ = matrix of stimulus coordinate estimates with elements $\hat{x}_{ik}$, $\hat{x}_{jk}$; matrix of stimulus and ideal point coordinate estimates with elements $\hat{x}_{ik}$, $\hat{x}_{jk}$, and $\hat{x}_{sk}$.

$\hat{\mathbf{X}}^*$ = rotation of the estimated coordinate matrix $\hat{\mathbf{X}}$: $\hat{\mathbf{X}}^* = \hat{\mathbf{X}}\mathbf{T}$ with elements $\hat{x}_{ik}^*$.

$\hat{\mathbf{X}}^\circ$ = matrix of coordinate estimates used as a starting configuration in an iterative MDS algorithm.

$\hat{\mathbf{x}}_s$ = vector of K ideal point coordinate estimates $\hat{x}_{sk}$.

x_i = coordinate of stimulus i along a dimension in a unidimensional space.

x_{ik} = coordinate of stimulus i along dimension k.

x_{iks} = coordinate of stimulus i along dimension k in the stimulus space of subject s.

x_j = coordinate of stimulus j along the dimension in a unidimensional space.

x_{jk} = coordinate of stimulus j along dimension k.

x_{jks} = coordinate of stimulus j along dimension k in the stimulus space of subject s.

x_s = ideal point coordinate for subject s in a one-dimensional space.

x_{sk} = ideal point coordinate for subject s along dimension k.

x_{sks} = ideal point coordinate of subject s along dimension k in the stimulus space of subject s.

$\hat{x}_{ik}$ = estimate of the stimulus coordinate x_{ik}.

$\hat{x}_{jk}$ = estimate of the stimulus coordinate x_{jk}.

$\hat{x}_{sk}$ = estimate of the ideal point coordinate x_{sk} for subject s along dimension k.

$\hat{x}_{ik}^*$ = coordinate estimate for stimulus i on rotated dimension k.

$\hat{x}_{ik}^{\circ}$ = initial estimate of the stimulus coordinate x_{ik} used in the starting configuration of an iterative MDS algorithm.

$\hat{x}_{jk}^{\circ}$ = initial estimate of the stimulus coordinate x_{jk} used in the starting configuration of an iterative MDS algorithm.

$\hat{x}_{ik}^c$ = estimate of the coordinate for stimulus i along dimension k computed in the cth iteration.

$\hat{x}_{jk}^c$ = estimate of the coordinate for stimulus j along dimension k computed in the cth iteration.

$\hat{x}_{ik}^{c+1}$ = estimate of the coordinate for stimulus i along dimension k computed in iteration $c + 1$.

$\mathbf{Y}$ = matrix containing hypothesized stimulus coordinates y_{ik}. $\mathbf{Y}$ is sometimes called a target matrix.

$\hat{\mathbf{Y}}$ = matrix containing estimates of hypothesized stimulus coordinates $\hat{y}_{ik}$.

y_{ik} = hypothesized coordinate of stimulus i along dimension k.

$\hat{y}_{ik}$ = estimate of the hypothesized coordinate of stimulus i along dimension k.

$\mathbf{Z}$ = matrix of standardized profile scores with elements z_{ik}; matrix of subject coordinates z_{sm} in a three-mode analysis.

$\hat{\mathbf{Z}}$ = matrix of subject coordinate estimates $\hat{z}_{sm}$ in a three-mode analysis.

$\hat{\mathbf{Z}}^*$ = rotation of the subject space coordinates in a three-mode MDS: $\hat{\mathbf{Z}}^* = \hat{\mathbf{Z}}\mathbf{T}$.

z_{ik} = standardized score for object i on measure k.

z_{sm} = coordinate for subject s along dimension m in a three-mode MDS subject space.

Author Index

235

Subject Index

Applied Probability and Statistics (Continued)

DAVID • Order Statistics, *Second Edition*

DAVISON • Multidimensional Scaling

DEMING • Sample Design in Business Research

DODGE and ROMIG • Sampling Inspection Tables, *Second Edition*

DOWDY and WEARDEN • Statistics for Research

DRAPER and SMITH • Applied Regression Analysis, *Second Edition*

DUNN • Basic Statistics: A Primer for the Biomedical Sciences, *Second Edition*

DUNN and CLARK • Applied Statistics: Analysis of Variance and Regression

ELANDT-JOHNSON • Probability Models and Statistical Methods in Genetics

ELANDT-JOHNSON and JOHNSON • Survival Models and Data Analysis

FLEISS • Statistical Methods for Rates and Proportions, *Second Edition*

FRANKEN, KÖNIG, ARNDT, and SCHMIDT • Queues and Point Processes

GALAMBOS • The Asymptotic Theory of Extreme Order Statistics

GIBBONS, OLKIN, and SOBEL • Selecting and Ordering Populations: A New Statistical Methodology

GNANADESIKAN • Methods for Statistical Data Analysis of Multivariate Observations

GOLDBERGER • Econometric Theory

GOLDSTEIN and DILLON • Discrete Discriminant Analysis

GROSS and CLARK • Survival Distributions: Reliability Applications in the Biomedical Sciences

GROSS and HARRIS • Fundamentals of Queueing Theory

GUPTA and PANCHAPAKESAN • Multiple Decision Procedures: Theory and Methodology of Selecting and Ranking Populations

GUTTMAN, WILKS, and HUNTER • Introductory Engineering Statistics, *Third Edition*

HAHN and SHAPIRO • Statistical Models in Engineering

HALD • Statistical Tables and Formulas

HALD • Statistical Theory with Engineering Applications

HAND • Discrimination and Classification

HARTIGAN • Clustering Algorithms

HILDEBRAND, LAING, and ROSENTHAL • Prediction Analysis of Cross Classifications

HOAGLIN, MOSTELLER, and TUKEY • Understanding Robust and Exploratory Data Analysis

HOEL • Elementary Statistics, *Fourth Edition*

HOEL and JESSEN • Basic Statistics for Business and Economics, *Third Edition*

HOLLANDER and WOLFE • Nonparametric Statistical Methods

IMAN and CONOVER • Modern Business Statistics

JAGERS • Branching Processes with Biological Applications

JESSEN • Statistical Survey Techniques

JOHNSON and KOTZ • Distributions in Statistics

        Discrete Distributions

        Continuous Univariate Distributions—1

        Continuous Univariate Distributions—2

        Continuous Multivariate Distributions

JOHNSON and KOTZ • Urn Models and Their Application: An Approach to Modern Discrete Probability Theory

JOHNSON and LEONE • Statistics and Experimental Design in Engineering and the Physical Sciences, Volumes I and II, *Second Edition*

JUDGE, HILL, GRIFFITHS, LÜTKEPOHL and LEE • Introduction to the Theory and Practice of Econometrics